MAKING HEN'S MEAT

A memoir

by

GARY SPENCE

SECOND EDITION - SECOND PRINTING
January 2005

Copyright © 2004 by Gary Spence. All rights reserved: No part of this book may be reproduced, stored in a retrieval system, or transmitted by any means, electronic, mechanical, photocopying, recording, or otherwise, without written permission from the author.

ISBN# 1-56411-348-5
YBBG# 0344

Cover Design: Ellen Spence
Photographic Restoration: Michele Spence

Published in the U. S. A.
By
CONQUERING BOOKS, L.L.C.
210 East Arrowhead Drive #1
Charlotte, N. C. 28213
(704) 509-2226
www.conqueringbooks.com

This book is dedicated to –
My darling wife, Susan, lover, companion and friend
My best friends, my children, Simon, James and Dominic and their wives, Ellen, Michele and Anne
My grandchildren, Jacob, Ethan and Megan, and step-grandchildren, Tyler and Lauren
My brothers, Michael and John, for keeping the home fires burning
My life long friends in England, Peter Thornton and Johnny Milnes for always being there for me
John Fell for showing me how to look at art, architecture and nature
Paul and Audrey Byrne for making the 1970's in Dublin into one long party
Albert Gubay and Peter Willers for teaching me that with time and patience it is possible to shag a mosquito
Eamon Halloran for filling my years in Bradford in the 1990's with music, laughter and brotherhood
My friends of 25 years in America, Deane Brunson, Becky Sippe and Chuck Sullivan for standing by me in the bad times as well as the good
Bobby and Gina Barnett for making my family feel like part of their family in Charlotte, North Carolina
And in memory of –
Sam Chippindale and Raymond Clegg for getting me started in the real estate business
Roger Suddards who spent his life being generous with his time and talents
Gerry Healy, class warrior, comrade and friend
Mont Kavanagh for showing me the meaning of the word civilized
Liz Bray for singing so sweetly and dying too young
My parents, Harold and Mary Spence, for striving to give my brothers and I a better start in life than they had.

INTRODUCTION

Since completing this book two years ago the time has flown by. My grandchild, Jacob, is now five years old and started kindergarten today. His brother, Ethan, is already three and it seems he was born only yesterday.

My youngest son, Dominic, married Anne Kelly in Charleston, South Carolina, on September 28th, 2003, and they have an adorable baby girl, Megan, who was three months old today, having been born two months prematurely.

It is four years since I quit drinking but I still think about having a drink every day. In January, 2003, with a lot of help from a Chinese acupuncturist and herbalist I did the impossible and quit smoking and have never had the slightest craving for a cigarette since quitting. To my amazement quitting smoking was a hundred times easier and more final than quitting drinking.

I have teamed up with my oldest son, Simon, and started a real estate investment company which we have called The Bradford Property Corporation after our home town in England.

This year I had my sixtieth birthday and I am amazed at how swiftly the years have passed. I remember my childhood so clearly. Today I bought a bumper sticker at the Smelly Cat Coffee House on 36th Street round the corner from my home in Charlotte, North Carolina. The bumper sticker sums up my feelings very succinctly. It reads "Inside every old person is a young person wondering what happened."

Gary Spence
Charlotte, North Carolina
August 20th, 2004.

PROLOGUE

On the 14th December 1997 Susan, my wife of 31 years, and I stepped off the train at Southampton and took a cab to The Post House Hotel. From the window of our hotel room we could see the ocean liner Queen Elizabeth 2 on which we would set sail the next day for New York. I had got drunk on the train so I went to sleep while Sue went for a walk around the town. We were emigrating to the United States for the second time. We had lived there previously from 1980 to 1990 and our three children Simon, James and Dominic had done a lot of their growing up there.

Simon, who worked as a management consultant for Solutions, Inc., was almost 31 years old and was married to Ellen Barnett. They lived on Thomas Avenue in the Plaza Midwood area of Charlotte, North Carolina and their home was our destination. James who was 28 years old had recently graduated from Manchester University with a Master of Arts degree in art history and was also living with Simon and Ellen until he found a place of his own. He was working at his old job at Quality Chrome developing and printing black and white photographs for professional photographers. Our third son Dominic who was 24, was with his new girlfriend, Finola Hingstone, in Bradford, Yorkshire, where we had been living for the preceding seven years, and was working as a commercial real estate agent.

We were traveling by ship because I had developed so intense a fear of flying that I could not contemplate an eight hour flight from England to America.

The next morning we boarded QE2 and quickly found our cabin, the cheapest one on the ship. We did not unpack but called the purser:
"Hello, this is Gary Spence", I said "we're in Cabin 5165 and I'm calling you about the upgrade you promised us."
"Good morning, Gary, everything is arranged. You're to be in 4095, on Deck 4 and a steward will be along shortly to move your bags. By the way how's Mark?"

"Mark is doing fine and he asked me to give you his regards and best wishes."

We settled into our stateroom and I gave Sue a hug. We sat together in silence but there was a bond between us, an understanding that this was a defining moment in our life. For the fourth time we were leaving one country to live in another. In 1970 we had left our homeland, England, to live in Ireland, taking with us our two children Simon and James. In 1980 we had left Ireland for the United States this time with three children in tow; our third child Dominic having been born in Ireland in 1973. In 1990 we had left the United States and returned to England bringing James and Dominic with us but leaving Simon behind; Simon had a steady girlfriend, Ellen, a good job and a nice house; his future was in America not England. And now seven years later we were returning to America leaving Dominic behind in England on this occasion. Surely this was the last move we would make.

There is something very definitive about making off, in the night as it were, to a new life in a new country. In his novel, Affairs of the Heart, Malcolm Muggeridge describes precisely how Sue and I felt:

> *It is always an alluring prospect to drop anything—a job, a love affair: to creep out in the darkness from a play just before the curtain rises. You walk out through those swing doors never to return: you buy a ticket at the guichet and go elsewhere; you shut a door behind you leaving forever unpaid bills, unanswered letters, uncompleted projects, dead love and dead desires. An illusory vista of release presents itself: on each voyage the sailor has the same sense of relief on seeing land disappear from sight but as soon as he can see it no more he is eagerly scanning the horizon for something to break the empty monotony.*

We had traveled on QE2 twice already in 1997, to and from the United States. We had been for a three month vacation at Simon and Ellen's expense. I had been hospitalized in Bradford, Yorkshire with heart trouble and psychiatric problems from 13th March to 1st May, 1997 and Simon and Ellen had offered me three month's convalescence in America. It was during that convalescence that we decided to return to the States permanently. This was how we had come to meet the purser and in conversation we had discovered that my nephew, Mark Spence, had been at school with him and they were old friends.

On 21st December we arrived in New York and took the train from Penn Station to Charlotte, an eight hour journey. Simon, James and Ellen met us at the station and took us to their home at 1816 Thomas Avenue. Everyone was ready for a drink and Simon handed me a bottle of Kaliber, non alcoholic beer. My cardiac specialist in England had told me to quit drinking unless I wanted my heart to deteriorate again. I had tried hard to quit but hadn't succeeded and Sue knew that as well as the couple of glasses of wine with dinner, which she and I had agreed was my limit, I was sneaking a few drinks during the day. I didn't want Simon to see my weakness and so kept up the pretence of drinking only non-alcoholic beer for the next few weeks. What I was in fact doing was opening the bottles of Kaliber, pouring off three ounces, adding a miniature of vodka and replacing the cap. Every time Simon handed me a Kaliber I was getting a double shot of vodka. This was crazy, knowing that my heart had recovered once from cardiomyopathy and that, each time I damaged it by drinking, the possibility of the damage being irreversible was increased. I really had every reason not to drink but also had an overwhelming craving for alcohol which I went to any lengths to satisfy.

The first thing Sue, James and I needed were cars. Charlotte is built to an extremely low density and because everything is so spread out it is impossible to get around without a car. There is no local rail or trolley service just a limited bus service. We couldn't afford new cars and I was nervous about buying second hand ones without an introduction so I phoned an old friend, an attorney called Deane Brunson, and asked him if he could recommend a used car dealer; I had a recollection that he had a client who sold cars.

"Well", Deane said, "as a matter of fact I've got three sitting in the parking lot outside my house in Riverhills".

"What have you got?" I asked

" There's a 1993 Buick Century which has only done 40,000 miles; it was my mother's and it hasn't been used since she died over a year ago. Then there's a high mileage Volvo that was my daughter's when she was at college; she graduated this year and as soon as she got a job she bought a new car; it's the same story with the third car, it's a Mercury Tracer and it belonged to my wife's daughter".

"When can I look at them" I asked

"Come over tomorrow at about 10am."

"Okay Deane, see you then."

I bought the cars for $11,000 and I took the Buick, Sue the Mercury and James the Volvo. This was one of those serendipitous strokes of good fortune that I seem to have just when things look bleak. And they were looking bleak; neither Sue nor I had a job and we knew it would be hard to find employment at our age. We had somewhere to live; Simon and Ellen had bought a new house on Midwood Place and planned to move in January 1998 leaving Sue and I living in their house on Thomas Avenue. James was moving with them to Midwood Place. All we had to do was give Simon the amount of his mortgage payment and we could stay for as long as we wanted. We paid a year's mortgage up front and also paid back $2,000 we'd borrowed to help out a friend a few years earlier. The only money we had was from the sale of our house in Bradford and between moving expenses, travel expenses, cars and the mortgage we had already spent over $30,000.

We went to Deane's office to pay for the cars on New Year's Eve and while Sue and I were with Deane, his partner Joe Griffin, who I knew slightly, came in and said hello. He then said to Sue:

"How would you like to be my secretary?"

"I'd love to" said Sue.

So they worked out a deal there and then and Sue started work on Monday 5th of January, 1998. Serendipity strikes again.

Now that Sue was working I was on my own again and had the opportunity to do some daytime drinking. I set off on foot to see if there were any local bars. I walked down Thomas Avenue to Central Avenue and took a right. The first bar I came to was Millie's right next to the railroad tracks. This was a private members' club (as were all bars in North Carolina selling liquor and no food) but a member signed me in and I filled out an application to join. The few people in the bar were well on their way to being drunk and to my surprise the bartender was openly drinking whiskey and was quite drunk himself. The reason I was surprised was that in North Carolina it is illegal for a bartender to drink while on duty and any that did usually did so surreptitiously. Something didn't feel quite right about Millie's so I asked if there was another bar in the neighborhood. They pointed me back the way I'd come to Elizabeth Billiards on Pecan Avenue. I remembered Elizabeth Billiards from my previous time in Charlotte. It used to be at the corner of 7th Street and Caswell but had apparently moved half a mile to the old ABC Liquor Store at the corner of Central and Pecan. It was no longer in the Elizabeth neighborhood but had retained the name. I walked back up Central Avenue and into Elizabeth Billiards. The place was dimly lit, there were half a dozen pool tables with no one playing, a long bar with a few customers and then an area with four or five dartboards.

This was another private members' club but I was signed in by Nikkie, one of the regular customers. I was made welcome by the bartender, Warren Stiles, and he and I were to become good friends. I had found my second home in Charlotte and this was to become my H.Q. for the next two and a half years. E.B.'s (as everyone called Elizabeth Billiards) didn't open until 3 p.m. but stayed open until 2 a.m. I needed a bar that opened before 3 p.m. and found that the Bayou Kitchen at 7th and Caswell opened at 11 a.m. To my surprise I found a bar further down Central Avenue called Happy Days that opened from 7 a.m. until 2 a.m. – the maximum permitted hours in North Carolina. I never made it there for 7 a.m. but I would often be there by 10 a.m. and on occasion 9 a.m. The morning crowd were mainly ex-army officers with good pensions who drank from 7 a.m. until 12 noon then went home and slept for the afternoon, woke up, ate dinner, and were in bed by 8 or 9 o'clock. This was their routine day in day out except on Sundays when the bar didn't open until 12 noon.

I registered with a doctor, Michael Friedland, and gave him the letters from my cardiologist and psychiatrist. He prescribed Librium for my mental condition and cut out all the other drugs. He gave me an echo test and the ejection fraction of my heart was at a very healthy 50%. When I was taken ill in England it had been as low as 12%, but with medication and abstemious drinking it had recovered to this level. He prescribed Gemfibrozil and Prinivil for my cholestrol and cardiac problems and told me I had to quit drinking.

In late January Simon, Ellen and James moved to Midwood Place and a few days later our furniture arrived from England.

One night Simon and Ellen, and Sue and I, went out with some close friends of Simon and Ellen, Jed & Paige Moody. We went to Thomas Street Tavern for a few drinks and when we got the tab Simon and I split it. We had agreed to go to EB's for a night cap and Jed said he would pick up the tab. When we were getting ready to leave Warren handed me a tab for $25 and I passed it to Jed. He looked at it and said:
"Call it $30 with tip so you and Simon each give me $10"
I went totally berserk and said;
"You tight fisted devil; you said you were going to pick up the tab."
"No I didn't" lied Jed
"You did you liar" I said and gave him a push.

He and Paige left in a hurry and Simon and I had to pay the tab.
When we got back to Thomas Avenue I said;
"I'll just walk down to see Jed," implying I was going to apologize
I knocked on Jed's door and when Paige opened it I said;
"Regarding the incident at E.B.'s I just want to say that I stand by every word I said. Jed is a tight fisted bastard."
I was interrupted by Simon physically picking me up and carrying me back to 1816 Thomas Avenue.

A couple of days later, at Simon's request, I wrote a groveling letter of apology to Jed and Paige.

In February I got a phone call from Dominic to say life in Bradford wasn't working out for him and he wanted to return to the States. I paid his airfare and two days later he moved into Thomas Avenue with us. Now the whole family was back in Charlotte, living within two minutes of each other. We renewed our friendship with Becky Sippe and Sue and I went on a week's holiday with her to our favorite beach, Tybee Island, Georgia.

James had a fulfilling year. In summer he started dating Michele Beck, who worked with him at Quality Chrome and who he'd known for several years. He secured a part time job teaching photography at Central Piedmont Community College and started there in September. Then he bought a little house on Brook Road just a few minutes from Simon and Ellen, and moved in at the end of January.

We knew we couldn't stay at the Thomas Avenue house indefinitely and we knew we couldn't afford to buy it from Simon and Ellen. Simon had bought it for about $80,000 but it had increased in value to nearly $200,000. We started looking at houses in NODA – the historic North Davidson Arts District - at the end of 1998. This was a mill village of single storey bungalows with floor areas of 1250 – 1700 sq. ft. built around 1905. The mill had closed years before and as former mill workers had moved out of the village to find work elsewhere the number of vacant houses and rental houses increased and the drug dealers and prostitutes moved in. The cinema on 36th Street began to show porno movies and then closed down. The shops in the village center between 34th and 36th Street on North Davidson closed one by one.

A few brave souls saw the potential to revitalize the area and put their money where their mouths were. Paul Sires and Ruth Ava Lyons, both artists, bought a block of property and opened the Center of the Earth Gallery. Across the street from them was Pat's Time for One More Bar and an art gallery opened on either side of it, the 23 Studio and The Wrightnow Gallery. K.C. Terry, an outrageous gay guy, bought a block of semi-derelict property at North Davidson Street and 35th and opened a restaurant, Fat City Deli. Other galleries opened but some were short lived. Paul McBroom bought the old cinema and adjoining property on 36th Street and re-opened it as the Neighborhood Theater, which became a venue for folk singers, bluegrass, country and western and blues music. More significantly he began to buy houses, remodel them and sell them at a profit. The houses typically cost $30,000 to $40,000 to buy, $20,000 to $30,000 to remodel and were sold for between $90,000 and $120,000. Other speculators copied McBroom and bit by bit the neighborhood was being turned around, with rental houses becoming owner occupied.

As we looked at NODA we had mixed feelings. The neighborhood was on the cusp, it could still go either way. Finally we took the plunge and bought 3033 North Myers Street with a 95% loan from First Union. The ground floor had been "McBroomed", new electrics, new air conditioning, two new bathrooms, a new kitchen, all walls newly sheet rocked and painted, new doors and windows, and the old heart of pine floors re-finished. It was ready to move into but we decided to spend some of our remaining cash on re-modeling the attic space as a master suite for Sue and I. Our old friend, the architect Adi Mistri, prepared sketch plans for us and helped in supervising the work. I employed all local labor and created a wonderful 900 sq. ft. suite for around $30,000. In May Sue, Dominic and I moved in. I used to joke that us moving into the neighborhood would ensure that the gentrification would speed up and it seemed as if I was right. Within months Boudreaux, a cajun restaurant moved into premises on 36th Street and Kelly's Vegetarian restaurant opened at Davidson and 34th Street. These were followed by Cabo Fish Taco at 35th and Davidson, the Smelly Cat Coffee house on 36th and the Mellow Mushroom, a chain restaurant, at Davidson & 36th. A new development of lofts and town homes was soon under way at Patterson and Davidson and the builder carrying out this scheme bought an adjoining fifteen acre site with plans to build two hundred houses. Across from Fat City a development of retail space and lofts is in progress and the owner of Pats Tavern and the adjoining galleries has sold to a leading developer who is to build retail and lofts. The old mill had been bought by a developer and refurbishment is in progress for office, retail and residential. House prices that only recently passed the $100,000 mark are nudging the $200,000 level and sales at between $140,000 and $180,000 are commonplace. The artists are being squeezed out as NODA becomes trendy and some of the entrepreneurs who made it all happen will sell their properties for a handsome and well deserved profit and move elsewhere to start the next NODA.

On 28th June my first grandson, Jacob William, was born at Carolinas Medical Center. We were there for the labor along with the father to be, Simon, and Ellen's parents, Bobby and Gina and her sister Kim. When finally the nurse came out of the labor room and told us a little boy had been born weighing 8lbs 6 ozs I burst into tears. It reminded me so much of the time thirty two years earlier when Simon had been born. I went down to the shop in the hospital foyer and bought him a soft toy and some balloons. I very quickly developed a deep affection for Jacob but began to realize what an impediment my drinking was to fully enjoying him. I was apprehensive about visiting in the evening because I didn't want Simon and Ellen to see me drunk; I knew I could never hold him when I had been drinking because of the danger of dropping him. I used to visit early in the morning before he went down for his nap and early evening after my siesta.

I needed to do something about my drinking but instead life for me now settled into a routine of drinking and sleeping. At 11 a.m. I would be in a new bar, Thomas Street Tavern, and drink three or four pints of beer then move on to the Bayou Kitchen where I would drink more beer and gin and tonics. Then I would go to Fat City and have a good laugh with the incomparable K.C. If I was still able to drive at 3 p.m. I would often go to E.B.'s and have a couple more drinks before heading home for some shuteye. I would set the alarm for 5.30 p.m. so I would be up when Sue arrived home at 6 p.m.. We would eat then I would fall asleep again and wake up between 9 and 10 p.m. when I would head out again to EB's where I stayed until 1 or 2 a.m. Then back home again praying I would not be stopped by the police. Often Dominic or some of my new found friends such as Sean Kelly or Joel Breckonridge would drive me home. Sometimes I would go to some other bars, such as Happy Days, The Penguin, Pat's or Bill's Pub, but the end result was the same; I was drunk twice a day, slept twice a day and only ate once between 6 – 7 p.m.. For the first time in my life I was no longer enjoying drinking. I was treating it like a job that I hated but couldn't give up. The only relief from this compulsive drinking was sleep.

Dominic took a job as a car salesman and James took a second part time job teaching at Winthrop University in Rock Hill, South Carolina. This was in addition to teaching at CPCC and between these two part time jobs he had more than a full time job.

For Thanksgiving, 1999 we went to Tybee Island near Savannah, Georgia, but this time with an old friend, the poet Chuck Sullivan and his partner, Linda Lindsay. James and Michele came down for a few days but found it hard to relax as Michele's mother was always on the phone relating the latest escapades of Michele's teenage son, Tyler.

I was drinking so hard and taking Librium as well that I inevitably became crazier and crazier and my behavior really got out of control. One day I walked into E.B's at 3 p.m. and Andy Smith was bartending. I ordered a pint of Guinness and as he handed it to me he said:
"That's on me Gary"
"That's one of the few true things you've ever said," I replied and threw the pint of Guinness, glass and all, straight at him and beat a hasty retreat. There was no reason for this behavior and luckily Andy forgave me and we became friends again.

One afternoon I was in bed sleeping when I awoke to find one of the boy's friends, Jack Curry, perched on the edge of my bed making a phone call:
"What are you doing, Jack, can't you see I'm kipping" I said
"I'm making a phone call" said Jack
"Piss off" said I and sprang out of bed and pushed him.
"You're not leaving fast enough" I said and spat in his face.
This kind of insanity become commonplace and my friends and acquaintances, even my son Dominic, were on edge whenever I was around. You just didn't know what to expect next. One night

Sean Kelly, Dominic and I, and a few others were in Fat City and as the night came to a close Sean said he couldn't afford to pay so he was going to skip out on his tab and come back and pay another day.

"No, you're not" I said and grabbed him by the throat and started shaking him. Dominic pulled me off him but here was another friendship almost down the drain.

Our family Christmas developed a predictable pattern. On Christmas Eve our family and Ellen's sister and parents together with Chuck and Linda gathered at our house for dinner. We had an English style Christmas dinner with crackers and paper hats and Christmas pudding with cream. We invited an English guy we had befriended, Pete, and he was very touched when we gave him a gift of English candies and groceries and a case of Pete's Wicked Ale. Chuck read his Christmas Poem inspired by his having been robbed of a new leather jacket at gun point the previous Christmas Eve; here it is:

<u>CHRISTMAS PISTOL: A POEM FOR THE SECOND MILLENIUM CHRISTMAS</u>

"You shall love your crooked neighbour
With your crooked heart...."
<u>*As I Walked Out One Evening.*</u> *W. H. Auden*

Just as Christmas Eve day was stealing
into night and Heaven was swaddled
in the birthing wounds of twilight

In step with the sprung rhythm
of my spaniel Hopkins
I walked out that evening
and we stopped on the corner
of the deserted street
 where the white paint was peeling
like welcome on the widow's shuttered house
just down from stained glass being kindled
in the windows of Whiting Street Baptist
and it was there that someone came

*out of nowhere nameless and first-born
of the dark blind-siding me
with the sight of him begging
Directions to a house with too many
numbers to be part of any neighborhood
there save in his imagination
and so what appeared to be was not---
was not only <u>any</u> Child in the manger
or not just <u>any</u> perfect stranger
desperately last minute stopping me*

*With his gun knocking on the door
of my temple's Temple of the Holy Ghost
as he carolled no blunt hymn
I had heard before
in which like any merchant
taking God's name in vain for the money
I was innocent of that night
he offers me a once in a lifetime bargain
he cuts me a heartfelt deal ending
with, "...or I'll blow your goddamn
head off, for Christ's sake!"*

*And so rifling my pockets he exchanged
those season's greetings for two or more
of Eternity's minutes tapping on my jaw
like the Little Drummer Boy
gone dark scarred and mad
his baton a Christmas pistol
in which the trembling behind my calm
knew that there is where the finale
of Advent waited down the blue black
tunnel in the cold chambered stable
in the still hollow-point crib*

*And in his chilling quest
I was blessed and penniless
as he was teaching me his shadow
I was teaching him mine*

*and all my attention was a single
prayer I was barely aware of saying
until finally above us and within us
Heaven shifted on its axis*

*As I gave him who came like a thief
in the night my coat my sister's gift
of deep chocolate leather with a likeness
of our blue-green world on the back
with the words <u>Save the Planet</u> stitched
in gold cursive thread beneath it
written there where its story was spun
in the stolen heavens of that Holy Night*

*And then he fled toward himself
and what he had learned
I can only guess
but as for me in my rich robbed heart
I have come to find that I was witness
to no less a treasure than this---*

*That for all anything ever taken from me
was worth there is nothing this Christmas
and every Christmas and every day given
but gift upon gift on this poor poor Earth*

On Christmas Day we all went to Gina & Bobby's for dinner which included game birds shot by Ellen's Uncle Bill. Not only had he shot them he made a fine job of cooking them.

The year 2000 dawned without any of the predicted upheavals to our computer dependent society. Had the problem been exaggerated or had the scare stories in the press ensured that all critical system were made Y2K compliant? I guess we'll never know. I was not much looking forward to the new millenium because I knew I would soon run out of money which meant my drinking would be curtailed and I'd have to get a job because Sue's income was not adequate to cover our living expenses.

In May we booked a house for a week at Sunset Beach in North Carolina; Sue and I, Simon and Ellen and Jacob, James and Michele and Michele's two children Tyler and Lauren made up the party. Ellen, Jacob and I went down the day before everyone else, with Ellen driving. Sunset Beach is beautiful but it had one drawback for me; it didn't have a bar or a liquor store. As soon as we got there I told Ellen I had to have a drink so she drove me back off the Island and dropped me at a bar in Calabash and came back for me two hours later. More and more it was becoming obvious how enslaved to alcohol I was.

When we got back from Sunset Beach I had completely run out of money. To keep drinking I resorted to theft. I would take one of Sue's checks from her check book and go to Thomas Street Tavern where I would pay my tab with the check and get $20 or $30 cash back to see me through the day. I would also do odd jobs for Ellen in the yard in the morning and sometimes she paid me $20. I even resorted to searching the drawers in my house and Simon's and James's houses for quarters, nickels and dimes to put together the price of a couple of drinks. When Sue's bank statement came I threw it away which postponed the denouement until one day a check bounced. Sue confronted me and I admitted I'd been stealing from her. She had bills of over $2,000 and no money. In desperation I called Simon and explained our plight. I asked him to lend me $2,500 and told him I was going to quit drinking. He and Ellen came to see me and before giving me the check Simon said:
"What's the plan?"
"What do you mean?" I asked
"How are you going to quit drinking?" he inquired.
"I'm going to give it a shot myself for a week or two and if that doesn't work I'll get professional help. You realize I'm an alcoholic, which means I have a disease which might need treatment"
"Alright" said Simon and handed me a check for $2,500.
I started crying and Susan and Ellen gave me a hug.
"I think Simon needs a hug too" said Ellen and for the first time for a long time Simon and I hugged each other

That weekend Simon, Ellen and Jacob, Bobby and Gina and Kim were going to stay in a house they had rented at a Methodist Retreat in the North Carolina mountains at Lake Junalaska. They asked me and Sue to go with them and Simon said he would pay for us to stay in a hotel at the Retreat Center. Being Methodist the whole place was dry which was fine by me. On my fifth day without a drink we went from Lake Junalaska to Asheville to a folk festival. I went to a bookstore and Simon bought me a book called "How Alcoholics Anonymous Failed Me". During the outdoor folk concert I got an overwhelming desire to have a drink. I made an excuse that I was going to the bathroom and headed for the nearest restaurant where I sank three pints of beer in ten minutes.

When I got back to Charlotte I was back to my old occupation of day long drinking but after two or three days of this I spoke to the director of Mercy Horizons Outpatient program, Bob Martin, and he arranged for me to go there immediately to meet one of his counselors, Susan. She explained that the program was designed to help people with alcoholism or drug addiction and that it involved a ten week intensive course, three half days and one evening a week. I told her I had noticed a lot of Alcoholics Anonymous material on the walls of the clinic and that this disturbed me because I understood A.A. had a religious program and I was an atheist. I then handed her the book "How Alcoholics Anonymous Failed Me". I think she was put out by my hostile and aggressive manner; it was unlikely the program would help me if I was not fully committed to it. She arranged for me to come in the next day at 9 am to see Brenda Yelton, the senior counselor. I then headed straight for the pub and tied on one almighty drunk just as I had done years previously in Ireland before being admitted to hospital.

Next morning Brenda Yelton listened to my story and said:
"I think that before you come into the out-patient's program you need to spend five days in the de-tox unit in Mercy Hospital, there is a danger of seizures if you stop on your own, without medical supervision, because of the quantity you drink and the length of time you have been drinking."
"When do you want me to be admitted" I asked.

"Right now," said Brenda, "I'll walk you over"
I will always remember the date, July 13th, 2000. The day I quit drinking for good. To help me with coming off alcohol they put me on a large dose of Librium, ten times what I was already taking. Gatorade, water and food were available in limitless quantities day and night. Alcoholics who quit drinking still have an incredible thirst and also begin to re-discover the pleasures of eating. Smoking was also permitted in the whole of the de-tox unit.

The next day an Alcoholics Anonymous meeting was held in the dining room and Bill, an old black guy, who conducted the meeting, really laid it on thick about the need for religion. He said;
"You will fail in this program unless you are washed in the blood of the lamb."
I had already read some A. A. literature and knew that Bill had it wrong; what the A. A. program suggested was belief in a "Higher Power" or " a God of my understanding". I joined A.A. at this meeting by picking up a white chip.

On 18th July I left the de-tox unit and reported to Brenda at the outpatients clinic. For the next ten weeks I attended the clinic every Monday, Tuesday and Thursday morning and Wednesday evening. Wednesday evening was a family event and I'm glad to say than not only my wife and sons attended but also my daughter-in-law, Ellen and James' fiancee Michele.

About three days after I joined the program I mentioned that I took Librium. There was consternation. This was an addictive drug and I absolutely had to give it up if I wanted to succeed in the program. Librium had a similar depressive effect to alcohol and it was felt that one would lead to the other. It seemed strange to me, if this were the case, that the de-tox doctor had prescribed massive doses of Librium for me whilst I was in the in-patients program. Nevertheless, I did as I was told and stopped cold turkey. This probably was not a good idea because for the next couple of weeks until I saw a doctor I suffered terribly from withdrawal symptoms.

The day after starting the out-patient program I received a call from an old friend, Miriam Diamond. Her husband, Harvey, had died a few weeks previously; we agreed to meet at her house the following day and Sue and I went there together. After we had talked for an hour or so Miriam asked:
"Do you need a job, Gary?"
"I do" I replied.
"My son, Steven, will be calling you and he will find something for you." she said.

The next day Steven called me and I went straight to his office and he offered me a job finding sites for his shoe retailing business. He provided me with a car and paid me a few hundred dollars a week. I started immediately and worked for him for about ten months when he laid me off. Dominic also went to work for him in a managerial position at $700 per week but also was laid off within a year. Nevertheless I was grateful to Miriam and Steven for being there when I needed help. Without a job to occupy my time it would have been much harder to stay off the booze.

Brenda Yelton introduced me to a doctor, George Hall, and after an hour's conversation he diagnosed me as suffering from bi-polar disorder (manic depression). It was amazing to me that none of the doctors I had seen previously in England and Ireland over a twenty five year period had made this diagnosis. He prescribed Zyprexa, Wellbutrin and Prozac. This combination of drugs has made me much more level headed. I no longer have my crazy episodes, neither do I have deep depressions anymore.

On 14th October, 2000, James and Michele were married in a beautiful outdoor setting at the River House in Ashe County. The wedding ceremony was performed by my friend, the poet, Chuck Sullivan, beneath a sycamore tree overlooking the New River. Chuck read a poem he had written that day and here it is:

THE PERFECT LIKENESS; THE OCTOBER WEDDING OF JAMES AND MICHELE

*Out of the clear blue marrying
awe of this field
of depth within the singular
branched murmuring of breezed tambourines
at play upon the trunk-freckled Cathedral
Behold of this old old unleaving sycamore
Autumn is coming and going of Age*

*Like a shimmering slip of a little flower
girl fleeing October's shifting fixed
river of promises running clean
through its heart vested in nothing
less than crisp caught flames
 of color falling to the lot of Earth
where in the spun troth of all their dances
leaves tremble like lovers taking their chances*

*And so James and Michele
in the striking nature of our fallen world
the wedding of your pledges will rise
to the occasion of all our hearts
in harvest here where beside us
and at our center
what is current becomes eternal*

*As on the holy cold clear and slowly
cobblestoned New River the procession
of witnessing leaves sails past us
on the speckled drift of her rippling
altar and with them watching over them
and us in the flowing focus
of the moment to be captured*

*When The River has nothing
and everything to do with Time
The Lord God in the wink of an eye*

*like any good wedding photographer
blends in with His surroundings*

*And then with the wind's fastest
most shuttering film and His Heart's
widest most trembling lens
He welcomes you
He takes your picture
He snaps you two into One
He silvers you in His Image
He prints you
He pronounces you*

*Man and Wife in the perfect likeness
of all the vows of light*

I knew being at a boozy wedding would test my resolve to stay sober. One of my former drinking cronies, Simon Oxford was there with his wife, Sue's sister Carol and their children, Tanya and Lorna. They had traveled from London for the wedding. I knew I would be very tempted to drink with Simon Oxford. I solved the problem of getting involved in drinking with Simon by going to an A.A. meeting both nights that we were at the River House and Sue went with me. We were joined at Saturday night's A.A. meeting by another of the wedding guests who was also in A.A.

We followed up the wedding with another "dangerous" activity; a trip to Tybee Island with the Oxfords and Ellen and Jacob. Once again I fell back on the local branch of A.A.. I got into the habit of regularly attending A.A. meetings and the Abutment Group, a meeting for alcoholics who also suffer from clinical depression, or bi-polar disorder. These groups do seem to help because when I quit going to them for a few months I became so depressed that I spent most of the time sleeping. I work part-time now as a courier/recorder for Deane Brunson's law firm so Sue and I are working together again. It would be good to earn more money but I am grateful for what I have got. I'm sober, generally I'm neither manic or depressed, I have grown spiritually since quitting drinking, and I am able to enjoy my family especially my grandchildren. Ellen and Simon had a second baby boy on 29th May, 2001, Ethan Benjamin, and Sue and I both think he is like our second son James Benjamin.

James sold his little house for a handy profit and together he and Michele, as man and wife, and Michele's children, Tyler and Lauren, moved into a new home in South Charlotte. James has been appointed as Chair of the Photography Department at CPCC and seems very happy. Dominic has found a girl friend, Anne Kelly, but still has not found the right job. I assume it is only a matter of time before he gets settled.

And so life goes on………one day at a time…….

Gary Spence, Charlotte, North Carolina, May 9th, 2002

CHAPTER ONE

"od thy foot up" Harold

My father, Harold George Spence, was born at home on July 8th, 1915. Home was Quarry Street, Heaton, Bradford, in the West Riding of Yorkshire. His mother, my grandmother, Bertha Harriet Spence, was 20 years old and unmarried having been born on 28th June, 1895. She lived with her parents John Sutcliffe Spence & Harriet Spence. Her father worked as a dyers laborer. Her three brothers, Alfred Brighty, Victor and Gilbert were all away in the army. Alfred Brighty was killed just a few days before my father was born on the first day of the Battle of the Somme. Alfred was in the Bradford Pals Battalion, the majority of whom were killed on the first day of that battle. Only two hundred and twenty three survived out of a total of two thousand. Victor was in the Royal Army Medical Corps (RAMC) and was not involved in the First World War being stationed in Ireland where British troops were struggling to hold on to this prize possession of the British Empire. He told me that on one occasion he was fired on while marching unarmed to church service in Fermoy, County Cork. My father used to annoy Victor by saying that RAMC stood for Rob All My Comrades not Royal Army Medical Corps. Father never knew who his own father was, something he bitterly regretted and resented all his life. His mother would only say it was a soldier, home on leave, that she had only met him once and didn't know his name.

There was no formal adoption or even fostering agreement but Harold was "given" to Mark Newbould and his wife Sarah Elizabeth, a childless couple, who also lived in Quarry Street. Mark had been born in Eastby near Skipton in the Yorkshire Dales in 1857 and was fifty eight at the time Harold was born. My father went to his grave not knowing who his father was. An old Heatonian, Percy Moorhouse, who would have been seven or eight years old when father was born told me after father died that everyone in Heaton knew Mark Newbould was Harold's biological father. This seems probable because not only did Mark and his wife bring father up they also provided him with a home and a job as a gardener when he left school in 1931. Mark Newbould's wife's maiden name was Greenwood. She was a member of a large old Heaton family. Unknown to father he had lots of relatives in the Parish where he was born, was to live almost all his life, and was to die.

When Harold was thirteen, in 1928, his mother, Bertha, married Ben Hartley, a man twenty years her senior and they went to live in Ben's house at 37 Rufford Street in Bradford Moor. They were married on 26th December, 1928. Ben was a textile laborer and Bertha a plush weaver. At this point grandmother claimed my father back from the Newboulds and he had three very unhappy years with her and his stepfather. Harold went to St. Barnabas Church School from the age of five to the age of ten when he transferred to Carlton Secondary School, on Tumbling Hill Street near where Bradford University is now situated. He failed to matriculate and left school when he was sixteen in 1931. This was the depths of the depression which had begun the year before. Bradford was the leading worsted textile town in Britain and the world center for the buying and selling of wool, alpaca, cashmere and silk. The depression hit hard in Bradford and father could not find a job. He used to say:
"I was born in a war, brought up in a depression, fought in a war – you kids don't know you're born".
He moved out of his mother's house and Mark Newbould took him back in and gave him a job working with him as a jobbing gardener; they worked together until father joined

Gary Spence

the army in 1939.

My mother, Mary Atkinson, was born at home on 17th October, 1915 and was named for her maternal grandmother. Home was a back to back house in Dudley Street in the Dudley Hill area of Bradford. Her father, Ashbel Atkinson, was born on 15th September, 1892 at Dacre Banks in the Yorkshire Dales. His father was called Joseph and his mother Hannah. His father and older brother were railwaymen. His mother and father were old when he was born and his father died before he was grown up. He had an elementary education and moved to Bradford at the age of fourteen where he was apprenticed to a farmer for seven years. The annual wage was £10.00 but he also received board and lodgings. The lodgings were a room in an outhouse and the food was very sparse. Grandfather told me all he got to drink was skimmed milk which in those days was considered unfit for human consumption and was usually fed to the pigs..

Ethel Moister, my maternal grandmother was born on 2nd January, 1892 in Shipley Fields Road, Frizinghall and later moved to Laisterdyke and went to Lawn Street School. Her father, Joseph, was a housepainter. At the age of nine she became a half-timer going to school in the morning and working at Gaunts mill in the afternoon. When she was fourteen she started to work in the mill full time as a burler and mender. Her walk to work took her past the farm where Ashbel Atkinson worked and they met, when they were both eigthteen, as he was driving the cows into the milking parlour. Soon they were courting and in March, 1915, Ethel discovered she was pregnant. Ashbel walked out of his apprenticeship and became a milk dealer for better wages and on 6th April, 1915 they were wed. Mother was born on 17th October, 1915 to be followed by her brother, Jack, and sister, Anne. Soon after Ashbel and Ethel were married Ashbel joined the Durham Light Infantry. He served in France in the First World War and suffered in a mustard gas attack.

Following a move from Dudley Street to Parsonage Road, Laisterdyke, Mary went to Lawn Street Elementary School where she was a quick learner and when she was ten, in 1925, her teachers persuaded her to sit the entrance exam for Bradford Girls Grammar School. She passed with high marks and was awarded a scholarship, which meant that no fees would be payable. Ashbel and Ethel would not let her go to the Grammar School. They saw no point in secondary education especially for a girl who would end up as a housewife. Anyway, they told Mary, they couldn't afford the school uniform. Mary stayed at Lawn Street School until the minimum age for leaving, fourteen, when she followed in her mother's footsteps and went to work in a mill. On 31st October, 1931 the family moved from Laisterdyke to 119 Haworth Road, the first house to be occupied on a large council estate about a mile from Heaton Village.

In 1937 Harold met Mary at a dance in St. Barnabas Hall on Rossefield Road just round the corner from Quarry Street. After the dance he walked her home to Haworth Road. Soon they were courting and were married on April 10, 1939 at St. Barnabas Church on Ashwell Road, Heaton. They rented 23 Quarry Street and moved in after the wedding. Just five months later Britain entered the Second World War and father volunteered for the Royal Artillery.

I was born on 25 February 1944 at Ilkley in Yorkshire. My mother, was evacuated from Bradford to Semon's Nursing Home, Ilkley because of the danger of bombing in Bradford. The Germans had only dropped a couple of bombs on Bradford but it was considered a target because of the textile mills and munition factories.

My grandfather, Mark Newbould, died in 1944, shortly after my birth, having been predeceased by his wife, Sarah, who died on 15th, August, 1941.

On 1 March my maternal Grandfather, Ashbel Atkinson, came to bring me and my mother home. He was by this time chauffeur to Neville Packett, a textile manufacturer, and had borrowed the car. A car was a rare sight on Quarry Street, where our house was, and it attracted the attention of the neighbours who came out both to look at the car and me. Inside the house my mother's sister,

Auntie Anne, was awaiting our arrival with my two year old brother Michael.

There was no father to greet me. He was thousands of miles away in Freetown, Sierra Leone, West Africa. He had been there six months and would serve there as a sergeant with the Royal Artillery for another year. My father had only been home on leave five or six times before sailing on the Mauretania to Sierra Leone. Both my older brother, Michael, who was born on 8th October, 1941, and I were conceived during leaves and were not to know our father until he was demobbed in January 1946, by which time Michael was five and I was two. In April 1946 another brother, John was born and the family was complete.

By any standards we were poor. My father was a jobbing gardener before the war working with Mark Newbould and earning about £3.00 per week. After the war he was employed as one of four gardeners by Sir Harry Shackleton (son of Shackleton of Antarctic fame) in Parsons Road, Heaton, Bradford at a wage of £4.00 per week. He supplemented this by growing plants and vegetables in two allotments at the top of Quarry Street and by working evenings and weekends doing jobbing gardening.

The house in which we lived had one room and a kitchen downstairs and one large bedroom upstairs which had been partitioned to create two rooms. My parents had the back bedroom and my brothers and I shared the front bedroom. There was a coal shed and an outside W.C. in a small back yard. There was no bathroom or toilet or hot water in the house other than that provided by a fire back boiler. Baths were taken weekly in a tin bath which was filled with hot water using a lading can. Due to the shortage of hot water my brothers and I were bathed in the same water. About 1950 my parents had a bath installed in the kitchen with a gas geyser for hot water.

The main room, called the living room, was used for sitting, playing, eating, baking and cooking, and when the weather was wet, which was often, for drying clothes on a clothes horse in front of the fire place. The fire place was a Yorkist Range, a cast iron fire place with an oven heated by the fire as well as a fire back boiler for hot water. Mother used to black lead this range every week. Although there was a small gas cooker in the kitchen mother always baked bread and made stews, pies and cakes in the range oven. Again, in about 1950, my parents had the Yorkist Range pulled out and replaced with a modern tiled fireplace. Now all the cooking had to be done on the gas stove.

There was no heating in the house other than the fireplace so the bedrooms were cold in winter. Ice would form on the inside of the windows and we would make spy-holes by placing a warm penny against the glass.

Growing up in Bradford we did not realise how bad the weather was; it rained almost every day and if it wasn't raining it "looked like rain" or it was "trying to rain" or it was "spitting". We also suffered from very bad fogs caused both by low cloud and the smoke from over a hundred mill chimneys and fifty thousand houses. This was before the Clean Air Acts and the only fuel being used at this time was coal which produced particularly harmful smog leading to a high incidence of bronchitis and other chest complaints. Most of the buildings in Bradford, built in golden mill stone grit, were completely black because of the smoke. When it snowed the surface of the snow would turn black within a few days. To try to give a picture of how bad the weather is in Bradford let me quote a passage written by an American visitor, George Tice, in the foreword to his photography book "Stone Walls – Grey Skies"

> "Thinking of the North of England I think of the weather. To say it rains there isn't sufficient. To say it is cold and windy isn't strong enough. Sometimes, walking up the hill from the Museum to the nearby college flat where I resided [in Bradford] I've leaned forward to see if I could fall on my face but the wind kept me from doing so…… I wore thermal underwear and many layers of clothing: shirt, pants, vest, jacket, gloves, scarf and a final layer of waterproofs, tops

> *and bottoms…… yet as I looked at the people about me, many were not even wearing a jacket and those that were never zippered them. Young and old alike dressed that way and appeared impervious to the weather. There are only three other places where I have experienced the coldness of winter as it was there: Leningrad, the Adirondack region of New York State; and northern Maine."*

Our little cottage was built of stone as were all the older houses in Bradford. Even the roof had stone slates. The floor downstairs was of stone flags. The steps to the bedrooms and to the small cellar were also of stone. The street itself was paved with stone cobbles. All this stone had been quarried locally, hence the name Quarry Street. Even the local pub was called "The Delvers"; a delver being a colloquialism for a quarry worker.

Despite our poverty we were not in the worst housing in Bradford and father had a job where he was able to grow vegetables and fruit, some of which he brought home. I never remember being hungry for long as a child but I do remember being afraid. That fear was of my father who had a violent temper. I never saw him hit my mother except by accident when she had placed herself between him and one of us children to prevent us from being hit. I do remember him threatening my mother with violence on many occasions:
"So help me Mary I'll lam you" he would say.
I never heard anyone else but him use the word "lam" but Harold did have a unique vocabulary. I suppose "lam" may have been a Yorkshire dialect word or short for lambaste. He hit me frequently from the age of five until I was about twelve. There was the slap across the head delivered in anger when I had done something that displeased him. I didn't particularly fear this, what I feared was his leather belt across my bare arse. Not only did this hurt, it was humiliating. I was made to pull my trousers and underwear down and lie across a chair arm. I would then be given from one to six strokes of the belt. There was one period when every Friday night about 6 o'clock he would give me six strokes of the belt. This was

Making Hen's Meat

a punishment for what he called "undetected crime" or "dumb insolence". I do not know where this sadistic streak came from; whether he was brutalized as a child or maybe by six years in the Army.

Most areas of Bradford were solid working class with row upon row of back-to –back houses built between 1850 and 1900, or in the outlying areas vast council estates built in the 1920's, 1930's, and 1950's. Heaton, where we lived, was different. Heaton was very middle class. This was where the mill owners, wool merchants and their managers and professional and clerical workers lived. Emm Lane, Park Drive, Parsons Road and Leylands Lane had magnificent detached villas; more modern and modest housing was to be found in the private housing estates such as the Duchy Estate. Here the houses were smaller but still detached or semi-detached and definitely a cut above Quarry Street.

The old Heaton Village center survived and was comprised of just five streets – Highgate, where the shops, the Baptist Chapel, and St Bedes Roman Catholic School were located, Ashwell Road where there were terrace houses on one side and back-to-back houses on the other. St. Barnabas Church and the Church School were also located on Ashwell Road as was the Bishop of Bradford's residence and Ashwell Farm. Dyson Street was a very short unpaved street with workshops on one side and back-to-backs on the other. Rossefield Road had terrace houses on both sides and the village hall - St Barnabas Hall. Quarry Street had a mixture of houses: three storey terraced, back-to-backs, and three groups of older "through" cottages in one of which we lived. There was also Drivers grocery shop and a dairy on Quarry Street.

You had to live in a place like Heaton in the 1950's or before to know that the social divisions were infinitely more complex than simply a working class/middle class division, and were based largely on the type of house you lived in. This was more important than being classified by occupation although that was a factor.

In Quarry Street alone there were at least four grades of housing, ranging from the three story terraced to the back to backs. Our cottage, because it was a "through" and had a tiny front garden and back yard fell between the two. In Quarry Street terms we were halfway up the social scale but in terms of Heaton as a whole we were definitely at the bottom. People who lived in the villas of Park Drive or the detached and semi-detached houses of the Duchy Estate saw only a working class street and were unaware of the finely drawn social distinctions within Quarry Street itself.

If you lived in a completely back-to-back housing area you didn't know you were poor because you had nothing to compare yourself to. Everyone around you was in the same boat. Living where we did, an island of workers occupying sub-standard housing, in a sea of business owners, managers, clerical workers, professionals and shop-keepers we were very aware of our poverty. How we envied the people with inside lavatories and bathrooms. Many of them had motorcars even as early as the 1950's. Some had refrigerators and washing machines and would you believe televisions on which they could watch one channel, the BBC, in black and white and broadcasting only in the evenings. A big boost in TV sales was caused by the coronation of Queen Elizabeth II in 1953. I clearly remember going with my family to my Great Uncle Victor's house in Eccleshill, a suburb of Bradford, to watch the coronation on TV. I remember the incredibly pompous Richard Dimbleby describing the scene in hushed and reverential tones. It seems as if the broadcast went on for five or six hours; certainly it was long enough to bore me and by brothers, Mike and John, to tears. We would much rather have been playing out.

My father used to give my mother £3.00 a week for house keeping. The rest of his wage he kept and he also kept all the money he earned from evening and weekend work. I rarely remember him without the price of a pint of beer or a packet of ten cigarettes. Out of the £3.00 my mother had to pay the rent (later a mortgage when they bought 23 Quarry Street from the landlord) rates, electric bill, gas bill, insurance man, milkman, coal man and feed and clothe a family of five, and save for holidays and Christmas. It couldn't be done so most of the time when we were

growing up mother had a part time job. She worked as a cleaner for Mrs. Milnes in Highgate and Mrs. Armstrong in Back Lane; she worked in an office at a textile factory; she worked as a shop assistant in Horrocks Bakery in Duckworth; she served lunches in a café on Broadway in the center of Bradford, she bartended at the Delvers and she worked the evening shift at Lister's Mill, burling and mending. I remember that whenever the subject of money came up between father and mother she would say:
"Harold I can't make hen's meat."
Twenty years later I realized that she was saying she couldn't make ends meet.

It is still a mystery how she juggled the finances and kept us afloat. I know that when it came to food we children and father came first. Many times she would say she wasn't hungry when the truth was there wasn't enough food for us all. She used to take me to the Co-operative Store down Heaton Road, a walk of about a mile, to do her weekly grocery shopping. Here she bought the basics, tea, sugar, butter, cheese, bacon, lard, flour, salt and so on. Cheese was sliced with a wire from a whole wheel and bacon was sliced on a Berkel machine. Food was rationed but this barely affected us because the available money could often buy less than the amount permitted by rationing.

Other food was bought locally at the shops in Highgate on a daily basis. This was the days before supermarkets and there was a surprising collection of shops in Heaton Village. On Quarry Street was Driver's grocery and greengrocery store. At the bottom of the street facing Highgate was Sowden's, tobacconist and sweet shop and on the opposite corner Leonard Atkinson's cobblers shop. Next door was Rhodes' bakery and grocery store. Across Highgate was John Lumb's Garage. A short walk past the graveyard brought you to Bartles which sold sweets, some groceries and tobacco.

At the other side of Sowden's was the Delvers pub and then Wade's Chemist shop and a few yards away Tom Holt's, the butcher, where my mother shopped for meat. Tom was a son of Annie Holt our next door neighbour. In the next block was a bakery and confectioners with a ladies hair dresser, Fasnacht's, adjacent. Another few yards down the hill was a draper's shop and next to that Eddie Baines' newsagent, sweet shop and tobacconist. Then there were three shops set back from the road, Crockett's Dry Cleaners, Joe Parson's fish & chip shop and Williams' green grocer, fish and game merchant. Behind these shops was the Kings Arms garage. The next block housed the Kings Arms pub and next to that was a post office that also sold fruit and vegetables. There was another garage opposite the post office operated by Harry Monk. At the corner of the next street, Ashwell Road, was Walker's, a high class grocery store, which sold freshly ground coffee and a wide selection of cheeses and cooked meats. Across from Walkers was Jack Tetley, another butcher. A small lending library on Rossefield Road brought the total number of business establishments in this small village to twenty three. It is a very different story today. Both butcher shops have gone as have all three grocery stores and the chemist. The drapers is no longer there nor is one of the sweet shops, the lending library and the drycleaners. They have been replaced by gift shops, a florist, antique shops, a fast food outlet and a restaurant. One of the butcher's shops has been turned into a private residence.

Eddie Baines, who ran the newsagents, sweet and tobacco shop on Highgate, was constantly miserable. I mentioned to my father that I'd never seen him smile. Father said the only time he had been happy was in the R.A.F. during the war. Just mention that to him and you'd see him smile. The next time I was in his shop I said: "What about the good old days in the R.A.F?"
He did more than smile, he positively guffawed. I have often wondered what it was about the R.A.F. that he had liked so much.

At the top of Ashwell Road was Ashwell Farm owned by the Tetley family who also owned the milk round in Heaton and one of the butcher's shops. Chicken used to be very expensive and was a real luxury. It cost more per pound than beef, lamb or pork and we only ate chicken once a year on Christmas day. I remember going to the farm to pick up our Christmas chicken one Sunday morning. Jack Tetley, the butcher, was plucking a chicken and it kept on clucking and he would hit it and tell it to 'be quiet'.

Making Hen's Meat

I thought he was plucking the chicken alive but he assured me that the clucking was some kind of nervous reaction that continued even after death.

The most enjoyable part of my mother's day was her walk to the shops to buy something for that day's dinner and tea. First stop was Tom Holt's butcher shop where she would buy a cheap cut of beef, skirting or shin or perhaps sausages or a slice of corned beef. She would also buy fresh eggs here. Next she would go into the baker's which sold potted meat and salmon spread. She would buy four ounces or if money was tight as little as two ounces. Then into Williams' the greengrocer, especially in the winter when father was unable to grow vegetables. Here she might buy a cabbage, a few onions, perhaps carrots or a turnip. I remember on one occasion when her budget must have gone awry that we just had a turnip mashed up for dinner.

If she was feeling flush, or if we had company coming she would go to Walker's and buy four ounces of boiled ham, sliced the thinnest possible, number 1 on the Berkel slicer. Sometimes she would shop at Drivers' on our street. A particular favourite was their stew pack, which contained a rabbit, potatoes, an onion and a few carrots.

This shopping trip would take at least an hour, and could take two, because all the way there and back she was meeting other women and stopping to gossip, about the weather, about husbands and children, about illness. This is where rumours were started and spread and for many of the women at this time this was their sole social activity.

The men, of course, had the pub. You would rarely see a woman in the Delvers or King's Arms except on Saturday nights or a special occasion such as a birthday or wedding anniversary. Even then they were not allowed in the tap room, which was a strictly male preserve Here the men would play dominoes and darts and find some respite from their wives and from the daily grind of their lives.

CHAPTER TWO

"on your way brother" Harold

I was a sickly child. When I was three years old I was diagnosed as having bronchial asthma, which plagued me until I was fourteen when it disappeared just as suddenly as it had arisen. This meant lots of house visits from Doctor Liversedge and weeks on end in bed or lying on the sofa in front of the fire. I was given doses of Effrylix and M & B pills.

By the time I was two my older brother Michael was going to St. Barnabas School so my early childhood memories are of me and mother and younger brother, John. My brother Michael had a pet rabbit but it was not kept in a cage, it had the run of the house and of the little front garden and back yard. It sometimes got out of the yard and would wander around Heaton but always came back home. One day it did not return and the next day Walter May, who lived across the street, came to our door to tell us Mike's rabbit had been in his allotment eating his lettuce and cabbage so he had killed it:
"But never mind Michael" he said "I've brought you a nice bowl of rabbit stew."

Until we were old enough to start helping father with his gardening we rarely saw him. Monday through Friday he left home before 8 am and returned just after 5 p.m. Once he had eaten his tea he would leave to work in the allotment or in someone's garden. In the allotment he had a greenhouse with a

Making Hen's Meat

coke fired stove and oil lamps for lighting. This meant he could be there even in the depths of winter when there was no day light after 4 p.m.. He would return about 8 p.m. when we were already in bed, wash, shave and change and go to the pub where he stayed until closing time, which was then 10 p.m..

My father was something of a magpie. He collected tools, screws and nails, scrap metal and pieces of wood wherever he could find them. As children we were brought into this collecting game and if we came home with a couple of nails or better still a piece of lead, father was very pleased. Once a year he would take the lead and other metals to a scrap metal merchant where he would get a few pounds for it. There were still quite a few horses pulling carts at this time and if one shit in Quarry Street or Rossefield Road I was sent with a bucket and shovel to collect the horse shit and bring it home. Father would take it to his allotment where he would add it to his compost heap.

Father used to save his cigarette butts or 'tab ends' as he called them. Every few months he would empty the tin of cigarette butts onto the table and we three boys had to take the paper off the butts and and place the tobacco in another tin. When the tin was full father would put a few slices of potato in with the tobacco to moisten it. A few days later out would come the tobacco tin and father would get out his Rizla papers and cigarette machine and roll himself a hundred cigarettes or more.

Quarry Street led from the main street, Highgate, to a track through the allotments which led to Heaton Woods and open country – a pocket of green between Bradford and Shipley. Behind Quarry Street was Heaton Hill, a recreation ground with swings, a roundabout and a rocking horse. There were magnificent views from the hill top of Baildon Moor and Ilkley Moor. On a clear day you could see all the way up the dales to Ingleborough, one of Yorkshire's highest mountains, a distance of forty miles. With the woods and the hill and nearby Lister Park, we had great places to play as children. We didn't realise how lucky we were at the time, but looking back on it we had some almost idyllic days in the long summer holidays.

Gary Spence

In the summer we often camped out on Heaton Hill, and my best friends and I, Duncan Moorhouse and Barry Dean formed a secret society called the Black Hand Gang. We pricked our hands with a pin then pushed the pinpricks together so our blood mingled. Now we were blood brothers with ties more tight than those of biological brothers. Because of the age difference I played and socialised very little with my brothers, we all had friends of our own ages. The Black Hand Gang built a den in the small wood at the top of Heaton Hill. This was built of wood which we 'found" and had a roof of lino. From somewhere we obtained a primus stove and a battered old frying pan. We used to make Be Ro puffs. This was a kind of pancake, the main ingredients being Be-Ro Flour and water. We discovered at a very young age that food eaten outdoors tastes wonderful.

A favorite play-ground for us especially in the long summer holidays (school closed for six weeks) was Heaton Woods, which was a ten minute walk from Quarry Street. The woods cling to the side of a steep ravine with a stream running through the flat bottom. The trees were oak, ash, beech and sycamore. There were no fir trees or other evergreens. In summer the woods were full of blue bells which is a sure sign of very old woodland. The woods were then owned by Bradford Corporation who upkept the paths and bridges across the streams. Often our mother would pack a picnic for us, banana or tomato sandwiches and if we were lucky a few biscuits and a piece of pie or cake. To drink we usually had lemonade or dandelion & burdock. We played for hours in the stream, building dams with rocks, sticks and leaves. We also played cowboys and indians and, of course, soldiers – English versus Germans.

On one occasion Barry Dean and I were walking on Shay Lane, which bisects the woods, when we found a large metal drum at the side of the road. Clearly marked on the side were the words, Prussian Blue Dye, and the name, address and phone number of the distributor. Barry suggested we use this find to dye the stream blue so we rolled the barrel down the hill, through the gate and down to the stream. We tried everything to burst open that drum.

We dropped rocks on it, we rolled it off the bank of the stream onto rocks which were half submerged in the water. We jumped on it, we beat it with sticks, but we never did succeed in opening it. We then had the idea of being good citizens and reporting the find to the police. We walked to Duckworth Lane Police Station and told the duty sergeant of our find. We were taken in a police car back to the woods and we showed the police where the drum was located. We had to pretend we had found it there as we did not want to admit that we had rolled it down the hill and into the stream. The police then drove us home. Mother was very worried when she saw me getting out of a police car and was relieved that not only was I not in trouble but I had done something good for once.

About a week later the postman delivered an envelope addressed to me. This was a great thrill as there was never any post for me. Inside the envelope was a letter of thanks from the chemical distributor explaining that the drum had fallen off one of their trucks and a reward of a pound note. I shared this with Barry Dean, ten shillings each. I gave my mother five shillings, because she was always hard up, and kept five shillings for myself.

Sometimes we would venture further afield and walk to Northcliffe Woods. We went down Highgate and Shay Lane. We passed through Heaton Woods and at the small hamlet called Six Days Only we turned right onto a track which led to a public right-of-way across a golf course and into the woods. One of the houses at Six Days Only was owned by the Gudgeon family, who had a small-holding where they grew plants and shrubs for sale. Brian Gudgeon, who was in the same class as me at school, would often join us. Next door to the Gudgeons an old lady made and sold nettle beer. She collected the nettles from the surrounding fields and made this drink which was supposed to cure all manner of illnesses. When we got to Northcliffe Woods we headed for a man made pond, rectangular in shape, the original purpose of which was by this time forgotten. The pond was filled with mud to a depth of about nine inches and in the mud lived hundreds, maybe thousands, of frogs.

Gary Spence

We had come prepared. We were wearing wellington boots and some of us were carrying fishing nets and the others had old screw top sweet jars which we had begged from Sowden's shop. For the next hour there was only one objective – to catch as many frogs as possible. As we walked through the mud frogs would be leaping in all directions and croaking furiously in alarm. Those boys who had nets would try to scoop up a frog which would then be dropped into one of the sweet jars and the top screwed firmly on.

We would walk home tired and mud splattered but happy with our catch of thirty or forty frogs. We stopped at my father's allotments and let half a dozen frogs loose among the plants. Father would be pleased because he was convinced that frogs ate slugs. The rest we divided between us and we would have three or four each. There isn't really much you can do with a frog but one thing you can do is race them. We would chalk a start and finish line on the pavement and would hold the frogs at the start line and then on a signal from the appointed referee would let them go. First past the finish line was the winner. We would touch them on the arse with our index finger to make them jump. Inevitably some would jump in the wrong direction but we held enough races for everyone to have a winner. Once when we were racing the frogs two bigger boys, aged about fourteen, who we knew vaguely, walked up and started watching. These boys were from Buxton Street near Lister's Mill in Manningham. Although this was less than a mile from Heaton, it was considered a very rough area by Heatonians, and we were always a little nervous when boys from this neighbourhood came on to our street.

One of the boys, John, said he knew something really funny you could do with a frog. He told us to get a drinking straw so I went down to Sowden's shop and Mrs. Sowden gave me one. I ran back up Quarry Street and gave the straw to John. He bent down and picked up a frog, then straightened up and holding the frog tightly, he stuck the straw up its arse. He put the other end of the straw in his mouth and started to blow. The frog swelled up like a balloon and he did not stop blowing until it was almost the size of a football:
"Now for the fun bit." he said.

Making Hen's Meat

He threw the inflated frog as hard as he could against the wall of a nearby house. Splat! went the frog as it burst open and fell to the floor, a sickening mess. John and his friend roared with laughter and wanted to blow up another frog. We were horrified and gathered up our frogs and ran to Barry Dean's house.

Although there were few cars, Quarry Street was a busy street. There were about fifty houses and as we lived close to the bottom end of the street most of the residents passed our house as they went to and from their homes. We knew who was coming by the sound of their footsteps and the time of day without looking at them. You hardly ever see a cripple these days, but in the 1950's it was commonplace. I suppose this was because of injuries sustained in the First and Second World Wars and malnutrition leading to rickets. In our street was Josh Pitts with one leg and Joe Craven walking with two sticks because his legs were twisted and you saw people with knock knees and bow legs everywhere.

Monday was washing day, not only in Quarry Street, but throughout the country. Until mother got an old second hand washing machine in 1954 everything was washed by hand in a peggy tub and using a washboard and then put through a hand operated mangle. If the weather was fine the washing would be dried outside on washing lines hung between the houses on each side of the street. There were no secrets about who wore what and how often they changed:
"Look at that, only one pair of knickers on the line" mother used to say "the dirty common woman".
You could be sure that as soon as the washing was hung out a coal wagon would want to deliver to one of the houses at the top of the street. All the women had to come out of their houses and hold up the washing lines with props so the wagon could pass underneath. There were dozens of coal merchants in Bradford and it seemed as if they all delivered to someone in our street. Some still had horses and carts, others motor wagons. As well as coal men quite a procession of people passed up and down the street. The yeast man came on Tuesdays. It seems hard to believe that someone could make a living selling nothing but yeast. It shows how much home baking was going on at that time. He delivered with a pony

and cart. Of course, the milk was delivered every day, initially from churns out of which a pint was dipped and poured into the proffered milk jug. By the mid nineteen fifties this had changed to bottled milk, but still delivered every morning in time for breakfast. The rag and bone men used horse and carts and we would see them everyday:
"Rags, bones, and any old iron" they would cry.
We had a rag bag at the top of the cellar steps and any clothes that were beyond repair would be put in it. Now and then mother would call out to a passing ragman and he would walk up to the door and weigh the rags with his spring balance. He would try to palm mother off with a balloon but she always insisted on cash.

Rington's Tea van used to come round selling tea in quarter and half pound packets. Then there was the paper boy after school delivering the Telegraph and Argus. We only got a newspaper on Sunday – The People – mother and father always read their stars, as written by 'Lyndoe'. Mother believed in astrology. She also believed in re-incarnation. Number seven and eight were lucky numbers and thirteen was bad luck. There was luck in houses – if you were having bad luck it was the house's fault and you'd have to move. If you broke a mirror it was seven years bad luck. If you spilled salt you'd better throw some over your left shoulder. If somebody gave you a knife you must always give them money, even a penny would do, or the knife would cut your friendship. If you walked under a ladder, you were in real trouble. My mother's birthday was 8th October, and father's 8th July, John's was 8th April, Mike's 17th October, - and didn't seven and one make eight. Mother was perplexed that my birthday was 25th February and there was no way, even for mother's convoluted mind, to make an eight out of this. Don't step on the crack between the flag stones:
"If you step on a nick, you'll be buried in a brick, and all the beetles will come to your funeral".

Every week the rent man came on Friday night. I remember occasions when the door was locked and the lights turned off and we all had to keep quiet until the rent man went away. The insurance man also came for his few pennies premium. This was

Making Hen's Meat

purely insurance to pay for a funeral. It was a matter of pride that no matter how poverty stricken life was, in death there had to be a decent burial, not just a coffin and a parson, but a nice reception. Mother loved a good funeral and her highest praise for the food was to say:
"They buried him with ham"

The insurance man had some bizarre illness that caused his right leg to jerk spasmodically as he walked. Watching him cross the road was like watching John Cleese in the Monty Python sketch – " The Ministry of Silly Walks". So severe was the twitching and jerking of his right leg that it seemed as if he was taking one step forward and two steps back.

A couple of times a year gypsies would come round hawking paper flowers and clothes pegs which they had made. There was always one who told fortunes and mother never failed to "cross the palm with silver", even if it meant digging into a jar on the shelf which contained rent money and electric money. Once a year a knife grinder came round. He rode a bike and attached to the front wheel was a pulley which drove a belt to turn the grindstone. We also had an annual visit from a French onion seller. He also rode a bike and the onions were strung from the handle bars and cross bar and even round his neck. I suppose that he had a truck around the corner as it would hardly seem worth his while to ride a bike with a few strings of onions from the nearest port, Hull, a distance of eighty miles.

The most frequent visitor was the doctor, Dr. Martin, and when he retired, Dr. Liversedge. The war time Government had introduced the National Health Service. All visits, treatments, hospitalisation and medicines were free. For the first time the working class had a chance to look after their health and they took full advantage of it. Although the Doctor's surgery was only a ten minute walk away everybody wanted and got a house visit.

CHAPTER THREE

*"there are three crows on yonder tree
and they are black as buggery"* Harold

By the time I was four years old father was taking me to work with him. He had left Sir Harry Shackleton's employment and was now the full time gardener at 'Maylands', a house on the corner of Parsons Road and Park Drive. The employers were Mr. & Mrs. Craven and the wage was £5 per week. I remember my first day going to work. Mother got me up at 7.15 a. m., washed me and dressed me in short trousers, a shirt, pullover and jacket and boots like father's. She packed a handful of tea leaves, some sugar and a couple of home made biscuits into an old army haversack that father always took to work. After a breakfast of Weetabix and tea father and I were off to work at 7.45 a.m. Work began at 8 a.m. I remember the warmth of my father's hand as we walked down Quarry Street, left on Back Lane and past Duncan Moorhouse's house. Then left again down Rossefield Road, past St. Barnabas' Hall. Another left and we were on Ashwell Road passing St. Barnabas' Church and the church school, which I would go to as soon as I was five years old. Right turn down Parson's Road, very steep and we jog-trot down the hill, across Wilmer Drive and now we're passing Sir Harry Shackleton's house where father used to work. Sir Harry was very rich indeed. He still lived in very much an upstairs/downstairs fashion with a butler, housekeeper, three maids, two chauffeurs for the two Rolls Royce's and four gardeners.

After four years at £4 a week father had asked for a pay rise and had been refused; so he quit the jobs and went to work for the Cravens. For the rest of his life he would be constantly changing employers as the only way he saw to increase his earnings. The other gardeners in Heaton nicknamed him 'the Happy Wanderer'. He had no time for Sir Harry because of his refusal of a pay rise and as we passed his house he came out with a fine piece of Harold speak
"Honi soit qui mal y pense – bugger you Jack, I'm alright" he said. I was to hear this saying hundreds of times in the ensuing years. 'Maylands' was a large house at the bottom of Parsons Road, so large that it was later converted to a Nursing Home; my mother died there. The only staff were a housekeeper and my father, no butler, no maids, no chauffeur. It was apparent that the Cravens only just had enough money to live here.

Separate from the house was a range of out-buildings, stables, by then used as garages, a saddleroom, used by father as a potting shed, a yard with a glazed roof – used for washing cars and a large heated greenhouse. Father and I went into the saddleroom and he hung up his pack. It was a warm day in May so we both took off our jackets and father put on his gardener's apron. This had a very large front pocket for holding a trowel and hand fork, pruners and string and whatever tools and odds and ends father thought he would need that day.

We watered the plants in the greenhouse and coldframes. There were perlagoniums (we called them geraniums), lobelia, allysum, fuschias, ageratum, antirrhinums all to be used for "bedding out" which father refused to do until June because frost was possible until the end of May. The only frost free months in Bradford were June, July and August.

Next we checked the kitchen garden where he was growing potatoes, cabbage, brussel sprouts, peas, runner beans, shallots, radishes, beetroot, and a few herbs, mint, parsley, sage and thyme. He also grew chrysanthemums, gladioli and sweet peas for cut bloom.   After tying up the sweet peas, disbudding some chrysanthemums and earthing up potatoes we turned to the main task of the day, mowing the large lawn.

Lawns at this time were maintained like putting greens and mowed twice a week. There was no motor mower just a hand propelled Qualcast mower with only a twelve inch blade. As soon as he'd mowed a strip round the edge of the lawn father got the long handled edging shears and trimmed the edges of the lawn. My job, he explained, was to pick up the grass which had been trimmed from the edges and deposit it in a bucket which he would take to the compost heap. I quite liked this job. Kneeling down and working my way around the lawn picking up the grass brought me close to a herbaceous border, then a border filled with hybrid tee roses and finally a steep rockery at the top of which was a terrace leading to french windows into the house.

I was fascinated by what I saw as I moved slowly round the lawn and was constantly fetching father to look. There were worms and slugs and snails, wire worms and earwigs, caterpillars and ants. Spiders webs stretched between plants. Father would squash the caterpillars between thumb and forefinger and cut the slugs in two with his pen knife. I learned the difference between good and bad in a garden. Slugs and caterpillars were bad, they lived on the leaves of plants; wire worms were bad, they attacked the roots of plants. Earthworms were good, they helped to till and aerate the soil and so were spiders for they caught flies and midges which were a nuisance.

Gardening became a way of life for me and my brothers, Mike and John. Father left "Maylands" when I was five years old and set up on his own account as a jobbing gardener, following in the footsteps of his father, Mark Newbould. He would work for different families on a regular basis. Some jobs were a day or two each week, some jobs were a day a fortnight or half a day a week. All told at any one time he would have about ten customers. This gave him a lot of independence which suited his temperament for if there was any problem with a customer he would simply pack up his tools and leave knowing he only had to find a replacement customer for a day or half a day. At this time in Heaton finding

Making Hen's Meat

work as a gardener was easy. There were lots of houses with big gardens and only about six full time professional gardeners. Amongst them were Willie Hagyard, who lived on Highgate, Harold May, who lived on Rossefield Road and Bob Nellist, who lived on that stretch of Highgate called Paradise Row.

The problem, once you were on your own account, was that you were often working for families who were themselves struggling to pay for the upkeep of their big houses and gardens. So the pay was low and sometimes you were kept waiting for your money. The pay in 1950 would have been about three shillings an hour, £1.4.00d a day, for an eight hour day, £6 a week for a forty hour week. This was not enough to live on so father had to work long hours, evenings and weekends. He could earn more money in the summer because the hours of daylight were longer but the winter was a struggle.

As soon as I reached the age of seven I was paid wages and my spending money of six-pence a week was stopped. The pay was three pence an hour but father increased it each year so that by the time I was in my teens I was getting two shillings an hour. I suppose father must have charged the people for whom he was working for my labor. Knowing him he probably made a profit out of us. Mike and John also helped him and he had a succession of other helpers usually recruited from the local pub, the Delvers. John Burdon and Roy Hardy worked for him evenings and weekends for years, and as time went by father would spend more and more time in the pub leaving the gardening to us brothers and his other help.

He grew plants in his two allotments and greenhouse and these he sold to his customers. There were geraniums, antirrhinums, lobelia and allysum, salvias & fuschias, coleus and chrysanthemums and for the winter, wallflowers. What he could not grow, he bought from other allotment holders or from one of the many nurseries in the area. He also grew vegetables and tomatoes for home use. Gardening supplies and tools came from the ironmongers in Duckworth or were delivered from the Cleckheaton firm of Charles Kershaw & Son. Fertilisers and insecticides came from the Heckmondwike Chemical Company or Peter Yewdall's agricultural supply shop on Thornton Road.

As well as doing gardens he also tended about thirty graves in Heaton Cemetery which was right behind our Quarry Street house and adjacent to Heaton Hill. The main entrance was from Highgate, catty corner from the Baptist Church and Sunday School and between Rhodes bakers and grocers and Bartles sweet shop and tobacconists. From a very early age my brothers and I helped in the graveyard. Father used to charge £1 a grave per year and for this he planted the graves with geraniums, lobelia and allysum for the summer and wallflowers for the winter. All the plants had to be carried on a gantry from the allotment, down Nog Lane, across Heaton Hill, down the steps onto Garden Street, past Roland May's hen-run, and through Nellist's builder yard.

The worst part of this job was watering the plants. The only tap was in Nellist's builders yard and we children would have to fill a two gallon watering can and struggle to carry it to whichever grave father was working on. If we needed refreshments or to go to the lavatory we would go home. The route we took was the shortest one – up the twelve foot high wall onto Heaton Hill, down Nog Lane to home. In the corner of the graveyard the wall was built on a natural outcrop of rock which went to a height of about six feet where there was a level platform. This was easy to climb onto and it was then only a six foot climb and over the top to a four foot drop onto the Hill. The graveyard provided the extra money needed for Christmas. In November father sent out the bills and before Christmas he would have about £30. This paid for toys for us kids, he gave mother extra money for food and he bought beer and a pint of whisky.

Bob Nellist also looked after about twenty graves in the cemetery. Apart from the ones he and father looked after the rest were mainly overgrown. Bob Nellist, who had grown up in Heaton with my father, was one of Heaton's most eccentric and best loved characters. He had been in the Coldstream Guards in the Second World War and stood well over six feet tall. He had long sideburns and a handlebar moustache. He was still using a horse

Making Hen's Meat

and cart when everyone else had switched to motor vehicles. He made a living as a jobbing gardener and went to work in the horse and cart. For weekends he had a beautiful pony and trap and his little dog always ran along side. When he was dressed up he was a sight to behold. He wore a three piece cavalry twill suit with lapels on the waistcoat and a long jacket with patch pockets. His trousers were narrow and did not have turnups. He wore a check shirt and dark brown tie and a brown bowler hat and brown boots. He looked as if he had stepped straight out of the Edwardian era. Unfortunately he was killed when a car ran into his horse and cart at Sandy Lane crossroads. His funeral was the biggest Heaton had ever seen and the next time the Church was nearly as full was for my father's funeral.

Many of the small towns and villages in and around the Yorkshire Dales had annual agricultural and horticultural shows and father always took the day off work to go to Bingley Show and Kilnsey Show. There were competitions for the best pig, sheep, cow, horse and so on and also for the best fruit and vegetables. There was horse jumping and at Kilnsey a dry stone walling competition, sheep penning and a fell race. Father always entered the competitions for the best cabbage, potatoes, tomatoes and sweet peas. He almost always won several prizes of a few shillings and this was spent in the beer tent. I remember one year his tomatoes were not quite ripe and the night before the show he slept with them in the hope that the heat from his body would hasten the ripening process. In the competition for potatoes, four potatoes had to be displayed and it was critical that these be identical in every respect, color, size and shape. One year father dug up all the potatoes in his allotment but could not get four that matched; he had three but needed a fourth one. In desperation he went to the wholesale vegetable market and bought a hundred weight of potatoes and sure enough he found the one potato he needed to win first prize.

Father had his own way of deciding whether or not to garden for a potential new customer. There were two deciding factors. First he would consider the build of the potential employer. The closer they were to his size the more the likelihood that he would take the job. This was because they were a potential source of clothing that would fit him. I never remember father buying any clothes apart from underwear, dungarees and footwear. Trousers, shirts, ties, jackets, suits, raincoats and overcoats were all hand-me-downs from employers. Here was this fellow earning £6 a week gardening, going out to the pub in a £50 suit, and he almost always put a suit on to go to the pub. Even if it was nine at night when he finished work he would wash and change into a suit before going out.

The other deciding factor was whether or not there was an outside toilet. My father's bowels were one of his big topics of conversation and taking a shit was always a cause for drama. Probably because of the amount of beer he drank he was often caught short. Even at home everyone had to clear out of his way if he had to go the lavatory:
"Hey up! Give me a straight run through" he would shout.

On one occasion he was going to work at the Laycock's house on Haworth Road and was standing at the bus stop by the Baptist Chapel when an urgent need to shit arose. He threw the spade and fork he was carrying over the chapel wall for later collection and set of at a sprint across the road to the consternation of the people waiting at the bus stop. The quickest way home was through the graveyard and he ran dodging the graves to the wall corner which he had to climb: "I was half way up the wall when it happened" he would say recounting the episode.
As if I had never heard the story before I would say innocently:
"What happened Dad?"
" I shit my britches of course you silly little bugger" he would say.

From the age of five we children were sent to the Baptist Sunday School every Sunday afternoon from 2 o'clock to 4 o'clock. I always thought this was strange because neither mother or father were churchgoers. Many years later my mother confided in me that this was when she and father made love. No doubt this was the routine for other parents, which is why the Sunday School was so full. Despite sending us to their Sunday School father had no time for the Baptists. This was because they were opposed to

drinking alcohol. Father was sure many of them were hypocritical and were secret drinkers:
"Front door of the chapel and side door of the pub – that's your bloody Baptists for you" he would say.

The Sunday School superintendent was Mr. Brayshaw, a tall stem figure, who we all disliked intensely. All the lads and lasses from Quarry Street used to go to the Baptist youth club on Tuesday night and I was also in the Boys Brigade which met on Thursday. On one occasion after youth club Barry Dean, Keith Robertshaw, Duncan Moorhouse and I were wandering around when we saw Brayshaw's car in the driveway of the manse next to the Chapel and we vandalized it as our way of getting back at him for the harsh way he treated us at Sunday School. We made scratch marks on the paint and then we removed the petrol filler cap and took it in turns to piss into the petrol tank. We threw the petrol cap into the graveyard.

That night about ten o'clock my father woke me up:
"Come downstairs" he said " we have a visitor".
My heart missed a beat when I saw the visitor was none other than the dreaded Mr. Brayshaw:
" Now Gary, Mr. Brayshaw has a question for you" father said.
"My car has been damaged and the petrol cap stolen" said Brayshaw "did you have anything to do with this?"
"NO" I replied immediately.

The next day at school Margaret Roberts, the Baptist minister's daughter, told me Brayshaw was so upset at the damage to his car that he was going to call the police and give them the names and addresses of all the boys at the youth club. Margaret thought he wouldn't call the police if he got the petrol cap back. I said I'd try to find out who had done it and tell them to bring the petrol cap and put it in the driveway where the car had been parked. Margaret could then "find" it and return it to Mr. Brayshaw. That day after school. Barry, Keith, Duncan and I went to the graveyard and were lucky enough to find the petrol cap and dropped it in the driveway to the manse as promised. We never heard another word about the matter.

Gary Spence

At the bottom of Quarry Street was Sowden's sweet and tobacco shop. Mr. & Mrs. Sowden and their son, Dennis, lived behind and over the shop. Their living room was a lean to single storey structure and from its roof protruded a chimney. One day Duncan, Barry and me were playing out in the street when we noticed that the smoke from the Sowden's chimney was particularly heavy:
"I'll tell you what" said I "Lets block their chimney up and smoke them out".
We needed something to block the chimney with and decided that a piece of turf, we called it a sod, would do the trick. I went home and got one of my father's spades and we went onto Heaton Hill and dug up a sod. We then climbed the fall pipe onto the Sowden's roof and put the sod across the top of the chimney. The smoke filled the living room and Mr. Sowden had to re-decorate. We were never caught and never told anyone what we'd done.

There was a favorite trick which we often played on Mischief Night. Mischief Night was on 4th November, the day before Bonfire Night or Plot Night. It was understood that on Mischief Night kids could play pranks without being punished for them provided no lasting damage was done. What we loved to do was to tie a piece of rope to the door knob on the front door of a house and tie the other end to the door knob of the house next door leaving about a foot of slack. We then knocked on both doors simultaneously and ran away. The first person to open their door could only get it open a foot and while they were trying to figure out what the problem was the second door would be opened with the result that the first door was slammed shut. There would then ensue a tug of war between the two neighbors with doors slamming in turn. We would watch from a distance and have something to laugh about for weeks.

CHAPTER FOUR

"you rubber nosed bugger" Harold

In 1952 my brother, Michael, passed the 11 plus exam at St. Barnabas School and started going to Belle Vue Boys Grammar School on Manningham Lane, a four-penny bus ride from home. For some reason most of the boys on Quarry Street failed the 11 plus and went to Drummond Road Secondary Modern School. Any that passed the 11 plus went to Belle Vue like Michael. The main difference between the schools was that at the Grammar School foreign languages were taught while at the secondary modern there was a greater emphasis on technical subjects and more time was devoted to wood work and metal work.

When I was almost nine my mother went to hospital for a hysterectomy or as she put it "to have everything taken away down there". She was in hospital for three weeks and I was sent to live with my maternal grandparents at 119 Haworth Road. My mother's sister, Auntie Anne, and her husband, Ron, were living there at the time.

I remember Uncle Ron and Auntie Anne taking me to the pictures at the Elite Cinema on Duckworth Lane. Uncle Ron was an engineer at the General Elecric Company on Bingley Road and was well paid. We went to the pictures in his car, an M.G.; I can still remember the smell of the leather seats and of Uncle Ron's pipe smoke. It was very rare for me to ride in a car and I was thrilled to bits by the whole evening. I had never been to the pictures at night before, only to the Saturday matinee at the Marlborough on Carlisle Road. I had ice cream in the cinema and on the way home Uncle Ron stopped at a fish and chip shop and

Making Hen's Meat

bought five portions of fish and chips. Grandma and grandpa were delighted to have a fish and chip supper which was a real treat for them and for me. Grandma's name for fish and chips was "greasy delights". I think fish and chips tasted so good then because they were cooked in beef dripping. Now most fish and chip shops use vegetable oil.

Grandma had a button box; a big tin box in which she had hundreds of buttons of all shapes and sizes collected over a lifetime. Whenever an item of clothing was being thrown away or sold to the rag man the buttons were always cut off and put in this box. I spent many happy hours sorting out these buttons on the kitchen table by size and color. There were endless variations to the fun that could be had from such a simple plaything. Although grandma was crippled with a twisted spine and chronic arthritis and walked with a stick she somehow still managed to cook. She used to make things specially for me – parkin (a kind of ginger cake) and toffee. She loved the toffee so much herself that she hadn't the patience to wait for it to cool and as soon as it was half set she was running cold water over it to speed up the setting process and to make it cool enough to eat. She used to put Tate & Lyle's Golden Syrup in the toffee instead of sugar which gave it a rich treacle taste.

On Sundays grandfather played a harmonium, a type of organ, the bellows of which he pumped with his feet. Grandma sang all her favorite hymns and they had their own worship service at home. I regret that I never learned to play a musical instrument. Michael played the trumpet in the school band and John played the violin. Years later he gave the violin to my son, Dominic, who was himself having violin lessons at school.

I was staying at grandma's when it was my ninth birthday, 25th February, 1953, and at school that day my brother John told me I was to go home after school as father had a surprise for my birthday. I couldn't wait for school to end and when 4 o'clock came I ran home up Rossefield Road to Quarry Street. Waiting for me was my first two-wheeler bike. It was second or third hand; it was an army surplus bike used in the war by paratroopers and it was made to fold up so a paratrooper could strap it on his back when parachuting.

Father had got it from my mother's brother, Uncle Jack. It had been used by my two cousins, Bruce and Stuart. The problem was I did not know how to ride a bike and grandma's house was two miles away. I wasn't leaving the bike at Quarry Street so there was nothing for it but to walk to grandma's wheeling the bike. This took me over an hour so it was 5.30 and dark by the time I got to grandma's. I was usually home by 4.30 as I rode on the bus. Auntie Anne was standing by the front gate anxiously looking for me and when she saw me she walked down Haworth Road and met me. She took over the wheeling of the bike.

When Saturday came Auntie Anne said she would teach me to ride the bike. Off we went with me balanced on the seat and Auntie Anne holding the bike upright and pushing. Up Haworth Raod we went, past the library and nearly to Thorn Lane, then back down we'd come. The bike gathered speed downhill and got away from Auntie Anne. I suddenly realized I was riding the bike unaided and was so surprised I promptly fell off grazing my knees and elbows. Auntie Anne took me into the house, washed my wounds and applied Germolene ointment and sticking plasters and out we went again to continue bike practice.

On Monday it snowed and when I got off the bus at Haworth Road two boys ,who I didn't know from Adam, jumped on me, knocked me down, rubbed my face in the snow and ran off. There was snow in my ears, up my nose and in my mouth and this brought on an asthma attack. I lay in the snow fighting for breath, wheezing noises coming from deep in my chest. Fortunately Auntie Anne was by the front gate of grandma's watching out for me to return from school. She came running down Haworth Road. He face was blood red with anger at what she had seen. She helped me to my feet and back to the house and mixed up some Friar's Balsam and menthol crystals in a bowl of boiling water. With a towel over my head I leaned over the bowl and inhaled the fumes. This was a folk remedy for asthma and bronchitis and it did seem to alleviate the symptoms. Soon mother was out of hospital and I returned home this time riding my bike while my father jog trotted alongside.

About this time father bought a New Hudson auto-cycle. This was somewhere between a push bike and a motor bike. It had a little 98 c.c. 2-stroke engine but it also had pedals. The engine wasn't powerful enough to go up steep hills so father had to pedal. Uncle Jack, my mother's brother, was a partner in a motor cycle dealership called Mobike Spares on Manningham Lane and had got the bike second hand for father at a cheap price. There was no pillion and the machine was definitely intended for one person. Father ignored this and tied an old sack onto a parcel rack located right behind the saddle. This was his idea of a passenger seat and my brothers and I regularly rode behind him, clinging on to him for dear life with our legs sticking out at each side because there were no foot rests. The newly found mobility enabled father to work further from home. Up to this time he had only worked at places he could walk to or no more than a five minute bus ride away. Soon he had jobs in Nab Wood, a residential area of Shipley, and in Baildon.

The year he got the auto-cycle we were told by father there would be no seaside holiday because buying the bike had used the money that had been saved up for the holiday. Then in July father announced there would be a holiday after all but not at the seaside. He had managed to get the use of a caravan from someone he knew at the pub. The caravan was sited about a mile beyond Knaresborough, a picturesque town on the River Nidd, about twenty five miles from Bradford. Mother and we three children went by bus to Knaresborough while father went on his auto-cycle.

When we arrived at the caravan park we were taken aback. It looked for all the world like a car-breakers yard. There were some caravans, mainly in a dilapidated condition, but there were also double and single decker buses, old railway carriages, even trams. Our holiday home for the week was a single decker bus which had had the seats ripped out and some rudimentary re-modelling work done to provide a small kitchen with a gas stove and a seating area, which converted at night time to a sleeping area. There was no piped water; water had to be carried from a communal standpipe a couple of hundred yards away. Lavatory facilities were in a communal block again several hundred yards walk from our 'caravan'.

There were no shops within walking distance so father went into Knaresborough every morning to bring back the provisions needed for that day's meals. Father timed his arrival in Knaresborough for 11 o'clock when the pubs opened. By the time he came back with the groceries he was quite merry and mother was furious because it was already past dinner time. Whether at home or on holiday mother was a stickler for meal times. Breakfast for father was at 7.30 am, and for us kids at 8.00 am. Dinner was at 12.15 p.m. except on Saturday and Sunday when it was at 1.15 p.m. and tea was at 5.15 p.m.. On week-ends father was never home at 1.15 p.m. for dinner - he was in the pub. Mother went ahead and dished up the dinner at about 1.30 p.m. and father's plate of food was put in the oven to keep warm. He would roll in around 2 p.m. and he and mother would have a row. About once a year he would turn up at 1 p.m. looking for his dinner. Mother would say it wasn't ready so he would storm off to the pub. In his eyes this made it quite in order to be late for dinner for the next year.

On holiday in Knaresborough there was very little to do and as it rained for two or three days we spent much of the time cooped up in the bus. When it was fine Michael, John and I would go down to the River Nidd which passed the campsite. We got a milk bottle and put some bread in it as bait, tied string around the bottle neck and threw it into the river. When we pulled it back in it would have a few small fish in it. 'Tiddlers' was our name for these fish.

One day, after dinner, we all went into Knaresborough to the cinema. Father made four trips into Knaresborough on his autocycle bringing mother, Mike, John and I in turn. The whole procedure took an hour. The logic behind doing this was to save the few pence that it would cost to ride the bus. Another day in Knaresborough was spent in a public park where there was a small zoo. We also visited Mother Shipton's Cave and the petrifying well. Mother Shipton was an 18th Century prophetess and many of her predictions had come true. She predicted the end of the world, but I can't remember what year was predicted. I do remember that there was a pub nearby called "The World's End". This pub had a beer garden and we sat at a table there drinking lemonade and eating potato crisps while father downed a few pints of bitter beer. The holiday in Knaresborough was very disappointing as we were used to going to the seaside. Our usual summer holiday was spent on the east coast of Yorkshire. The most popular resorts for Bradfordians were Blackpool and Morecambe on the west coast in Lancashire. Father was a dyed in the wool Yorkshireman and that was why we always holidayed in Yorkshire. I think he also liked the rugged beauty of the Yorkshire coastline with its towering cliffs and secluded coves. He liked to have a harbor close at hand and almost every town or even village on the Yorkshire coast had a harbour and a small fleet of fishing boats called Yorkshire Cobles. I remember well the different places where we stayed, Skipsea, Bridlington, Thornwick Bay on Flamborough Head, Runswick Bay, Whitby and Staithes. We stayed in a rented caravan or small house or flat. All the cooking and cleaning was done by mother so it was never really a holiday for her. We never ate a single meal in a restaurant. I don't know if this was for financial reasons or if it just never occurred to my parents.

When I was eleven years old I went on holiday with my friend Barry Dean's family. We stayed in a caravan at Barmston on the Yorkshire coast. It was a real treat for me to be on holiday with one of my best friends instead of family. Barry's father, Harold, was an interesting guy. He had a succession of jobs. One moment he was a taxi driver the next he was a milkman. He was caretaker at St. Barnabas Hall and used to spend his afternoons playing cards with Joe Craven and a bunch of old codgers who were members of the Men's Club. Then suddenly Harold Dean launched an estate agency selling houses all over Bradford. He very quickly became one of the biggest agents in town. He used to smoke Wild Woodbine cigarettes which were the cheapest brand available and were very strong:
"Why do you smoke Woodbines?" I asked him

"Because they're very smooth and cooling to the throat" he replied.

My father was for many years secretary of the Bradford & District Professional Gardeners' Association. They met once a month in a reserved room in a pub or hotel. After a business meeting they would have a lecture from a specialist in a particular area of horticulture. These lectures were often accompanied by a slide show. One of father's tasks was to book all the speakers a year in advance and then have a Syllabus printed and distributed to all the members. In the 1950's there were about fifty members and a normal attendance would be twenty five to thirty. As time went by the numbers dwindled and to save the society from extinction amateur gardeners were allowed to join and, mainly for father's convenience, meetings were moved from the center city to the King's Arms in Heaton.

CHAPTER FIVE

"you're nothing but a blue eyed closet" Harold

My schooling really began at home. I was taught to read by mother before I started school. From the age of five to seven years I was off school a lot with bronchial asthma and migraines accompanied by bilious attacks. No matter – I stayed in bed and read and read and read. My favorite books were Enid Blyton's Famous Five and Secret Seven series. The school sent work home for me to do and despite my absences I was able to keep abreast of the curriculum. When the annual exam results came out I was usually in the top five of my class. When I was nine I moved up into the top class, Standard Four, and shortly after my tenth birthday I sat the 11 plus exam. When the results came out I had passed and when the school exam results came out I was top of the class. It's been all down hill since then. My parents were very proud of my achievement and my paternal grandmother gave me £5 which was not much less than father's wages for a week. I wanted to go on a spending spree but my parents insisted I buy Premium Bonds.

As my first secondary school choice I picked Carlton Grammar School, not Belle Vue. I didn't want to be in the same school as my brother Michael as I didn't want teachers comparing us. Father was very pleased that I had picked his old school and when I was accepted by Carlton he went to the pub to celebrate. The school building father had gone to had burned down and Carlton had re-located to the old Bradford Grammar School building on Manor Row, close to Bradford city center. Unlike my primary school, which was coeducational, Carlton was a boys only school.

At that time it was normal to segregate the sexes as puberty approached. In September 1954 I started attending Carlton Grammar School. There were about six hundred boys at the school ranging in age from ten to eighteen. Most left at sixteen, at the end of their fifth year, after they had taken the standardized test known as the Ordinary Level General Certificate of Education. A handful of boys stayed on in the sixth form for two years. These were the boys who planned to go to college or university, and they had to pass the Advanced Level G.C.E in three or four subjects.

I was the youngest boy in the school and at four foot three inches the smallest. This didn't mean I escaped the initiation ceremony of being 'racked'. Some of the older boys would grab hold of you in the playground and carry you to a flight of steps leading from the yard into the gymnasium. They would deposit you on the landing about six feet above yard level. There was a safety railing on the landing and you would be suspended by your hands from this railing. To prevent you from letting go and dropping to the ground one of the boys would put his hands tightly over yours. This could last from five minutes to fifteen minutes. The more you struggled and shouted and cried the longer the punishment would continue.

There was one corner of the school yard which could not be seen from any of the school windows. This was known as smokers' corner and a crowd of about twenty boys would gather here at morning and afternoon break and at dinner time to enjoy a smoke. I soon joined them and was smoking two or three cigarettes a day from the age of ten. There were about a hundred boys in each form at school and these were streamed into three classes, A, B and C. according to their perceived ability. This streaming could not be done until the first year was complete so the three classes in the First Form took their initial from the Form Master. I was in Mr. Singleton's class so this was known as One S. Fred Singleton was a very easy going person and I enjoyed having him as my form master. I ran into him again after I had left school and discovered he was a left wing Labor Party Member.

My French teacher, and form master in Two A was Alex Eaton. He used to bring his guitar to school and we would sing songs in French. He usually threw in a couple of folk songs or even a song about the I.R.A. such as "Johnson's Motor Car". After leaving school I met him again and discovered he was a very active member of the Campaign for Nuclear Disarmament and a former Communist Party member. At the time he was teaching me in 1955 I believe he was still in the Communist Party.

I joined the Frobisher Club (a geography club), the Dramatic Society and the Boxing Club. After being beaten up three weeks in a row, I quickly dropped out of the Boxing Club. The Dramatic Society put on the annual school play and my first part was as a member of the crowd in Julius Caesar. My first speaking part was in the Devil's Disciple where I played Essie. I have often wondered since whether the English teacher, who ran the Dramatic Society, got some sexual pleasure from watching teenage boys dressing as women. The school was divided into four houses and I played soccer for the Brown House XI.

I was supposed to eat school dinner and my mother gave me the money to buy a dinner ticket each day. The food was cooked elsewhere at a central kitchen and brought to the school in large insulated metal containers. I found the food to be almost inedible although a lot of the boys loved it. Consequently I stopped going to school dinners and would spend my dinner money on buying one or two cigarettes at the sweet & tobacco shop across from the school and either a bar of chocolate or some broken biscuits from Woolworths in nearby Darley Street. We used to love going to Woolworths , because it was one of the first self-service stores and easy to shop-lift from. Another favorite haunt was Busby's Department Store on Manningham Lane very close to the school. I would often wander round John Street Open Market or Kirkgate Market Hall.

There was an old guy called Mr. Geary who lived in a small cottage in Paradise Row. For some reason we called him 'Tough' which he seemed to like. He was a professional magician and we used to visit his house and he would entertain us with tricks and

give us sweets and pop. On one occasion I was there alone and he offered to show me some tricks. He stood behind me and put his arms over my shoulders and started showing me a trick involving tying knots in a piece of string. He told me to put my hands behind my back and concentrate on watching his hands. I felt something oddly familiar touching my hands and turned round to discover 'Tough' had his dick out and had been rubbing it against my hands;
"What do you think you are doing?" I asked
"I'm sorry" he said "my fly must have been open and it just popped out"
I never visited him again but one of the local lads, called Beresford, became his assistant and used to travel to Blackpool and other seaside resorts where 'Tough' was booked to do magic shows. 'Tough' even had the balls to go and see Beresford's parents and tell them that, to keep the expenses down, they would have to share a bed in the boarding house where they stayed. Beresford always seemed to have plenty of money while he was 'assisting' Mr. Geary.

In the summer holidays in 1956 I went to stay for two weeks with Big Grandma and her brother, Uncle Victor, at 13, Norman Avenue in Eccleshill. His wife had died and my grandmother's husband, Ben Hartley, had also passed away. Grandmother had moved in with Uncle Victor as a companion/housekeeper. I remember watching cricket on television with Uncle Victor. He took it very seriously and kept score on his own score card. A cricket match at that time could last five days so he had ample time to teach me to keep score. When the cricket was over he took me out to his garage which he used as a store room and workshop as he had no car. He made me a pair of stilts by screwing wooden foot rests on two broom handles. I was amazed how quickly I learned to walk on stilts.

We always called my father's mother big grandma because she was fat and my mother's mother little grandma, because she was of short stature. When I was at Uncle Victor's, big grandma did most of the cooking. She was not a good cook. She had bought a pressure cooker which was the 1950's equivalent to a microwave.

It was a large metal container with a series of compartments inside into which could be placed the separate ingredients for a meal, meat, potatoes, vegetables etc. A small quantity of water was added and the lid screwed tightly on. Then it was plugged in and switched on. As the water turned to steam the food was cooked rapidly, usually in about twenty minutes. As the one thing big grandma had plenty of was time there seemed little point in this rapid mode of cooking. I can still remember the bland taste of those steamed dinners.

About once a year we would be invited by big grandma to go for tea. My father hated this but usually managed to arrange to be there from about 3 p.m. to 7 p.m. on a Sunday when the pubs were shut so at least he wasn't wasting valuable drinking time. The meal was always the same, one thin slice of boiled ham, lettuce, half a tomato, one slice of cucumber with bread and butter and a cup of tea. Pudding was always tinned fruit salad with Carnation Milk. Father would look at his plate then look at grandmother and say:
" I see you've killed the fatted calf again".

When I was nearly thirteen in 1957, Dr. Singer, who taught Latin and German at Carlton Grammar School, announced in January that he was organizing a three week trip to the south of France in August. The maximum number was twenty boys and he and another teacher, Mr. Kendall, would be going along to supervise. I begged mother and father to let me go but they said they couldn't afford the cost which was £10 plus spending money of £5. There were six months before the trip so I told Dr. Singer I would be going. Then I made sure to work gardening at least five or six hours on Saturday to earn ten shillings. I was earning £2 a month and in six months I would have £12. I saved even more by getting Uncle Jack, who worked close to my school, to give me a ride there on his motor bike and by walking home this saved eight pence a day, which in six months was £4. I had a total of £16, more than enough for the trip!

We went by train from Bradford Exchange Station to London where we changed stations and boarded another train to take us to

Newhaven. At Newhaven we took the ferry, Lisieux, to Dieppe. In Dieppe we boarded an express train to Paris. I had never even been to London before so it was a tremendous thrill to see both London and Paris in the same day. In Paris we changed stations again and boarded the night express bound for Labenne on France's Atlantic coast near the Pyrenees. From Labenne we went by chartered bus to the camp near the village of Hossegor. Apart from some central administrative buildings the whole camp was under canvas. We twenty boys and Mr. Kendall were all to sleep in one large tent. Dr. Singer and his family had separate accommodations. There were large numbers of Algerian children at the camp as well as poor French kids from the major cites. I suspect that the camp was government financed. Dr. Singer was a friend of the Directeur and I think the £10 cost probably covered the fare and the food and accommodation were free.

The camp was situated in rolling sand dunes surrounded by pine forests and about a mile from the village of Hossegor and half a mile from the beach – La Plage Blanc. After breakfast of bread, butter and jam washed down with bowls of café au lait we were free to do as we pleased provided we were back for lunch at 1 o'clock. My school friend, Alan Hepworth, and I would walk to Hossegor where there were two or three pavement cafes. We found there was no problem about buying beer and cigarettes. We felt very grown up and contented to be sitting in a sidewalk café drinking ice cold beer and smoking Gauloises. Elvis Presley was playing on the juke box singing 'Love me Tender' and for the first time I began to be attracted to the opposite sex. There was a beautiful sixteen year old girl called Monique who was a camp monitrice and I developed quite a crush on her.

One day walking back from Hossegor we spied an apple orchard. The sight of those big red juicy apples was too much for us and we decided to scale the six foot high fence and raid the orchard. Unfortunately I slipped climbing the fence and fell back to the ground. The fence was topped with barbed wire and this got caught in my shirt and I felt an excruciating pain in my stomach. I had three gashes about three or four inches long. I was afraid to ask Mr. Kendall or Dr. Singer if I could get medical help, so for the rest of the holiday I was in some pain. Before we got home the cuts were almost healed but I still have the scars.

In the afternoons we usually went to the beach and were supervised by Monique. The temperature climbed to over 100F. while we were there and some of the boys got severe sunburn. I did not get burned but I did get a touch of sunstroke and spent two days in the camp hospital.

One day we went by bus to the town of St-Jean-de-Luz where we ate a picnic of bread, cheese, salami, ham and fruit. From St-Jean-de-Luz the bus took us first to Biarritz and then to the Pyrenees where we were taken up a mountain, La Rhume, on a rack and pinion railway. At the top was the Spanish border and there was a small shop selling souveniers. Some of the boys bought Spanish guitars. It was a perfectly clear day and it was a wonderful experience to look south and see Spanish peasant farmers down in the valley and to look north and see the whole sweep of the Bay of Biscay with Bayonne and Biarritz clearly visible.

One day we went by bus to a bull fighting ring. It is largely assumed that bull fighting is an exclusively Spanish sport but in the Basque region of France it is equally popular. The bull fight we attended was a special show for children and the bulls were not killed but we saw a great display from the picadors and matadors and, especially for us, a group of clowns. The highlight of the event was an International 'Soccer' Game between French and English schoolboys in which I took part. Goal posts were erected at either end of the bull ring and the 'ball' was a real live bull. Each team had to try to drive the bull between the opponent's goal posts. The final score was nil/nil, or victory to the bull.

All too soon the holiday was over but it sparked a wanderlust in me that has never been satisfied.

Michael was now sixteen and had left school and was working for Dallas & Co., Insurance Brokers. Father gardened for Colonel Dallas at his house on Parsons Road, next to Maylands, and had used this position to get Mike an interview. Within a few months of starting work Mike bought himself a Vespa motor scooter and this gave him a lot of independence.

About this time I realized that the Church of England youth club, St. Barnabas, had much better facilities than the Baptist Youth Club. And the girls seemed far prettier, and certainly better dressed and groomed. I started going to St. Barnabas Church and to the Youth Fellowship. I threw myself into this with great fervor, especially when, to my surprise, I was accepted as an equal by people who I thought would have looked down on me because of where I lived and because my father was a gardener.

On Sunday I went to church morning and evening and then to the Youth Fellowship. On Tuesdays I went to confirmation classes. My decision to be confirmed into the Church of England had a lot to do with the fact that Susan Jowett was also going to confirmation class. I used to walk her home and kiss her goodnight. On Thursdays I went to the youth club. On Saturday night there was often a dance at St. Barnabas Hall; the remaining nights I would go to the tennis club behind St. Barnabas Hall. I didn't play tennis but just sat in the open fronted pavilion talking to my new friends.

Just as everyone in the world remembers where they were when J.F.K. was killed so every Englishman remembers where he was when most of the members of the Manchester United football team were killed in the Munich air crash of 6th February, 1958. I had just left Horsfall playing fields near Odsal Top and was walking to the bus stop when a passer-by told me of the disaster. It was hard to comprehend that so many of the cream of English first division football had died in a single event. Carlton Grammer School had no playing fields of its own so we were bused each week to Horsfall playing fields to play soccer in the winter and cricket in the summer. We also had regular training in athletics. The only sports I was any good at were soccer and the long jump, which was amazing considering my short stature.

CHAPTER SIX

"where t'crows fly backards road to keep t'muck out of their eyes" **Harold**

By this time my brother, Michael, was seventeen and working, and John was twelve and attending Carlton Grammar School with me. My mother was pressing my father to move to a bigger house. She thought it was wrong that we three boys, rapidly growing into young men, were sharing a bedroom. Eventually she convinced him, just as she had convinced him to buy 23 Quarry Street for £300, when the landlord they rented from had offered to sell it to them. The house they bought was 12 Ashwell Road, just two streets away from Quarry Street, but a far superior house and a far superior address.

The house was a terrace house built in 1910 and because it was built on a sloping site it was four storeys at the back and three storeys at the front. Entering from the back yard there was a large room which father commandeered for storing tools and equipment and as a workshop. On the ground floor was a small sitting room and a dining kitchen. On the first floor were two bedrooms and a bathroom and there were two further attic bedrooms on the second floor. They paid £750 for the house, having sold 23 Quarry Street for the same amount. The price they paid was cheap because the house had been neglected and had not been painted or decorated for thirty years. Father set the whole family to work and we painted and wall papered the whole house from top to bottom. Night storage heaters were installed on the ground floor and lower ground floor. There were four fire places in the house and in the attics we were provided with electric radiators.

We moved in on my fifteenth birthday, 25th February, 1959, and for the first time mother gave me a cigarette after all the work was done. This seemed like an acknowledgement that she now regarded me as grown up. Mother and father took the front bedroom and John the back one. Mike and I each had an attic. After sharing a room for the whole of my life I was over the moon to have a private place to call my own.

By this time father had got rid of the auto-cycle and had a 350 c.c. ex-army Ariel motorbike. He decided he wanted a sidecar so the whole family could travel together. When Uncle Jack told him the price of a sidecar he decided he would build one himself. He enlisted the help of Norman Cockroft, a carpenter who lived on Quarry Street and who father drank with in the Delvers. Father got a chassis cheap from Uncle Jack. The sidecar was built out of marine plywood with a sheet of aluminum for the curved front. There were three seats, one behind the other and a canvas top to keep the rain out. Now the whole family could go out together with mother riding pillion and we three boys in the sidecar.

The summer trip to the seaside was now made using the motor bike and side car. Previously father had got someone he knew with a car to drive us there and fetch us back. Sunday afternoons were now seen as opportunities to visit the Yorkshire Dales. Skipton, the gateway to the dales, was only twenty miles away, but until father got the motorbike and sidecar the only time I would go there would be on Easter Monday. The youth club always went on a hike on Easter Monday. We would get the bus or the train to Skipton or Ingleton or some other suitable starting point and would then walk ten or fifteen miles. We would usually end up in a village pub and then get the bus or train back home.

Father's favorite dale was Littondale. This was a dead end dale with two villages, Arncliffe and Litton. Father particularly liked Arncliffe having camped there with mother when they were courting. We would walk by the river, have a picnic in the church yard and visit the blacksmith's forge. Father was also fond of the village pub, the Falcon. Many years previously, when I was four years old, we had spent a week in Arncliffe. Mother and father and baby John stayed in a gypsy caravan and Mike and I were in a tent. I remember we went to watch a cricket match between teams from Arncliffe and Litton. This was played in a field behind the pub so father was able to keep himself supplied with beer. Father befriended one of the local sheep farmers, Mr. Metcalfe, and went off with him shooting rabbits. I remember them returning like big game hunters with a long wooden pole between their shoulders with a dozen rabbits hanging from it by their back legs. They sold most of these to the landlord of the Falcon, Marmaduke Miller, but kept back one each for home cooking. Mother made a rabbit pie next day. Another day father took all the family to watch Mr. Metcalfe dipping his sheep, and we then went and sat beside an old drovers road that ran across the fells and watched a motorcycle scrambling race.

Much of father's life revolved around pub opening times. The pubs were open from 11 am to 3 p.m. and again from 5.30 p.m. to 10 p.m. (later extended to 10.30 p.m. and then 11 p.m.). No travelling could be done when the pubs were open; that would be wasting valuable drinking time. On Sunday the hours were 12 p.m. to 2 p.m. and 7 p.m. to 10 p.m. On our Sunday trips we would always arrive at our destination by 12 p.m.. Whether it was Arncliffe or Ingleton, Kilnsey or Malham, Appletreewick or Bolton Abbey, Embsay or Eastby, father would be in the pub as the door opened. If there was a beer garden we would sit out there, if not mother and we children would have to walk around the village until father had had his fill of beer. It never occurred to anyone in the 1950's not to drink and drive. If caught speeding or in some other infraction of traffic laws a common plea was that the driver was drunk, and sometimes this would be grounds for being let off!

Father went to the pub every night from 8.30 p.m. or 9 p.m. until closing time. On Fridays he wouldn't work after 5 p.m. so he'd be in the pub by 7 p.m. again until closing. On Saturday morning he would work but he'd be in the pub at 12 p.m. and drink until 2 p.m. when he went home for dinner. In the afternoon he would

sleep but would awake at 5.20 p.m. in time to have a quick wash and brush up and be in the pub by opening time. Sunday was a repeat performance. His summary of the weekend was:
"Friday night is little ale night, Saturday night is big ale night, Sunday is all ales day".

Mike and father were often at cross purposes at this time and this would lead to them fighting especially on Friday or Saturday night when they had both had too much beer. Usually no blood was spilled and it ended in a few minutes with Michael either leaving or going to bed. On one occasion things got out of hand and as Mike was getting the better of things, father sent me to fetch a friend of his, Syd, who lived across the street. Syd managed to calm them down. On another occasion when father got a bloody nose he called the police. The policeman who arrived was well known to us. His name was Brian and he drank in the Delvers. He gave Mike a talking to and when he could see there was going to be no further trouble he left. A week later another fight broke out and father told Mike he had to find somewhere else to live. He went on his Vespa scooter to live in Eccleshill with big grandma. She lived alone now, Uncle Victor having died of a heart attack in 1957. I suppose Mike stayed at grandma's for a couple of weeks and then, much to mother's relief, returned home.

Shortly after moving to Ashwell Road we got a fourteen inch television. In Quarry Street we had a television with a nine inch screen and to make the picture bigger a magnifying glass was hung in front of it suspended on two strings. If a war movie was on father would be glued to the set and no one was allowed to talk. He would even miss the pub to watch anything about the Second World War. He loved "The Cruel Sea" and "The Dambusters" and devoured the series "Victory at Sea". He wasn't too keen on American made war movies because they emphasized the role of the United States forces in winning the war. He used to say:
"The trouble with the G.I.'s is that they are overpaid, over-sexed and over here."

Before TV we used to listen to the radio a lot. I remember listening to "The Navy Lark" and "The Goon Show" with Harry

Secombe, Peter Sellers, Spike Milligan and Michael Bentine. Another favorite was "Workers Playtime" and "Have a Go Joe" with Wilfred Pickles, his wife Mabel and Barney Colehan. There was a ventriloquist, Peter Brough, and he had a dummy called Archie Andrews. He had a weekly radio show called "Educating Archie". Its hard to believe that we took this seriously, but we did. Television was not good for Peter Brough's career. He moved his mouth when ventriloquising and now that we could see him as well as hear him – well, you get the picture.

A popular television show was the 6-5 Special on Saturday evening. This featured singers such as Cliff Richards and Tommy Steele, and jazz bands such as Acker Bilk's band. This was right at the time when crooning was giving way to rock 'n roll. My father and his generation thought there was no one better than Bing Crosby or Frank Sinatra. In 1956 when we were on holiday in Bridlington the whole family went to see Bill Haley and the Comets in 'Rock Around the Clock'. The audience went wild. Teenagers were dancing in the aisles. The manager stopped the movie several times and went on the stage to call for calm. Father was disgusted and made us leave before the end. The big influences on teenage music at this time were, Buddy Holly, Chuck Berry, Little Richard and Jerry Lee Lewis. I remember in Latin class we had to make up something original in Latin and write it on the black board for the teacher to translate. When my turn came I wrote:
" Edepol, magnae pelae ignis".
The teacher translated this as:
"Oh dear me, large burning spheres"
"No sir" I said "it's Goodness gracious great balls of fire!"
This was a line from one of Jerry Lee Lewis's best selling records. The class comedian, I liked to be the center of attention.

Bradford had a great little concert hall, St. George's Hall, and I used to go every year when the Halle Orchestra, a world famous symphony orchestra, were visiting from Manchester. I remember seeing Acker Bilk and his Jazz Band play there. On the same bill were Sonnie Terry and Brownie McGhee, two black blues singers from the deep south who twenty years later I saw perform at Spirit

Square in Charlotte, North Carolina. They got such an ovation and so many curtain calls that Acker Bilk, who was due to perform another set, asked Sonnie and Brownie and the audience if it was alright for him to accompany them. In 1958, when I was fourteen, I saw Paul Robeson perform. He must be the greatest singer of the twentieth century and I had tears in my eyes when he sang "I Stand Here". How much more it would have meant two or three years later when I had become politically aware.

I went to see Bradford City football team at their Valley Parade ground with my brothers in about 1958. I have no recollection of who they played but I do know they lost. The only player whose name I can remember is Flockett. The crowd called him Frankenstein Flockett because he was so ugly. We watched the match from the Spion Kop end and standing in front of us was a man wearing a pac-a-mac. These were plastic mackintoshes which folded up to a small size and could be carried in a pocket. I was smoking and I touched the back of the man's coat with my cigarette. Immediately the plastic melted and a hole about half an inch across appeared. This gave me an idea and I proceeded to burn more holes in his coat until they spelled out the words "I am a cunt". We three boys and a whole section of the crowd nearly died laughing at this.

In my fifth year at grammar school I was so busy with the youth club and chasing girls and going away for weekends that I totally neglected my school work. I just didn't do much homework and took the consequences. I went away for a weekend to Highfield House on Ilkley Moor with the youth fellowship and for a week to Squires Gate Holiday Camp near Blackpool. I was in a pantomime – Jack and the Beanstalk at St. Barnabas Hall and this meant evenings were taken up for weeks with rehearsals.

I was also in hospital for a week in 1959. One of my balls had been getting bigger than the other one since I was fourteen and soon it was about the size of a tennis ball. I thought my other one should be the same size as I was in puberty and I'd heard that your balls grew bigger. I told my father about the problem and he had a look. He went pale and told me it wasn't that one ball was too

small it was that one was too big. He sent for the doctor and I remember him arriving when we were all eating dinner. Dad told him what the problem was and instead of taking me somewhere private to examine me Dr. Liversedge said:
"Stand up Gary and drop your trousers"
With the rest of the family watching he grabbed my balls and started kneading them:
"Yes, yes, you've got a hydrocele" said the doctor " I'll send you to see a specialist at the Bradford Royal Infirmary and he'll decide what needs to be done".
The specialist said I would need a small operation to drain the fluid and to stitch up the hole in the internal wall of the scrotum that was permitting the fluid to enter. This was portrayed by him as something very minor. I didn't think that having my ball bag cut open was minor at all.

After the operation I discovered I had three clips and seven stitches and a temporary plastic drain had been installed. I had lots of get well cards from friends, especially girl friends in the youth fellowship. Visitors were always asking to look at my stitches but of course I declined to show them. I developed a sweat rash on my balls and I remember Norman, a male nurse, coming round to put talcum powder on them:
"Here you are Gary" he would say, "Knacker Lacquer, adds luster to your cluster."

Around this time the Vicar of St. Barnabas, Rev. Kay retired. A few days after his retirement I was walking past the lych gate when I heard a shout in a very posh voice:
"Hello, do be a good chap and come and help me!"
I looked over the gate and saw a figure halfway up a fifty foot oak tree with a saw in one hand and clinging on with the other. But not just someone, this man was wearing a Roman Collar and a black cassock which he had tucked down the top of his trousers. I walked towards the tree:
"Who are you?" the tree figure roared.
"I'm Gary Spence and I live down the street at number twelve" I replied.

Making Hen's Meat

"Well, I'm the new Vicar, Arden Constant, and I'm in a bit of a pickle, I climbed up the tree to saw off a dead branch and now I can't get down again" he said.

"How did you get up there, where's the ladder?" I asked.

"I told you, I climbed the tree but it looks as if I do need a ladder to get down, I'm sort of stuck you know"

"Alright, hold on tight, I'll be back" I said.

I ran down Ashwell Road to Mr. Dodgson, the plumber's house, and asked if I could borrow a ladder.

"What on earth for?" asked Les Dodgson

"The new vicar's stuck up a tree". I answered.

"I'll have no more of your silly tricks, Gary" he said, and slammed the door in my face. I knocked on the door again

"Honest, Mr. Dodgson, the vicar is stuck up a tree in the churchyard"

"Alright" he said "I'll be there in a few minutes, but you'd better be telling the truth."

I ran back and told the vicar that help was on its way.

Before long Mr. Dodgson arrived pushing an old hand cart with a triple extension ladder roped on it. He looked at me, he looked at the tree and the vicar and said

"Well, I'll be buggered!"

Soon the vicar was down on the ground and Mr. Dodgson was hurrying off.

"Well Gary, we need a drink after all this excitement" the vicar said "come down to the vicarage"

We went through the back door into a large kitchen with a farm house style table and he got out two glasses and poured out two bottles of beer. After my third beer I said goodbye and walked home a little the worse for wear. No sooner was I through the door than mother said:

" Where have you been, you've been drinking"

"I've been with the new vicar" I said.

She couldn't be convinced, but later she realized it was true when Rev. Arden Constant became a regular in the King's Arms and Delvers.

By this time one of father's regular customers was Raymond Clegg. He was about my father's age and they'd grown up in Heaton together. His mother and father used to run the King's Arms pub and he had been brought up there. Harold and Raymond both played soccer on the church field behind St. Barnabas Hall. Raymond Clegg had done very well for himself. He had risen to the rank of Captain during the Second World War and afterwards went back to his old job as an Estate Agent. He and his friend and neighbour on Leylands Lane, Harry Hartley, had become partners in the firm of S. H. Chippindale and Co., a firm of commercial estate agents in Bradford. The principal of the firm was Sam Chippindale who lived in the biggest house in Heaton, The Ryddings, on Emm Lane opposite Lister Park. By 1955 Raymond Clegg was having a new house built on a site he had bought on Toller Lane and when he moved in he asked father to do the garden. This was not the usual garden maintenance job, what was involved was creating a garden from scratch. This was a major challenge and father jumped at it. Here was a chance to put into practice all he had learned in twenty years of gardening.

The Clegg's garden project involved the building of a rock garden, building retaining walls, making a terrace, creating lawns from scratch, making a rose garden, a herbaceous border and a kitchen garden and building a greenhouse and potting shed and conservatory. Father reveled in this. He seemed to enjoy mixing and laying concrete and building a stone wall as much as he enjoyed any of the gardening tasks. For three years he worked at Clegg's a day a week plus evenings and weekends. At weekends I was usually with him. I became quite adept at mixing concrete and mortar by hand. There were no landscape architect's plans for this garden. The ideas were all in father's head and were being constantly modified as problems were encountered.

Raymond Clegg tried to keep abreast of what father was planning, after all it was his garden and he was paying all the bills. Often he and father would get at cross purposes because father was doing a poor job of communicating. This is where I became invaluable, at translating Harold-speak into language and concepts that Raymond Clegg could understand. More and more Raymond

Clegg would come to talk to me in preference to father. He even started inviting me into the house and giving me a bottle of Whitbread beer while father continued working outside.

One day in January 1959, Raymond Clegg asked me what I planned to do when I left school. I told him I had hoped to go into the sixth form and go to university but mother and father wouldn't hear of it. They thought I should go to work and start contributing to the family finances. Raymond said that he and his fellow directors had decided that they had to start planning for the future of the firm by taking on some young assistants. These assistants would sign articles of pupilage (similar to an apprenticeship) for a term of five years. The pay would be small but one day and three evenings a week the articled pupils would attend Bradford Technical College at the expense of the firm to enable them to pass the exams of either the Royal Institution of Chartered Surveyors or the Association of Landed Property Agents.

He explained that Sam Chippindale was bringing his son, Howard, into the firm and Harry Hartley was bringing in his step-son, Tim Edlin. He and Albert Ramsey, the other two directors, had only daughters so he was inviting me to come and be his articled pupil. At that time it would have never occurred to anyone to bring their daughter into this kind of job. The only professions open to women were nursing and teaching. A prerequisite for student membership of the Royal Institute of Chartered Surveyors was passes in four subjects in the General Certificate of Education (ordinary level) to include Maths and English.

I accepted his offer and told him I would be taking the G.C.E. in June and would have the results in August and should be able to start on September 1st. We shook hands on it and drank another Whitbread. My mother and father were over the moon. They had always wanted me to have a better start in life than them, and they thought this job offer was infinitely preferable to going into the sixth form and then to university. They were probably right and in any event there was some doubt about how well I would do in the G.C.E. exams. The sixth form might not be an option.

By this time I had been confirmed into the Church of England but I was not really a committed Christian, although I went through the rituals of church attendance, bible study and Sunday School. On Saturday nights I would often go into Bradford City Center and listen to the public speakers who positioned themselves around Forster Square and at the corner of Cheapside and Broadway. A particular favorite of mine was Harry Goldthorpe. Goldthorpe was a middle aged man of stocky build with a shock of red hair. He was a powerful speaker and had a commanding presence. He was a left wing socialist and had been the leader of the Bradford Unemployed Workers Association. This had been formed in 1921 under the influence of the fledgling Communist Party. Goldthorpe had accused the Communist Party of mismanaging the finances and wrested control of the movement from them. He wrote a book, "Room at the Bottom", which dealt with this subject at length.

Goldthorpe reserved much of his venom for the traitors to socialism in the Labour and Communist Parties. His main platform, however, was atheism. His was not a passive form of atheism; it took the form of a rabid, raging, anti-Christian ethic. Goldthorpe was very straightforward:
"Jesus Christ never lived." he would shout.
"If Christ did live then he died on the cross and the priests and parsons have been living off it ever since" he would say.
When a woman started speaking on a Christian theme nearby Goldthorpe would amuse the crowd by shouting:
"There she goes again, the bloody Virgin Mary".
Much as I was amused by Goldthorpe, I did not take him seriously.

I was more interested in what the Charismatic Christians had to say. I was confirmed into the church and was a regular churchgoer but religion had not affected the way I lived. These Christian speakers were talking of the need to be born again and of total surrender to Jesus Christ. They began to make an impression on me and I would get into long conversations with some of them. One of them gave me a book entitled "What Would Jesus Do?" The book proposed that Christians when confronted with decisions should use their knowledge of the Bible to answer the question – what would Jesus do? – and make their decisions accordingly. This was a very logical and attractive idea to me. I considered myself a Christian but I was not really acting out Christ's teachings. Here was a very simple way of solving the problem.

By this time I had become a regular weekend drinker. Saturday night was definitely pub night and I started to go to the bar of the Alexander Hotel on Morley Street. This bar was very popular with young people, in particular underage drinkers. The legal age for drinking alcohol was eighteen but anyone over the age of fifteen had no problem getting served in the Alex, as we called it. Johnny Milnes who lived in Highgate, Heaton was also a regular at the Alex.

Johnny was in the same class as me at St. Barnabas School, but he obtained a scholarship to Bradford Grammar School and we had very little contact from the age of ten to fifteen. Now we became firm friends and after the Alex we would usually end up at a party at someone's house.

Johnny and I often used to go to the Student's Club which was in a dimly lit cellar across the street from the Odeon Cinema and next door to the Alassio Coffee Bar. This was a jazz club and featured live musicians and principally traditional jazz and blues. The musicians used to drink on the stage and were often as drunk or drunker than the audience. A particular favorite of mine was George Melly who used to take swigs of gin straight out of the bottle as he sang the blues. When he was in Bradford he used to date a Communist Party member who went by the soubriquet of Dirty Alice. The club was owned or managed by Paul Hockney, brother of David Hockney, the artist. A group of art students were regulars at the club including Peter Falkingham and John Seaton.

Johnny and several of his close friends were members of the Campaign for Nuclear Disarmament. CND was a rapidly growing nationwide organisation promoting a policy of unilateral nuclear disarmament for Britain and an end to nuclear testing by all nations. Applying the simple test of "What would Jesus do?" I decided he would join CND. "Blessed are the peacemakers" was a very persuasive argument.

CHAPTER SEVEN

"tales I heard at my mother's knee and other low joints" Harold

The first CND meeting I attended was held at the Mechanics Institute and I was amazed at the odd collection of characters present.

The secretary was Alec South. He was a prominent Quaker and a member of the Independent Labour Party and owned a wholesale paint and wallpaper company. What was surprising about him was that despite being a Quaker he drank copious quantities of beer, smoked cigars and lived with his secretary. He was a committed pacifist and gave everything he had to the peace movement.

Kenneth Hockney, father of David, the artist, and Paul, a future Lord Mayor of Bradford, was also present. He was a diminutive chap like a little sparrow. His specialty was producing the most horrific blown up photographs of injuries caused by the atom bombs at Hiroshima and Nagasaki. He made these into placards to give to people to carry on demonstrations.

Another member was Anthony Cadbury, the black sheep of the Cadbury chocolate family. He was another Quaker and a member of the Vegetarian Society and sometimes seemed to be confused as to which meeting he was attending. We would be discussing a demonstration to be held in Leeds and he would chime in about the benefits of eating alfalfa sprouts.

Also there was Ron Florey a painter and decorator from Pudsey with very left wing views. He became a supporter of the Chinese Communist Party and investigated the possibility of emigrating to China with his family. This came to nothing so he got a job as a traffic warden in Bradford and was horrified to discover that this involved being sworn into the police force.

Joe Corrina was a suave well dressed man in his fifties, with slicked back silver hair and a neatly trimmed mustache. Corrina was the mainstay of the Bradford Humanist Association. He was an avowed atheist and often introduced Harry Goldthorpe at his public meetings in Forster Square. Joe ran a cats home at Odsal Top and was the author of a book called " Cats My Line". He had his own little publishing company and as well as publishing "Cats My Line" he had also published Harry Goldthorpe's book "Room at the Bottom". You would have expected there to have been friction between Alec South and Joe Corrina; one a practicing Quaker, the other a militant atheist, but on the contrary, they had a mutual admiration society going.

Then there was Dennis Edmundson. Committed as he was to the CND cause and lots of other causes Dennis couldn't hide his profound interest in the opposite sex, particularly the young girls who were in YCND. Dennis lived about five miles outside Bradford in a place called Wilsden and had acquired an old van so he could get to and from the many meetings which he attended in Bradford. He never failed to give us all rides home and would try to contrive to have a pretty girl as his last stop. He used to write poems and give them to these girls. I remember one that began:

> *"Jane, Jane, my darling Jane.*
> *From loving you I'll ne'er refrain.*
> *'Tis for you we fight this fight*
> *To turn the darkness into light"*

There were also a couple of school teachers, Alex Eaton, who had taught me at Carlton Grammar School and Colin Siddons, who taught at Thornton Grammar School.

Also present were George Harrison, Jim Wigglesworth and Maurice Bennett who were engineering workers active in the Amalgamated Engineering Union and members of Bradford Trades Council.

Harry Wright and Bernard Doyle were there. They were both salesmen and close friends. They spent most mornings drinking coffee and playing chess at a café in the center of Bradford. Once a week Harry had to submit a report of all the sales calls he had made; this was necessarily a work of fiction and Harry would spend hours poring over the telephone directory to get the names and addresses of companies he could say he had called on.

Peter Thornton, who was at the meeting, was a plumbing contractor with his own business in the Manningham area of Bradford. He and his wife, Jean, were originally from Roberttown in nearby Spen Valley and Peter had served as a Labour Party councillor, but had been expelled from the Labour Party because of his support for the Peace Movement. I was quickly to learn that their home at 40 St. Paul's Road was the unofficial headquarters for the Bradford left.

Every Tuesday evening the Youth Campaign for Nuclear Disarmament met at 40 St Paul's Road. There would usually be about a dozen people there. Johnny Milnes and John Sanderson were always there as were some very pretty girls; Christine, Mavis, Jane, Pam, Penny and Felicity are the ones I remember.

People were always dropping by the Thornton's house which was the base for a loose association of left wing people called the New Left. Coffee or tea was always available and people would sit and talk for hours on end. Harry Wright was there most nights and a frequent visitor was Bob Cryer who was to become the Labour Member of Parliament for Keighley and then for Bradford North.
The New Left was composed of left wing Labor Party members and former members of the Communist Party who had left the party following the crushing of the Hungarian Revolution in 1956. They had their own journal edited by Edward Thompson and John Saville, called initially The New Reasoner and then New Left

Review. The New Left was not a political party but a loose association of left wing people most of them claiming to be marxists. In effect it was a talking shop without a specific program of action.

In Bradford supporteers of the New Left raised the funds to buy an old Victorian house at 6 Edmund Street near the city center. This was brought back to habitable condition thanks to the efforts of a few people most notably Harry and Isobel Wright and Peter and Jean Thornton. I remember working there night after night, scraping wall paper off crumbling plaster, and then painting. Once these premises were ready for use they became the meeting place for both CND and YCND, the Anti-Apartheid movement and many other predominantly left wing groups, including, surprisingly, the Communist Party. The premises were simply called The Left Club.

My father was vehemently opposed to CND and made no attempt to understand its policies. He had been in the army for six years and apparently enjoyed every minute of it. If he had not had family responsibilities he said he would have signed on for a twenty year stint in the army at the end of the war. He perceived CND as a being hostile to the army and that was all he needed to know. He also thought it was a Communist Party 'front' organization. We had many arguments which could probably have been avoided if I had kept my own counsel. Instead I acted and spoke provocatively and often drove father to the brink of violence and sometimes beyond it. On one occasion he told me to get out of the house and grabbed me by the scruff of the neck and pushed me out of the front door which he then locked behind me. In a moment of uncontrollable anger I swung my fist at the door breaking a glass panel. A piece of glass cut one of my fathers fingers and he had to go to the hospital. He claimed to be unable to bend that finger for the rest of his life.

A few weeks after joining CND I went on their annual Easter march from the weapons research center at Aldermaston to Trafalgar Square in London. This was a very impressive march attracting tens of thousands of participants. The march lasted three days and each night we camped out in a virtual tent city. For Alec South the march was a pilgrimage. He soon developed blisters but insisted on walking all the way. When we reached the campground each night he collapsed. When he heard I was going to the nearest pub he asked me to bring him back four pints of beer. I did. Never have I seen anyone so grateful for beer. He guzzled down the four pints in about thirty minutes.

On the way back on the chartered bus I was talking to Jean Thornton and told her my father was convinced that CND was full of Communists and was nothing more than a Communist front organization. I said I hadn't met a single member of the Communist Party since I had joined CND and it was obvious that the leading members in Bradford, such as Alec South and Joe Corrina were not remotely close to the Communist Party:
"You have met members of the Communist Party" Jean told me.
"Who for example?" I said.
"Well me for one" said Jean.
I was dumb-founded. This was the height of the Cold War and I had been influenced by television, radio and the newspapers into believing that Communists were agents of a foreign power infiltrating the schools, universities and workplaces to do harm to the British economy. I don't know what I expected a Communist to look like, but certainly not like Jean Thornton. Jean was a vivacious red haired woman in her early thirties, married with five children and exuding tremendous warmth, and sympathy. I was utterly charmed by her and had often stayed up talking with her for hours after her husband, Peter, had gone to bed.

She was from a working class family but thanks to the Workers Education Association and years of meetings and classes given by the Labour Party (from which she and her husband, Peter were expelled) and by the Communist Party, she had obtained a very well rounded education. She was equally at home talking to me about the history of the British working class or Picasso's Blue Period or the art of Utrillo. I can honestly say I loved Jean Thornton, not in a sexual way, but as a warm, kind hearted individual. And now I had to reconcile these warm feelings with the knowledge that she was in the Communist Party. I asked her how as a member of the New Left she could be in the Communist Party. She told me the Labor Party was hopelessly reformist and if you wanted to change society you had to belong to a party that embraced a policy of socialism. She didn't agree with those people who had walked out of the Communist Party because of the misdeeds of the Soviet Union. She thought it right to stay in the party and work for the changes envisioned by the New Left.

One of the C.N.D. members, Kevin Baxter, suddenly joined the R.A.F. He said he was going to try to recruit for C.N.D. in the armed forces. This sounded like a crazy scheme and within a few weeks Kevin was back in Bradford having gone absent without leave. He brought with him a radio transmitter built into a suitcase. Where he had got it from I do not know but it did not look like R.A.F. equipment, there was something very Heath Robinson about it. It was supposedly tuned to broadcast on the same frequency as BBC television and the idea was hatched of broadcasting live after the 11 o'clock news and just before close down. Alex Eaton, my former school teacher, and I agreed to take on the job of broadcasting and prepared a message which began with the words:
"Do not turn off your TV set. The following message is from the Bradford Branch of the Campaign for Nuclear Disarmament"

Alex and I lugged the transmitter to the highest point we could get access to -Wrose Reservoir on Wrose Hill. We made our broadcast at 11 p.m. but no one heard it. Either the transmitter was a dud or was tuned to the wrong frequency. The transmitter was returned to its home under Jean & Peter Thornton's bed.

In the spring of 1959 the United States were proposing to carry out some tests of the H-Bomb and CND launched a campaign in opposition to this proposal. Obviously, we had little chance of having our viewpoint put forward by any of the newspapers, TV or radio so we had to resort to other means. CND would not resort to any illegal activity or even peaceful direct action but individual members and the more militant Committee of 100 did so.

As a means of getting our message across a group of us decided we would go out armed with paint and brushes and write slogans on walls around Bradford. We assembled at the Thorntons, about fifteen of us, and divided into groups of three, two to paint and one to drive and act as look out. Bob Cryer was one driver with his trade mark Armstrong Siddeley Saphire limousine, Peter Thornton was another, Dennis Edmunson was there with his old van and Keith Jennings who drove for a fire extinguisher company had brought the works van. The fifth driver was Harry Wright.

I went with Keith Jennings and Jim Wigglesworth, both of whom I had now discovered were in the Communist Party. Our designated area was Thornton Road, Great Horton Road and Little Horton Lane. We would find a place to paint and while Keith watched out Jim and I daubed the slogans. The agreed slogan was "NO H TESTS , EAST OR WEST" but Jim wouldn't paint this. He was only prepared to paint "NO H TESTS" because as far as he was concerned the Soviet Union should have the right to test nuclear weapons to prevent the Americans from gaining a military advantage. This theory of a "people's bomb" was a major cause of friction between Communist and non-Communist members of CND. We were just finishing painting our last slogan on a wall on St Enoch's Road at about midnight when a passing motorist stopped a couple of hundred yards past us and started to turn around.

We jumped in the van and sped off with the car in hot pursuit. Keith Jennings did some hair-raising driving and we managed to shake off our pursuer. Jim Wigglesworth was singing his favorite song "The Anthem of the Soviet Air Force". He used to love to sing this on CND marches to annoy the non-political and pacifist elements. The bit of it I remember is:

> *"Fly higher and higher and higher*
> *Our emblem the Soviet Star*
> *We're the first people's air force in the air...."*

Life was getting busy as summer of 1959 approached. I had meetings of CND and YCND every week , and often I would attend a public meeting. I had been elected secretary of YCND and this meant I had to keep the minute books and other records. I was still spending time at St. Barnabas Tennis Club and Youth Fellowship and I was helping father gardening to earn some cash for a planned return visit to France, this time with Johnny Milnes. I was also trying to do some revision for the upcoming GCE examinations, as my job with Raymond Clegg was dependent on passes in four subjects to include English and Maths. Maths was my weak spot especially calculus. I totally failed to understand what it was about.

The weekend after I had been out painting slogans Johnny Milnes, John Sanderson and I went to Bishop Auckland in County Durham. We were going to a party being thrown by Charlie Radcliffe who we had met on the Aldermaston March. We hitch-hiked to Bishop Auckland up the AI. At the party where there was plenty of beer I told the story of the slogan painting in Bradford. Mike Corner, who was secretary of Bishop Auckland CND and a reporter for the local paper, suggested we go do some slogan painting in Bishop Auckland.

Charlie supplied us with a gallon of white paint and some brushes and John Sanderson and I painted slogans all around the town center including on the windows of Marks & Spencer and on the local Labor Party H.Q.

We weren't back at the party for long when the police arrived. They hadn't had any difficulty tracing us; they simply followed the trail of spilled paint. They asked to look at everyone's hands and of course John Sanderson's and my hands were covered in paint. We were arrested and taken to the police station where we both made statements admitting that we had painted the slogans and stating we had done so in protest against the upcoming US Nuclear tests. We were charged with "conduct likely to cause a breach of the peace" and released on bail. A couple of weeks later we attended court where we were "bound over to keep the peace of Her Sovereign Majesty, Queen Elizabeth II."

CHAPTER EIGHT

"wait small" Harold

In June I sat my GCE examinations in seven subjects, English, English Literature, French, German, History, Geography and Maths. At the end of June I had what I thought was my last day of school. My final school report contained a note from my form master which read "Able but Idle".

A few days later Johnny Milnes and I set off to hitch-hike around France. We had both just read Jack Kerouac's "On the Road" and considered ourselves members of Britain's beat generation. Our hitch hiking got off to a bad start. We got a bus to the outskirts of Bradford on Wakefield Road. This was in the days before motorways and we had to hitch-hike from Bradford to Wakefield and then join the A1 for London just before Doncaster. We made the mistake of accepting a short lift and ended up being dropped just outside Wakefield at Nostell Priory. We thumbed for hours but nobody stopped. In desperation we each stood on opposite sides of the road and thumbed in both directions. We were prepared to accept a lift in either direction to anywhere. Eventually a car stopped heading back to Bradford and we gladly accepted the lift. We were too embarrassed to go home so we headed for the Alexander Hotel, this being Saturday night. We managed to get an invite to a party in Bingley and full of beer we crashed out on the floor and awoke early on Sunday morning.

Making Hen's Meat

Once again we took a bus out of Bradford and were lucky enough to get a lift all the way to London. We spent Sunday night at Charlie Radcliffe's flat in Islington – he had moved to London from Bishop Auckland. Next morning Charlie showed us to the Dover Road and we met up with another hitch hiker called Ernie. He was a squaddie in the British Army and was heading to Paris like us. He had been on leave and was on his way back to SHAPE, Supreme Headquarters Allied Powers in Europe. It was virtually impossible for three people to get a lift together, sometimes it was difficult for two, so we split up and met again at Dover where we got the 12 noon ferry to Calais.

We then hitch-hiked to Paris and met up in a café in La Rue des Huchettes in the Latin Quarter. This area was full of coffee bars and jazz clubs and was a mecca for beats like us. There was an international crowd in the cafes and clubs and spilling out onto the streets. We ran into Christine and Mavis from Bradford YCND but they had plans and didn't hang out with us for long. Lots of people were wearing long baggy sweaters and jeans with twelve inch bottoms. Some had moccasins on their feet and some were barefoot. We met up with a crowd of English boys and girls who told us they had found an abandoned warehouse a few streets away and we were welcome to stay there with them. We were short of money and were traveling light, just a haversack with a change of clothes and a sleeping bag, so we were glad of a free place to stay.

On Monday morning we ate bread and cheese for breakfast washed down with a glass of vin ordinaire and agreed to walk with Ernie to the place where he had to catch the service-men's bus to SHAPE. On the way we stopped at the Louvre and spent a couple of hours looking at the paintings. When we arrived at the bus stop Ernie asked us why we didn't come to SHAPE with him; the cigarettes and beer were cheap as they were duty free and the food was free for servicemen. We were very unsure about this but Ernie told us not to worry, everything would be alright. And everything was. Nobody asked to see a pass or any kind of identification when we boarded the bus. When we arrived at SHAPE the bus was waved through by the sentry on the gate. Ernie took us to his barrack room and pointed out a couple of spare beds and told us we could stay if we wanted to.

We went to the mess hall and had a free dinner and then to the NAAFI where we spent the afternoon drinking duty free English beer. This all seemed a little unreal to me and Johnny. Here were two members of CND, close friends of Communist Party members and we were inside Supreme Headquarters Allied Powers In Europe. We often wondered how many other people were in there who weren't supposed to be. We stayed one night in SHAPE and then headed back into Paris and took the metro to its furthest southern point where we began hitch hiking with the object of reaching Nice and St. Tropez. We split up after agreeing to meet at the Youth Hostel in Nice and I made it there the same day. Johnny was already there and we walked down into Nice from the Youth Hostel, which was situated in the hills overlooking the Mediterranean. Nice was full of well heeled people. The shops, cafes and restaurants were expensive. Johnny and I had about £10 each to spend in a planned two to three week period and we just could not afford to eat in Nice. Once again, as in Paris, the best we could do was to buy bread and cheese and steal grapes from a vineyard and apples from an orchard.

We decided to hitch to St. Tropez just down the coast and found it much more to our liking. There was an area of town that was reminiscent of the Left Bank in Paris with a crowd of young people from all over Europe and America, all like us looking for cheap food, beer and wine and hoping to hear some good music. Rock and roll had not yet completely taken over from the crooners and the favorite music of the avant garde in London, Paris, St. Tropez, and even Bradford was jazz. Both traditional jazz and modern jazz had a big following. The Modern Jazz Quartet, Dave Brubeck and Miles Davis were very popular. After a day roaming the streets of St. Tropez and making new friends we slept on the beach. When we awoke Johnny & I had an argument. I have no recollection of what it was about so it must have been something trivial. I decided to head off but Johnny was going to stay in St. Tropez for a few days.

Earlier in the year a French girl called Roselyne Delpanque had been to England on an exchange visit and stayed with a friend of mine, Judith Smith. I had become very friendly with Rosie and remember taking her to the Thornton's house to show her off to Jean Thornton. On the way back we were walking through Lister Park when Rosie said she was going to take a piss. I was about to show her where the public toilets were when to my surprise she pulled up her skirt and pulled down her pants, squatted down and took a piss right where she was. I couldn't imagine an English girl doing this but to Rosie it seemed perfectly normal. I liked her for this. Anyway, Rosie gave me her address and said I could stay with her anytime I wanted.

My destination on leaving St. Tropez was clear, I was heading for Rosie's. She lived a long way from St. Tropez, in a small town called Jeumont, near Maubeuge, on the Franco-Belgian border, just off the main Paris to Brussels highway. First stop was to be Paris which I hoped to make in one day. I made the same mistake I'd made when first leaving Bradford and accepted a short ride which only took me about ten miles out of St. Tropez. There I was dropped on a dead straight flat stretch of road. I could see at least a mile in each direction. Hitch hiking is a real emotional roller coaster ride. The elation when you see a car stopping, especially if it's a Mercedes or a Ferrari, the depression when nothing will stop for you; the contradictory feeling when you are offered a ride of just a few miles; part of you tells you to accept it when another voice is telling you to refuse it and wait for a better ride to come along.

This day nothing stopped for me. The cars were whizzing by me at sixty or seventy miles per hour. and even if someone had wanted to stop it really wasn't a practical proposition. Morning grew into afternoon and afternoon into evening and still nothing stopped.

I had eaten the last of my bread and cheese and drunk the last of my water. I had nightmares of dying of hunger stranded at the roadside. I only had enough money left to pay for the ferry back to England and maybe one day's food. I desperately needed to get to Jeumont. As darkness approached I started walking and after about one mile I came to an isolated farmhouse and I went and knocked at the door. In my schoolboy French I explained my predicament and asked if they had somewhere I could sleep. They told me I could either sleep in the barn with the horses or in the back of a 2CV Renault van parked in the farm yard. I opted for the van. No sooner had I rolled out my sleeping bag and begun to struggle into it than the back of the van opened and there stood the farmer's wife with a steaming bowl of coq au vin and a big hunk of bread and a glass of wine to wash it down. Never had food tasted so good.

The next morning I was up at dawn, awakened by the crowing of a rooster, and without stopping to say goodbye made my way back to the highway. I lit a Gauloise and sat down on my pack by the roadside. It was 6 a.m. and I didn't expect much traffic. The first car to come into view was a convertible VW bug with the top down although the sun was only just up and the morning was still chilly. I got to my feet and started thumbing and to my surprise the VW screeched to a halt about a hundred yards in front of me. I started running towards the car and the driver slipped it into reverse and gunned the car towards me. He said:
"Paris?"
I said:
"Paris" and I climbed into the backseat of the car. The driver and his companion were two young Parisians, about twenty years old, who had been holidaying in St. Tropez. They were anxious to get back to Paris and drove straight through stopping only for petrol. It was too noisy with the hood down to make any attempt at conversation so I just dozed in the back seat thanking my lucky stars for this five hundred mile ride.

We arrived in Paris in the early evening and because I was so low on funds I decided to carry straight on to Jeumont. I took the metro to the furthest point I could go in the direction of Brussels and started hitch hiking just as the sun began to set. A car stopped within minutes and I climbed in next to the driver. He was obviously drunk and as soon as we set off he put his hand on my thigh and began fondling me. I told him I didn't like what he was doing and he removed his hand and soon pulled into a roadside café. He was very apologetic and bought me some food, a glass of wine and cigarettes.

When he went to the lavatory I beat a hasty retreat and started thumbing again. Once again a car stopped almost immediately and I slid into the front passenger seat. We hadn't gone a hundred yards when the driver put his arm around my shoulder and started stroking my hair. I told him I didn't like this and asked him to drop me off, which he did. It was obvious I had got myself onto a stretch of road that was frequented by rent boys and twice I had been the victim of mistaken identity.

By now it was almost dark and there was very little traffic. I decided to sleep right there on the grass verge at the side of the road and resume my journey next morning. As I was spreading out my sleeping bag a car stopped and the driver asked me where I was heading for . I told him Jeumont near Maubeuge. He said he was on his way to Brussels and would take me all the way. This was a wonderful end to a great day. Two lifts from St. Tropez to Jeumont.

I arrived at Rosie's house about mid-night and was having difficulty explaining to her father who I was and what I was doing arriving at their house in the middle of the night, when Rosie came down the stairs rushed up to me and kissed me on both cheeks. Her English was better than my French and she soon explained to her parents and to her young sister and two young brothers who I was and what I was doing there. I was made very welcome by the whole family and stayed five days. There was a fete taking place in Jeumont and there were bands playing in the streets, dancing and singing, carousel rides and all the fun of the fair. The first night I was there Mr. & Mrs. Delplanque took me out with their family to a bistro where we ate steak and pommes frites and while they drank wine they bought me beer which they thought was appropriate because I was English. I was surprised to see them giving the boys, who were aged about eight and ten, wine mixed with water. The restaurant was full of families and there was a very happy festive atmosphere. I thought how different this was from life in Bradford. My parents had never taken me to a restaurant, in fact the first time I ate out was a few months before when Jean and Peter Thornton took me to a Chinese restaurant on Godwin Street in Bradford.

The next day I was at the fete with Rosie when I was surprised to hear someone shouting "Gary Spence" from across the square. It was a girl from Bradford, Rosemary, who was dating Johnny Milne's brother, Tony, and who later married him. She was on an exchange visit and was with the French girl with whom she was staying. The girl's parents were very strict and no smoking or drinking was allowed and they had to be home by 9 p.m.. They smoked and drank that night alright and they were home closer to midnight than 9 p.m.. I didn't see Rosemary again until I got back to Bradford and she told me her and her friend had got into terrible trouble for being out late and arriving home drunk.

Although Mr. Delplanque was an engineering worker in a factory and had built the little house they lived in himself they seemed to have a better quality of life than my family in Bradford. The last meal of the day for my family was tea at 5.15 p.m. with maybe a couple of cream crackers and a cup of tea before going to bed. Eating was a purely functional activity, something to be done quickly and without ceremony. For the Deplanque family the evening meal was an event. It began at 7 p.m. and would last until 8.30 or 9 p.m.

Even though they may not have had much more to eat than my family in Bradford, they ate at a more leisurely pace and divided the meal into five or six courses. Where we would have our meat, potatoes and vegetable on one plate they split these up into separate courses. I remember having a course of petit pois in a butter sauce. This would have seemed strange in Bradford but here it seemed perfectly natural. The children were drinking wine mixed with water and Mr. Delplanque had bought litre bottles of beer for me.

I packed up to leave the following Friday morning and to my surprise Mrs. Delplanque gave me a train ticket to Calais. A few hours later I was on the ferry to Dover. The sea was very rough and I had a bad bout of seasickness.

I met someone on the ferry who was travelling to London by car and he offered me a lift. I was in London by about 4 p.m. and once again stayed with Charlie Radcliffe. On Saturday morning I was up early for the last leg of my journey, from London to Bradford. I caught the tube to Hendon Central and then a bus to Apex corner. This was regarded as the start of the A1 and was a good place to hitch because there was a roundabout which stopped the traffic flow. The first vehicle to come into view was a green Austin A35 van. I thumbed furiously but the van passed by, then stopped a few hundred yards up the road. The van made a U turn and came alongside me and stopped. The van was driven by my father and mother and John were passengers. It turned out that while I had been in France father had got rid of the motor bike and sidecar and bought this little van second hand and very cheaply. His mother had given him £100 and apparently with the motor bike and sidecar thrown in as trade this had done the deal.

I still remember the license plate numbers after forty five years; the motor bike was ARN 629 and the van SAK 606. Raymond Clegg had a holiday house on the Island of Anglesea overlooking the Menai Staits on the North Wales Coast. He had loaned this cottage to the family for two weeks and after spending four or five days there they had decided to spend three days in London with my father's cousin Geoffrey (Uncle Victor's son). They were now on their way back to North Wales and asked me if I would like to go with them as there was plenty of room for me. I declined as I was anxious to get back to Bradford. This was Saturday and I was thinking of going to the Alex to see what was happening. I refused their offer of a lift as they would be taking the A6 and I wanted to go North on the A1.

The strange thing was that none of us were particularly surprised to see each other but looking back it had to be a million to one chance that we would be on the same stretch of road at precisely the same time; I was supposed to be in France and they were supposed to be in North Wales and there we were on the A1 just north of London. It seemed to be an odd series of coincidences that on this one trip I had run into Christine and Mavis in Paris, Rosemary in Jeumont and my family in London.

I soon got a lift all the way to Bradford and when I arrived home there was mail for me. I had passed the GCE in four subjects, English, History, French and German. I had also been awarded a Carlton Grammar School Leaving Certificate in English Literature and Geography. The problem was I hadn't passed in Maths which was a prerequisite for the job with Raymond Clegg. On Sunday morning I walked to the Clegg's house and explained to Mr. Clegg what had happened and told him I could stay at school for one term, take my maths GCE again in November, and if I passed join him in January, 1960. This was fine by him, he was very pleased that I had passed four GCE's at the age of fifteen and was sure I'd pass maths next time.

When father got home from North Wales I told him I had failed maths and was going back to school to take it again. He was very sympathetic having failed to matriculate himself due to his weakness in maths and, like me, particularly calculus. He went to see a neighbor, Mr. Copley, who taught maths at St. Bedes Grammar School and he agreed to give me some tuition for a fee of just £1. I went to his house twice a week for an hour and he set me extensive homework. These classes ensured that I passed the examination at the second attempt which meant the job with Mr. Clegg was mine.

Mother took me to the Co-op Emporium on Sunbridge Road in Bradford and bought me my first ever suit, she also bought me shirts and ties, underwear and shoes and socks. Everything was paid for with her Co-op dividend certificate which she received once a year as her share of the profits of the Bradford Co-operative Society. This scheme paid dividends related not to the share holding but to the amount of money spent at the Co-op during the preceding year. This was one of the reasons why mother bought her groceries at the Co-op every week.

CHAPTER NINE

"don't thee thou me" Harold

In January, 1960, a month before my sixteenth birthday, I went to work for S. H. Chippindale & Company in Howard House, Bank Street, Bradford. The office hours were 9 am to 12.30 p.m. and 2 p.m. to 5.30 p.m. Monday to Friday and 10 am to 12 noon on Saturday, but I had every Thursday off to attend Bradford Technical College. I loved the job so much that I often worked until 6 p.m. or 7 p.m. and then went straight from work to night school or to one of my meetings.

S. H. Chippindale and Company worked exclusively for the Arndale Property Trust Ltd. a publicly quoted company founded by Sam Chippindale and Arnold Hagenbach. Arndale came from the first three letters of ARNold Hagenbach's name and the last four letters of Sam ChippinDALE's name. Shortly after I joined the company S. H. Chippindale and Company was acquired by the Arndale Property Trust and its name changed to Arndale Developments, Ltd. There were four directors, Sam Chippindale, Harry Hartley, Raymond Clegg and Albert Ramsey.

Sam Chippindale was a very down to earth Yorkshire man with no airs and graces whatsoever. His one concession to his millionaire status was that he drove a Rolls Royce with a personalized number plate, SHC 333. The other directors drove 3.8 Jaguars and were very well paid for the time. Their annual salary was £5,000 or about £100 a week at a time when my father was probably making about £10 a week. In addition they received an annual profit share. They were very well off. Albert Ramsey was a very quiet person and he was prudent with his money. He had a very attractive stone built house on the outskirts of Leeds and his wife and two daughters were well provided for. He had acquired a sizeable shareholding in the Arndale Property Trust and was a very shrewd investor. Both Clegg and Hartley lived life to the full, with foreign holidays, second homes and the very best of food and drink. It was not unusual for Raymond Clegg to buy a round of drinks for everyone in the Delvers and whenever he saw me in a pub he bought me a drink. Harry Hartley was such a lavish tipper that his nickname was "scattercash".

They certainly didn't scatter any cash in my direction. The first thing I had to do was sign Articles of Pupilage which bound me to work for them for five years and bound them to provide for my education in all aspects of the property business. Raymond Clegg told me that it was usual for Articled Pupils to pay for the benefit of being trained but as they knew that my parents were unable to do this there would be no payment required. He had even persuaded his colleagues that I should be paid and the salary would be a miserable £10 per month. After deductions I had about £8 a month which I gave to my mother and she gave me back ten shillings a week. I was no better off than I had been when at school, so I still worked some evenings and Saturday afternoons and Sunday morning with father to get money for beer and cigarettes.

Arndale Property Trust was a property investment and development company specializing in shopping centers. When I joined them they had just completed schemes in Kenton and Longbenton in Newcastle, the first phase of a three phase development in Shipley near Bradford and had under way the first phase of a complete new town center for Jarrow on Tyneside. Some sites were assembled over a long period of time. They spent twenty five years piecing together their site in Market Street, Manchester where the Arndale Center is now located. Similarly, they spent a few years assembling sites in Crossgates, Leeds, Walton Vale and London Road in Liverpool.

The majority of the bigger schemes took place on land compulsorily purchased by the local authority and designated as a comprehensive development area. As most of the developments were in towns in the North of England and Scotland almost all of the councils from whom Arndale leased land were controlled by the Labor Party. These Labor councils loved to compulsorily acquire and demolish all the old shops and slum property in the town center and then lease the land to a developer. Not only did this municipalisation of land seem to them like nationalisation, they were also acquiring the property of, and effectively putting out of business, their Conservative opponents. The situation that had prevailed from 1951 and was to continue until 1964 was ideal as far as Arndale was concerned; the Tory party in control of the national government and fiscal policy with Labor majorities on the councils of the northern industrial towns and cities.

Raymond Clegg was responsible for developments in Jarrow, Shipley, Lancaster, Lytham St. Annes, Rushden, Goldthorpe and Morecambe at the time I became his assistant. His job was site acquisition, leasing, managing the building contracts and generally overseeing all aspects of the development process. In the morning he would have his mail brought to him when he arrived at 9 am and would let me read through it with him and ask questions. He would then call his secretary in and dictate replies to the various letters with me listening as he dictated. We then usually went to one of the sites to check on development progress and to meet potential tenants.

Everyone used to wear white shirts or blue shirts with white collars to the office. Not just Arndale's office but all offices everywhere in Britain. Then suddenly in the 1960's everything changed. Raymond Clegg who was an impeccable dresser came to work wearing a pink shirt. I asked mother for the money and bought myself a pink shirt. I was ready to leave for work next morning and father saw my shirt:
"You can take that pink shirt off and put on a white one. No son of mine is going to work looking like that." he said.
"It's the fashion, dad, everyone's wearing them." I said.
"Everyone except you" he said and ripped the shirt off my back.

The secret of Arndale's early success was their close working relationship with the property department of the variety store chain, F. W. Woolworth & Co. At this time, before the development of the major supermarket chains, the key to a successful development was to secure a Woolworth Store as the anchor tenant. With Woolworths signed up letting the remaining shops was comparatively easy. Sam Chippindale seemed to have the inside track with Woolworths and carried around with him a list of all their stores with the towns where they wished to relocate to bigger premises highlighted. He also knew in which towns or suburbs they wanted to acquire completely new sites. Woolworths struck a hard bargain. They required a 199 year lease at a peppercorn rental (i.e. zero rent). They would then build their own store but they would use the same architect and builder as Arndale so that the completed scheme was architecturally unified.

Almost all the construction was carried out by Leslie & Co., a subsidiary of Bovis, and most of the major schemes were designed by outside architects, usually Shingler & Risdon of London. Smaller schemes were designed by the company's staff architect, Gerry Baxter, and he also approved tenant's shop fitting plans and prepared drawings and specifications for refurbishment schemes. He also attended monthly site meetings to check on the progress of the works.

Raymond Clegg was a great guy to work for. He let me sit in on every meeting he had, he took me on all his site visits, he took me to appointments with city officials and the managing directors of retail companies. I attended every project meeting for all his jobs. He really did seem to want to teach me everything he knew and I was very keen to learn it.

At this time all the Arndale schemes looked alike regardless of where they were located. They were generally in situ concrete framed buildings with brick facades and marble pilasters on the face of the columns at either side of each shop. They were usually two storey with the upper floor used as storage. The first floor windows were metal and were painted a turquoise color called Arndale blue.

A young architect, John Fell, joined the firm shortly after me and was determined to change this cookie cutter approach to architecture. He was only twenty two years old and like me was brought into the firm by Raymond Clegg. Raymond knew John from the Delvers and had know his father, Jack, and uncles, Arthur and Laurie, all his life. John and his father lived on Ashwell Road in the same block as me so I had been acquainted with him for years. John's first project was in Lancaster, about fifty miles from Bradford and ten miles from Morecambe, a seaside resort that was so popular with Bradfordians it was known as Bradford-by-the-Sea.

The scheme involved the construction of a shopping parade with frontage to two streets with two floors of offices over. John's proposal involved the use of the usual in situ concrete frame but instead of cladding this with brick and marble to hide the structure, John proposed that the structure should be visible and that the aggregate in the concrete should be exposed. It was remarkable that a young man of twenty two would be given total responsibility for a project of this size. What was even more remarkable was that Raymond Clegg stood behind John Fell and ensured that the project was built with the honesty he intended. Arnold Hagenbach, Chairman of Arndale, wrote to Sam Chippindale to say that he had seen the scheme in Lancaster and in his opinion it was the 'Rolls Royce of Arndale developments'.

I spent a lot of time with John Fell because as well as working on the same projects in the office we also traveled to sites together. John had a company car, a Ford Anglia, and we had great fun on the trips to Lancaster, Lytham St. Annes and Rushden, where we had schemes under construction. Sometimes for a laugh I would sit on the floor of the car and operate the accelerator with my hand while John steered. He would give me directions- "faster, faster" or "slow down". John talked to me at length about architecture and I soon became familiar with the work of the Bauhaus Movement, Le Corbusier, Frank Lloyd Wright and Rennie

McIntosh. As well as giving me an appreciation for art and architecture, John also opened my eyes to nature. It's amazing how little I appreciated nature considering that I had lived close to woods and open country and worked in gardens for years.

John would be driving along when he would point excitedly and say:
"Look at that marvelous tree"
He would screech to a halt and he and I would pile out of the car and take a photograph. The couple of years I spent working closely with John Fell were a very important part of my education. I learned to see and feel in a new way.

About this time father took me to join the Oddfellows. This was a self-help benevolent society that provided life insurance and sick-pay. It was an old established organization and had a ceremony similar to the Masons for new members. Father had been a member since he was sixteen and I suspect that Mark Newbould was a member before him. It was a vital organization for self employed people such as my father.

At the same time as I was being educated at work and at Bradford Technical College, I was receiving a different kind of education in my spare time at evenings and weekends. I went to night school two nights a week but the other five nights were taken up with political activity. One night a week was CND, another YCND, I would attend public meetings at the Left Club, go to the Topic Folk Club on Fridays and would spend an increasing amount of time with Jean and Peter Thornton, Harry Wright, Bernard Doyle, Bob Cryer, Johnny Milnes and other left wing socialists. The first thing to go was my religion which I quickly jettisoned when I had been convinced that rather than God creating man in his image, man had created God in his.

I soon became a convinced socialist and was reading the works of Marx, Engels and Lenin. I was particularly impressed with Lenin's "What is to be Done" which outlines the need for and the tasks of the Bolshevik Party. It was obvious to me that the Labor Party was hopelessly reformist and that under the entrenched leadership of the right winger Hugh Gaitskell it was impossible to think of the Labor Party as a party which would change society. The Communist Party, I learned from my New Left friends, was also compromised. It had defended all the actions of Stalin and supported the frame-up trials in the USSR and the crushing of the 1956 Hungarian uprising. It had abandoned its revolutionary platform and adopted as its program "The British Road to Socialism", which envisaged a transfer of power from the capitalist class to the working class via the ballot box by achieving a majority in the House of Commons for the Communist Party in unison with left wing Labor M.P.'s.

There was no precedent for the ruling class in any society surrendering power without an armed struggle and in any event the prospect of the Communist Party winning ten million votes, the minimum necessary to achieve a majority in Parliament was ludicrous. The number of Communist M.P.s fluctuated between zero and two and it was considered a major victory if a candidate obtained enough votes to save his deposit. A typical vote for a Communist Party candidate was between fifty and two hundred votes; a similar number of votes would be cast by mistake for any name on the ballot paper. It seemed to me that a new party was needed that espoused marxism-leninism and the traditions of the Bolshevik Party. I talked about this with members of the New Left and it was clear we were at cross purposes. They were interested in building a broad left coalition based around organizations such as CND and had no thoughts of developing a marxist party.

I asked Jean Thornton why she was still in the Communist Party. Her reply was that for a genuine socialist there was really nowhere else to go. Here was a party with thirty thousand members and a daily newspaper; included in its ranks were many leading academics and a hard core of workers many of whom held key positions of leadership in the trade union movement. She thought the party needed reforming, it needed to get back to its revolutionary roots and it needed to re-examine Soviet history and its own history from an objective marxist standpoint. Join the Communist Party in order to change it seemed to be what she was proposing. I joined the Young Communist League; I would not be eligible to join the Communist Party until I was eighteen. Most of the YCL members in Bradford were the children of Party members, people like John and William Baruch and Joan Siddons. Before long I was elected as secretary of the Bradford YCL and was also elected to the Yorkshire District Committee, which in turn elected me to the Yorkshire Executive Committee.

Shortly after I joined the YCL Raymond Clegg asked me into his office and sat me down across the desk from him:

"Are you a member of the Communist Party?" he asked

"No, I'm not" I said, which strictly was true.

"Well Police Inspector Rose who lives next door to Harry Hartley has told Harry you are. I will take your word for it for now but if I find out you've lied to me you will be out of a job."

My eyes were opened as to how the police were tapped into the old boy network to deprive militants of employment. Another lesson learned.

Sam Chippindale and Arnold Hagenbach went on a long trip to Australia in 1960. They were looking for development opportunities and bought several sites for shopping centers while they were there. They appointed John Graham & Co. of New York, Seattle and Honolulu as consultant architects for the first scheme in Australia. At John Graham's invitation Sam Chippindale visited two of his developments, the Ala Moana Center at Waikiki, Honolulu and the Lloyd Center in Portland, Oregon and was overwhelmed by these covered centers.

When he returned home Sam Chippindale called a meeting of the whole firm and showed a film about covered mall centers. This was the future as far as he was concerned; total segregation of pedestrians and vehicles and a climate controlled environment for year round shopping comfort. Add to this large free car parks and he felt certain he had a winning formula. In the States many of these centers were being built in out of town locations where land was cheap and vast surface parking lots could be built. What Sam Chippindale had in mind was something different; he proposed to build this kind of scheme in town centers with underground or roof top parking and servicing and integrated bus and rail links where possible. It was back to the drawing board for every major scheme that Arndale had in the works. From Manchester to Leeds, Bradford to Basingstoke all proposals were to be revamped in line with the new policy. The problem was that no British architect had any experience with this type of development. Chippindale solved this by recruiting from John Graham's Seattle office a British national, Percy Gray, who was a member of both the American Institute of Architects and the Royal Institution of British Architects. Percy's job was to do all the original concept sketches for every development and then ensure that the appointed architects stayed with the agenda. At this time almost all Arndale's schemes had Shingler & Risden as the architects , so Percy only had to supervise one firm.

Sam Chippindale agreed to pay for a new cricket pavillion for Woodhouse Grove School in Apperley Bridge, Bradford, which his son, Howard, had attended. An architect, John G. Poulson, did all the architectural work gratis and at the ceremony to open the pavillion Sam Chippindale was to meet him for the first time. Poulson pitched for Sam's business by explaining his own modus operandi. He visited local authorities, and told the councillors and officials that he would design them a town center redevelopment scheme free of charge provided they hired him as the consultant who would advise them on the selection of a developer to carry out the scheme. He would then have the developer appoint him as the scheme architect and earn his fees that way. He told Sam that he had dozens of councils already tied up and that he had the town councillors in his pocket. He spoke of close associations with leading members of both the Labor and Conservative Parties. If Sam Chippindale would give him all his architectural work then he would ensure that Arndale was appointed as developer in all the towns where he held sway.

He took Sam Chippindale to look at his office in the small market town of Pontefract. By any standards it was impressive. Poulson had a staff of over three hundred working shifts and providing not only architectural services but also a full consulting engineering service. Sam Chippindale told his colleagues that he proposed to fire Shingler & Risden and replace them with Poulson. Shingler &

Risden would be paid whatever fees were due to them calculated on a quantum meruit basis. Clegg & Hartley were hotly opposed to the proposal; they thought it was wrong in principle to fire Shingler & Risdon, who had done nothing wrong, and predicted delays and cost over-runs on jobs under construction as Poulson's staff took over.

Chippindale overruled Clegg and Hartley and Poulson was appointed. Shortly afterwards Clegg and Hartley resigned and set up their own business. Whether there was any connection between Poulson's appointment and their resignation I cannot say. Several years later John Poulson and T. Dan Smith, a leading member of the Labour Party in the north east, were arrested, tried and sent to jail for corruption.

Another Chippindale recruit was Colonel Kenneth Post, formerly Chairman of the National Trust. He was hired as a 'consultant' and used to come down from London to Bradford two days a week. He obviously had a low opinion of the food in Bradford because he used to bring a wicker picnic basket containing his lunch. His job was to pull political strings and I clearly remember one case in which he was totally successful. Arndale had built a four story office block speculatively in Jarrow as part of the town center redevelopment. It is a brave or foolish man who builds office space in Jarrow where demand hovers between nil and zero. The only hope was to get the Ministry of Works to lease the space for a Government Department. There was vague interest from the Ministry of Housing and Local Government but we had never been able to finalize a deal. Colonel Post wrote a letter to Geoffrey Rippon, the Minister for Housing and Local Government. It went something like this:

> "*My Dear Geoffrey;*
>
> *I am advising the Arndale Property Trust in connection with some of their developments.*
>
> *They have been talking to the Newcastle office of the Ministry of Works about leasing some*

space to your department in their Jarrow Town Center Development.

They are not making much progress and I wonder if you would be a good fellow and try to speed things up.

Yours ever,

Kenneth

Col. K. Post "

Four weeks later the lease was signed. This is a prime example of how the old boy network functioned.

Ron Jennings and Des Longbottom were appointed to the Arndale Development board to replace Clegg and Hartley and Longbottom took over Hartleys schemes while Jennings became an assistant to Chippindale, working on major schemes throughout the country in particular Arndale's first covered center in Crossgates, Leeds. I was left with Clegg's project in Jarrow to complete and the final lettings in Lancaster, Goldthorpe, and Shipley. Subsequently I became Des Longbottom's assistant.

Howard Chippindale, Sam's son, joined the firm in 1962. Growing up in Heaton I had known Howard and he had attended the Baptist Sunday School with me. I became great friends with him and he became part of the crowd that met on Saturday nights at the Alex. Although Howard had a company car – an Austin A40 – he, like me, was paid a miserly wage and so he and I had to resort to a little subterfuge to try to level the playing field. The firm had an account for petrol at the Turf Garage on Bradford Road and the Turf sold cigarettes and both Howard and I smoked. We would get cigarettes and have them put on the account as petrol: if anyone had ever calculated how few miles to the gallon Howard's car was doing they would have been in for a big surprise. Although Howard's father was teetotal he had a cocktail cabinet in his office and on Saturday nights on the way to the

Alex, Howard and I would go to the office and help ourselves to a few drinks. That way we had a buzz going before we got to the Alex and could spend less on beer.

Until I got my own company car – an Austin 1100 – which was after Clegg left I used to travel around a lot with Howard. I would walk down from Ashwell Road to Howard's house, The Ryddings, on Emm Lane and he would give me a ride to work. From Howard's house it was about a quarter of a mile to the bottom of Emm Lane and we had a contest to see who could get the car's speed up to over 60 m.p.h. and stop at the bottom of Emm Lane by using the gears. Use of the brakes was not permitted. My recollection is that the manufacturer provided two new engines for that car because of the abuse Howard and I gave it.

Next to Howard House was another building owned by Arndale, Swan Arcade. This was a Victorian building which fronted three streets, Market Street, Charles Street, and Broadway. There were four arcades running through the building connecting the surrounding streets. The ground level was comprised of shops and there were three or four upper levels of office space. These were mainly let to wool merchants and there were lots of one and two man offices. Chippindale's plan was to demolish the building and replace it with modern shops and offices. He tried very hard to buy the Wool Exchange on the opposite side of Market Street with a view to demolishing it and merging the two sites with a development that would have involved either the closure of Market Street or building over it at first floor level. This scheme would in turn have been linked by pedestrian walkway to Brown Muff's Department Store.

When he found he could not buy the Wool Exchange he appointed the American architects, John Graham & Co., and they designed a scheme for the Swan Arcade site with a basement car park, shops on ground floor & first floor levels, a roof garden over the shops and a seven storey office building. The offices known as Arndale House were to have sealed windows and be air conditioned. They were the first and probably are still the only air conditioned offices in Bradford and became Arndale's new headquarters. At the time there didn't seem to be anything particularly wrong with demolishing Swan Arcade and there was very little outcry. In retrospect it was a sad loss for Bradford as was the subsequent demolition of Kirkgate Market by Bradford Council to make way for an Arndale Center.

The Arndale offices on the seventh and eighth floor of Arndale House were to be divided up using planters and I managed to secure the contract for father to both do the initial plant up and the subsequent watering and maintenance. He also got the job of looking after the roof garden. A couple of years later he was awarded the contract for the interior landscaping at Arndale's first covered mall at Crossgates in Leeds. This was much easier work than being out in all weather digging someone's garden or clipping hedges and as he got older he relied more and more on this type of indoor work.

After Swan Arcade was demolished the caretaker, a man called Maurice, who would have been in his sixties, moved into the offices in Howard House and was given a job as a messenger and general factotum. He and Bob Salter, Arndale's clerk of works, used to regale us with stories about the First World War and about things that had happened in their lifetime. Maurice told me that in the First World War his commanding officer was the owner of a mill where Maurice worked before joining up. Maurice hated him because of the way he ill treated his workers. When they got to France and were advancing across no man's land Maurice says he killed him by shooting him in the back. He said this very matter-of-factly and when I questioned his veracity he assured me that what he did was commonplace.

One of my favorite stories Maurice told concerned his time as caretaker at Swan Arcade. One of the tenants complained to Maurice that there was a pile of shit in one of the office corridors upstairs. Maurice went to investigate and sure enough there was a pile of distinctly human shit "still steaming" said Maurice. He cleaned it up. The next day a call came from another tenant. Sure enough another steaming pile of shit in a different corridor. This went on for months and they were never able to catch the culprit who they nicknamed "the Phantom Shitter".

In 1960 Grandad Atkinson died – he had Parkinson's Disease – but the doctor said his premature death (he was only sixty five) was attributable to having been gassed in the First World War. Grandma moved into 12 Ashwell Road with us as she couldn't manage alone. Not only was she crippled with arthritis she had now developed ulcerative colitis. Our dining kitchen was converted into a bedroom for her and a toilet and shower were installed. The kitchen and dining area was moved to the basement which put an end to father's workshop. Grandma only lasted until 1962 and she was buried in the same grave as Ashbel in Heaton Cemetery.

In the summer of 1960 I took two weeks holiday and was off again hitch hiking to France. This time I went alone and I had definite objectives in mind. Roselyne Delplanque had been to stay with us earlier in the year and I planned to go back to Jeumont and spend a few days with her. I had met two other exchange students, one, Jean Pierre, lived on the outskirts of Paris, the other one, Marianne, lived in Clermont Ferrand. I was very lucky with lifts and got to Paris in one day and made my way by metro to Jean Pierre's house. I knew that Jean Pierre and his family were Communist Party members because he had been staying with the Baruch family in Bradford when I met him and he told me so. For some reason I was expecting a modest house so I was surprised to discover that these Communists lived in a mansion. I had a pleasant couple of days there with a beautiful room and excellent food but I never really felt relaxed. I never felt I was en famille as I did with the Delplanques.

When I arrived in Clermont Ferrand I found that Marianne's parents owned a small hotel close to the town center. I was given a very small windowless room by Marianne's father who was surly and did not make me welcome. Marianne ignored me so after a couple of days I headed to Jeumont. As in the previous year I hitched straight through Paris and made it to Jeumont in one day. The Delplanques were very hospitable and I had five very enjoyable days with them. I was never to see them again and when I wrote several years later they replied and told me that Roselyne was married and had children and was living in Nice.

By 1961 I was becoming very busy indeed. I was secretary of YCND, an active member of Bradford CND, a member of the Yorkshire Committee of 100, and secretary of the Bradford Branch of the Young Communist League. Every night was taken up with a meeting and I had completely stopped studying for my Chartered Surveyor exams. Once Raymond Clegg left Arndale I was too involved with work to take a day a week off to go to technical college so I had started a correspondence course run by the College of Estate Management. The idea was that I would do this in the evenings but by the time I had worked all day, been to meetings, and ended up in the pub for a few pints the last thing I felt like was studying.

My brother, Mike, started dating a girl called Liz York, who he had met at a dance at St. Barnabas Hall and on 18th November, 1961, they were married at Haworth Road Methodist Church. Liz lived on Marriners Drive off Emm Lane and her father was manager of the Bradford branch of the Yorkshire Insurance Company. I think he was unhappy about Liz marrying a gardener's son but, fair play to him, we all went to a hotel after the wedding and there was no shortage of sandwiches, cake and champagne.

When John was getting ready to leave school in 1962 father tried to find him a job, as he had done for Michael and I, but without success. There was an advert in the newspaper from Henry Cullingworth & Sons, wool merchants for an office boy and John applied. Father actually went with him to the interview and he got the post. John never liked the job and after a couple of years said he was quitting. Once again father intervened and spoke to Sam Ludbrook, the head gardener at Lister Park, and got John a job as one of thirty gardeners at the park. John never really fitted in and was in trouble with the other gardeners because he was the only one who would not join the union. Finally he was warned he must join or suffer the consequences. He didn't join and one of the

Making Hen's Meat

gardeners knocked him to the ground then jumped on him and stabbed him with his pen knife. After he returned from the hospital the first thing John did was join the union. One day Sam Ludbrook told a Polish gardener called Walter that he was sacked and he should get his personal things and leave:
"First I get shovel" said Walter.
"Alright, get the bloody shovel" said Sam.
Two minutes later Walter re-appeared with the shovel and hit Sam Ludbrook over the head with it knocking him to the ground. Only then did he leave.

CHAPTER TEN

"haben sie any ale gegotten, as they say in Wales" Harold

In 1962 a boy of about seventeen who went to Bradford Grammar School and lived in Calverley, between Leeds and Bradford, started showing up at YCND and CND meetings in Bradford and at public meetings organized by the New Left, Anti Apartheid, the Communist Party or any other left wing group. His name was Tony Whelan and he was a member of a Trotskyist organisation called the Socialist Labor League. He used to sell their weekly newspaper "The Newsletter" and their monthly youth paper "Keep Left".

He made no bones about the fact that he had been sent to work in Bradford by the Leeds Branch of the Socialist Labor League in order to gain recruits. I was a prime target and I was interested to hear what he had to say because I had the same objective as him, a socialist government. He and I started spending time together. After meetings he would go with me to the Alassio Coffee Bar opposite the Odeon Cinema or maybe to a pub for a pint. He used to write me long letters sometimes handwritten, sometimes typed in black, sometimes in red. These were historical treatises dealing with events in Russia in 1905 to 1917 and the subsequent history of the Communist Party of the Soviet Union.

In the simplest possible terms what he was saying was that after Lenin's death with Stalin's rise to power the Communist Party of the Soviet Union abandoned marxist principles and a bureaucracy came to dominate the party and society. Stalin had framed up and executed the majority of the leaders of the 1917 revolution and had arranged for Trotsky's assasination in Mexico City . Stalin had developed the theory of socialism in one country, which was in opposition to the teaching of Marx, Engels and Lenin who had always held that socialism and communism could only be built on an international scale. The interests of the bureaucracy in the Soviet Union became all important and the Communist Parties in the capitalist countries became nothing more than mouth-pieces for the CPSU. Their sole concern was defense of the Soviet Union and they had abandoned a revolutionary perspective.

Trotsky and his followers believed that the Communist Parties could not be reformed from within and that it was necessary to create new Parties and a new international – The Fourth International – which was established in 1938. The Socialist Labor League was the British section of the Fourth International. Whelan persevered with me and eventually after meeting Cliff Slaughter, who was a lecturer at Leeds University and the party's main theoretician, I agreed to join. Slaughter had been recruited to the Socialist Labor League after he resigned from the Communist Party in 1956 following the crushing of the Hungarian uprising.

About this time I met Janet Crawford at the Topic Folk Club and walked her to her bus in Forster Square. We stopped in the doorway of Sports & Pastimes shop on Cheapside and kissed and cuddled for half an hour. Soon Janet became my girlfriend and she joined all the organizations of which I was a member. Both Janet and I were virgins and we decided to have sex together. With some trepidation I climbed the stairs to my attic with Janet. It was a very unsatisfactory experience for me but Janet thought it was beautiful. I guess it must have grown on me because before too long I was having sex at every opportunity, exclusively with Janet for a while, but soon with others. Janet and I broke up some time later and she started dating another member of the Socialist Labor League,Trevor Holdsworth, whom she later married.

She calligraphed a poem for me by a Russian poet, Vaptsarov as a sort of goodbye gift. This is it:

Spring

My Spring, my white spring
Still unlived, still unfeted
Still only a daydream
Skimming the poplars
Not caring to stay here

My spring, my white spring
You'll bring thunder, I know
Rain and hurricane too,
To restore many hopes
And wash bloody wounds.

How the skylark shall sing
As it soars high above us,
Our work gladness bring,
And all men be brothers.

My spring, my white spring
Let me see your first flight
Call the dead squares to life
Let me but see your sun,
And then –
On your barricades die.

I started dating another of the girls who was in the Socialist Labor League, Pamela, and one night she came to my house on one of those rare occasions when mother, father and John were out for the evening. I was assured nobody would be home before 10 p.m. At about 9 p.m. the door to the sitting room suddenly opened and there was mother. We were just about to make love. I do not know who was more embarrassed me, Pamela or mother. A few minutes later there was a knock at the door and mother came in with two cups of coffee. Pamela left shortly after to catch the bus home and although we continued dating for a while things were never the same and we never tried to make love again. One night I was due to go out with Pamela selling the young socialist paper

around the pubs in Bradford when I noticed there was a movie on at the Civic Theater which I'd seen a good review of. The movie was called Fellini's 8 ½. Pam and I decided we would go to the movie and sell Keep Left the following day. As we were leaving the Civic Theater we ran into Cliff Slaughter and his girl friend, Diane Davis, who had also been at the movie. This was slightly embarrassing because I had been talking to Cliff in the afternoon and had assured him I was going out selling Keep Left that evening. I asked Cliff if he'd like to go for a pint and when he said yes I asked him if he wanted to go somewhere sophisticated or somewhere bawdy:
"Definitely bawdy" Cliff replied.
We went to the Old Crown in Ivegate, a pub favored by the Irish and also the haunt of small time criminals and prostitutes. Cliff asked me if I had understood the movie and I said not really.
"Well" said Cliff "this was Fellini's ninth movie but he never finished it so he called it Fellini's 8 ½. Fellini is a marxist and his struggle to make this movie is similar to our struggle with the revisionist Socialist Workers Party in the U.S.A. Just as we are struggling to defend marxism against empiricism so Fellini is struggling to use the marxist method in movie making."
"I see" I said, although I didn't.

At this time the majority of the Socialist Labor League's members were operating as an organized faction in the Labor Party and particularly the Young Socialists, the Labor Party's youth organization. This was a highly secret operation because SLL members were barred from membership. Within three years of entering the Young Socialists the SLL had a majority on its National Committee. Socialist policies were adopted and the YS organized marches, demonstrations and lobbies of parliament against growing youth unemployment. The Trotskyists via the Young Socialists were for the first time in their history mobilizing large numbers of youth around socialist policies.

In 1963 a bitter dispute broke out at Denby's Dyeworks in Lower Baildon and the strike lasted two years. Every week I joined the picket line at 7 a.m. and sold the Newsletter which was enthusiastically received because it always contained an article

telling the truth about the strike. I usually wrote these articles and Mike Banda, editor of the Newsletter, gave me the nom de plume Geoff Penn. The strike could have been won and won quickly if the members of the National Union of Dyers, Bleachers and Texitile Workers who worked in other dyeworks had been brought out in sympathy. Left to fight alone the Denby workers had a bitter struggle. Truck loads of scabs were bused in to keep the plant running and a large force of police was always present to ensure they got in and out of the plant unscathed. Security men with alsation dogs patrolled the grounds and the chairman of the company produced a shot gun when workers approached his home. Les Herd the National Secretary of the union did little or nothing to help the strikers. At a demonstration in Shipley market square organized by Bradford Trades Council in support of the strikers Mr. Herd quoted the bible:
"Blessed are the peacemakers"
War was being waged on his members and this "leader" wanted to make peace.

One Saturday night a benefit concert for the strikers was held at East Bierley Labor Club and Jack Gale, a leading member of the Socialist Labour League in Leeds came over to help me sell the Newsletter and Keep Left. There was a concert with all the artistes giving their services free. The highlight of the show was a strip tease artiste and Jack got very aroused, particularly as the stripper removed every stitch of clothing and ended the act totally naked:
"What did you think to the shop steward?" I asked Jack.
"I haven't seen the shop steward," he replied.
"Yes, you have, the stripper is the shop steward" I said.
"So you mean to tell me the shop steward is a woman and a stripper?" asked Jack.
"No" I replied "A man and a stripper. The shop steward is a female impersonator".

I quickly recruited most of the Bradford membership of the Young Communist League into the Socialist Labor League, the exceptions being John and William Baruch, sons of died in the wool Stalinists, Lou and Hilda Baruch. I didn't even try to win over the Baruch brothers as I knew they would have reported me to the District Organizer and I would have been expelled. Other members of the YCL in Leeds were also recruited and before long we had three members on the Yorkshire District Committee. All three of us were elected to the four person executive committee. The SLL was so busy with the Young Socialists that they never really worked out what to do with their few members in the Communist Party. Tony Whelan was either a police agent or mentally unstable or both for in early 1964 he went to the Labor Party regional office in Leeds and gave them a list of names and addresses of SLL members who were in the Labor Party and Young Socialists. He also went to see Bert Ramelson, Yorkshire District Organizer of the Communist Party and gave him a list of SLL members who were in the Communist Party. Ramelson sent for me and asked me point blank if I was in the SLL. I said no but he did not believe me and rather than wait to be expelled I left the YCL and the Communist Party and in 1964 we formed a Bradford branch of the SLL and of the new independent Young Socialists.

The Labour Party, under Harold Wilson, had won the 1964 General Election and were threatening to close down the Young Socialists so the SLL moved to make the Young Socialists a body unconnected with the Labor Party, an open revolutionary youth movement. We had some success in Bradford in recruiting young people on the Buttershaw and Holmewood housing estates. These forces were turned toward the trade unions on a national scale and an objective was set to launch a daily newspaper before the end of the decade. It was a fact that the fight against the right wing had been fought very successfully and that the tactic of "entry" into the Labor Party, first advocated by Trotsky had been successful.

Gerry Healy, National Secretary of the SLL, had this to say in an internal bulletin:

> *"Not only was this work most successful but it proved that by maintaining a strong independent revolutionary organisation and combining faction work with serious activity amongst youth in the local areas it was possible to win over the forces*

necessary to defeat the Labor Party bureaucracy. We established in practice a united front from within with those youth who were moving to the left, whilst at the same time we exposed the role of the fake lefts in the fight against the right wing. This in our opinion, is how Trosky advocated the entry tactic"

I was very impressed with Gerry Healy, who was a formidable character. He was born in 1913 in Ballybane, County Galway, Ireland, and as a child witnessed the murder of his father, Michael, at the hands of Britain's infamous militia, the Black and Tans. He left Ireland at the age of fourteen and joined the merchant navy in Cardiff, Wales, having completed a course as a ship's radio operator. He soon became a member of the Communist Party which had a strong base in Cardiff, particularly amongst the seamen. He received his education in the Communist Party and as a seaman became a valuable asset to the Communist International acting as a courier in a secret network all over Europe. As part of this work he studied the Lloyds Register of Shipping and saw something which puzzled him greatly. He recalled this as follows:

" Soviet cargo ships from Batum were dropping half their cargo of oil in Genoa and the other half at Barcelona. I asked Communist Party leader, Harry Pollit, how it was that the Soviet Union was shipping oil to Mussolini's Italy to fuel their Caproni bombers in Spain and Abyssinia. Pollit told me to see William Joss of the control commision who said 'These are Trotskyite questions' I replied that I had never read a word of Trotsky in my life; Joss said 'if you persist with this then you will be expelled;' I persisted and I was expelled".

Healy then started to listen to Troskyists speaking at Hyde Park Corner and to read their papers and pamplets and joined the movement in 1937.

In October, 1964 Gerry Healy decided that the way forward for the movement was to appoint full time organizers for the Socialist Labour League and the Young Socialists in the major conurbations. He believed that this would quickly lead to a further influx of youth who would provide the finances necessary to pay these organisers. He appealed, in a letter to the membership of the SLL, for volunteers. I volunteered. Gerry Healy came to Leeds to interview me and others. He asked me what I had read by Marx, Engels, Lenin and Trotsky. Then he asked me if I had a driving license and I said I had. That seemed to clinch it and he told me I was to work in Manchester and my wage would be £9 a week. I handed in my notice at Arndale and told mother and father I was leaving to go to Manchester. You would have thought it was the other side of the world instead of just thirty miles away. Mike had left to get married, now I was leaving, the house was emptying. Father said:
"We might as well have stayed in Quarry Street".

I was dating a girl called Joyce Stockdale who was attending Bradford University and lived in a flat owned by the Thorntons in St. Pauls Road, Bradford. She had been recruited to the SLL in Leeds where she was in the YCL. Her parents were old time Communist Party members. She and I had both been on the YCL District Committee and we had worked together politically before we started dating. We had been drifting apart for a few months and with the move to Manchester imminent we agreed to bring the relationship to an end.

My first week as a "professional revolutionary" was spent in Liverpool. Mike Farley, National Secretary of the Young Socialists, and Reg Perry worked for the SLL full time in Liverpool. I don't think they were paid. They signed on as unemployed and drew the dole. They had three very active Young Socialist branches in Liverpool and they also had a lot of influence in one of the dockers' unions, the National Association of Stevedores and Dockers. A leading shop-steward in the docks, Peter Kerrigan, was a Trotskyist. Once they had shown me the ropes I went to Manchester and attended my first meeting of the Manchester Branch of the SLL.

There were about ten members, amongst them were Chris and Hilary Sames, who used to be students of Cliff Slaughter at Leeds University, Mike Hughes an engineering apprentice and Secretary of the National Apprentices Movement, a Trotskyist controlled organization, Tiny, a building worker, Ralph Williams, who was a psychiatric nurse and Susan Salkey, a seventeen year old school girl. I was immediately attracted to Susan. She was about 5'2" tall and weighed about 10 stone. She had a great figure and long straight dark hair. She wore spectacles which for some reason I found attractive. She was dressed in a green tweed two piece suit with a very short skirt which showed off her legs to great advantage. I knew right away that I wanted her to be my girl friend and within a couple of weeks I was meeting her off the school bus in central Manchester and taking her to Yates' Wine Lodge on Market Street for a glass of marsala or commandaria.

To my surprise I discovered that the Manchester members under the leadership of Chris Sames were still in the Labor Party and the Labor Party Young Socialists. The rest of the movement had exited the Labor Party and were operating the Young Socialist branches openly as the youth movement of the SLL. I immediately wrote to Gerry Healy about this and asked his opinion about me having a showdown with Chris Sames. Healy replied by saying that I was undoubtedly right on the political issues but rather than have a showdown with Sames he would get Chris and Hilary to move to London and I could then re-direct the branch. He sent me a copy of a letter to Chris Sames asking him to move to London to assist at the centre with theoretical work.

We obtained premises in the Collyhurst neighborhood of Manchester and in Salford and formed two branches of the Young Socialists. We sold our newspapers outside major engineering companies and at Salford Docks. Progress with recruiting was slow and, after I had been in Manchester for about ten weeks, I received a letter from Gerry Healy telling me that, due to the response being less than anticipated, they could no longer afford to pay me and I should look for a job but he wanted me to stay in Manchester. By this time Susan and I were totally involved with each other, and I knew I had found the love of my life. I was therefore very happy to stay in Manchester so I could see Susan every day.

The first time I went to Susan's house in Prestwich was just after her grandmother had died. Susan was Jewish and although her parents had long since stopped going to temple they still observed Jewish customs and traditions. When I arrived at the house, Susan's parents and relations were there praying. All the mirrors were covered with sheets and there was a very solemn atmosphere. Susan and I went into the small parlor, a room the family never used. I remember we ate a box of chocolates and were sitting on a sofa kissing when her father, Reuben, came in. He went berserk and told me to leave the house for daring to touch his daughter. I pointed out she was seventeen and had the right to make her own mind up who her boyfriend was but Reuben was adamant, Susan was to stop seeing me. We didn't take the slightest notice and went on seeing each other every day.

At this time I was living in a little flat over a washing machine repair shop on Mill Street in the Manchester suburb of Bradford. Susan would spend the night with me and tell her parents she was staying with her friend, Frances, whose father was the vicar of Ashton-under-Lyne. I took a job as a clerk in an office in Shude Hill in central Manchester. I truly hated this job and was always taking days off sick. When I didn't go to work I would take the bus to North Manchester Girls High School, where Susan was in her final year. I would ride the school bus into the city center with Susan and forty other girls. I remember one afternoon after school Susan got drunk in Yates' Wine Lodge and we wandered up Market Street to Picadilly Gardens to catch a bus to my flat. I stopped to buy some contraceptives and gave these to Susan to put in her school bag. A policeman stopped the traffic so we could cross Market Street and to my amazement Susan started blowing up one of the contraceptives like a balloon. The policeman just looked at her and laughed.

There was a coin-in-the-slot electric meter in my flat and I was always short of money for this meter. It took shilling pieces and I

discovered that a half penny with one side filed flat would operate it. I used to take piles of half pennies down to the landlords workshop in the cellar and use his vice and file to convert my half pennies for use in his meter. The bath tub in my apartment was old and rusty and discoloured and Susan and I bought a can of white paint and repainted it. When the paint was dry I ran a hot bath and soaked myself for half an hour. When I got out of the bath tub Susan looked at me and started laughing uproariously.
"What's so funny" I asked
"It's your arse" she said
"What's wrong with my arse"
"It's covered with white paint"
We had used oil based paint and the hot water had melted it. I could never take a bath in that flat again.

My 21st birthday was on 25 February, 1965 and my mother baked me a birthday cake and sent it through the mail. That night after the Young Socialist meeting we all went to the pub and celebrated my birthday with pints of ale and slices of birthday cake.

My mother and father came to visit in March and I introduced them to Susan. Susan told me father had taken her to one side and asked her to "Look after Gary". She took this to mean have sex with me, but I thought he meant no more than what he said. Sue thought my father was lecherous and I began to see a side of him I had not previously been aware of.

Someone gave us an old van for the use of the Young Socialists in Manchester. We called it Betsy. We never had the money for petrol and were always running out. We spent as much time pushing that van as driving it. I used to carry a rubber tube with me so that I could syphon petrol out of somebody's car if I got the chance. The way this worked was to park the van so its petrol filler cap was close to the one on the other vehicle. Then drop the tube into the target vehicle's tank put your mouth over the tube and suck. You then had to get your mouth off the tube before it got full of petrol, and stick that end of the tube into Betsy's filler. Nine times out of ten you got a mouth full of petrol but it was worth it to get a free fill up. One night we saw a Ford Cortina parked in a back alley near Tiny's house in Salford and pulled up next to it. I put the tube in the petrol tank and sucked – just then I heard the door of the house open and someone came out. I dropped the tube. We all jumped into Betsy and off we went. About half an hour later I went back to see if I could retrieve my syphoning tube only to discover that when I had dropped my end of the tube the other end had remained in the car's petrol tank and a full tank of petrol had emptied into the street. I thank God I wasn't smoking when I made this discovery.

The National Committee of the Young Socialists called for a lobby of parliament in February 1965 to demand the payment of a pensions increase promised by Harold Wilson as one of his General Election pledges. The idea was to unite trade unionists with pensioners under the banner and leadership of the Young Socialists. We campaigned amongst the Young Socialists in Collyhurst and Salford and booked a forty seat motor coach to go the lobby.

When the day came only four of us turned up, myself, Susan, Tiny and Mike Hughes. We had to tell the bus driver we didn't need his services. We had no money to get to London by bus or train so decided we would look for a car to steal. There was no question of using Betsy, she wouldn't have made it twenty miles, never mind two hundred. As we were walking around looking for a car that was open and had the keys in the ignition we saw a taxi pull up outside a club. The taxi driver left the cab with the engine running while he went into the club to locate his customer. The four of us immediately jumped in the cab and with me driving headed for the M6 and London. We stopped at Knutsford Services on the M6 and there we met a crowd of Young Socialists from Glasgow on their way by coach to London. We hitched a lift on their coach and left the taxi at the service station.

One day I was with Tiny who was out of work at the time, and we were both penniless and hungry. I said lets hitch hike to Bradford, at least my mother will give us a meal. We arrived in Bradford a couple of hours later and mother cooked us a breakfast of bacon, sausage, egg, tomatoes, mushrooms and baked beans with toast and tea. I asked mother to give me some money and she gave me ten shillings which was all she could afford. I took Tiny to meet Jean Thornton and after I'd brought her up to date on all the happenings in Manchester and we'd agreed on what a traitor Harold Wilson was Jean asked me if I needed some money. I told her a pound would come in handy:

"Here, take this" said Jean and handed me a five pound note.

We decided since we were in funds we would get the train back to Manchester. We rode the bus to town and walked to Exchange Station. We went to the ticket office and asked for two single tickets to Manchester. I reached into my pocket for the fiver and it wasn't there. I searched every pocket and could not find it. Reluctantly I handed the tickets back. It's still a mystery where that fiver went. Tiny and I were so deflated as we hitched our way back to Manchester and poverty.

In June Susan took her Advanced Level GCE examinations and was confident she would pass at least two of them. She had been for an interview and audition at the Laban Art of Movement Studio in Addlestone, near Weybridge in Surrey and her acceptance was conditional on her passing at least two "A" levels. She was to study modern dance. I couldn't bear the thought of being separated from Susan so I wrote to Gerry Healy and asked him if I could transfer to London and he replied saying that he was glad to have me in London. He told me he wanted me to live in the East End of London and be in the East London branch of the Socialist Labor League. Susan was to be in the Croydon branch in S.W. London, the closest branch to Addlestone. It was impossible to be farther apart in London.

CHAPTER ELEVEN

*"once upon a time when the birds shit lime
and the monkeys chewed tobacco
the little pigs run with their fingers up their bum
to see what was the matter"* Harold

I moved to London in July, 1965 and found myself a room in Forest Gate, East London. I got a job as a coffee roaster's laborer at C. Miles & Co. in Whitechapel. This was a terrible sweat shop. I was the only Englishman there apart from the owner. The foreman was German and the other workers were Irish, Polish and Pakistani. My job involved mixing raw coffee beans of different types, country of origin and so on into specific blends as required by customers, some of them coffee merchants, others delicatessens and coffee bars.

Some of these customers had been doing business with C. Miles since its foundation in 1762 and C. Miles had cheated them consistently for the whole two hundred years. There were two ways of cheating; the first was to add chicory to the blend. Chicory was much cheaper than coffee and no matter what the recipe called for anywhere between 10% and 20% chicory would be added. The second way of cheating was on the shrinkage. When coffee beans are roasted they lose moisture and therefore weight. If 300 lbs of coffee beans is roasted the shrinkage might be 10% - 30 lbs so you end up with 270 lbs of roast coffee. C. Miles & Co. would say that the shrinkage was 20% - 60 lbs and would only deliver 240 lbs of roast coffee to their customer and keep 30 lbs for themselves. On an annual basis the amount of coffee stolen by this company could be measured in tons.

After the coffee was roasted and ground it had to be delivered all over London from the City to the West End and Soho. The driver left and I was offered the job. Anything rather than working in a hot dusty roasting shop shoveling tons of coffee everyday. One day I had to deliver a sack of coffee beans to a coffee merchant in Fenchurch Street. I parked the van and set out across the street with a sack of coffee weighing about 75 lbs on my back. I was half way across the street when my belt snapped and my trousers fell down. I had the choice of putting the sack down and pulling up my pants or shuffling to the side of the road. I opted to shuffle. Horns were blowing and taxi drivers were shouting ribald remarks.

In September Susan moved to college in Addlestone and the first weekend she got the train to Liverpool Street Station where I met her and we got the tube to Leytonstone. I had moved from Forest Gate to Leytonstone when I got behind with my rent. I did what was called a moonlight flit. I took her to my one room bedsitter and we had a passionate reunion. Very few copies of the Newsletter or Keep Left were sold by us that weekend. We got very involved with the Young Socialists and the Socialist Labor League in London. Gerry Healy relented and let Sue spend her weekends working with me in the East End. Before relenting he told me off for "stealing Tiny's girlfriend". Sue claimed she wasn't Tiny's girl friend but apparently Tiny had told Gerry otherwise.

On Christmas Eve I was driving the company van across Tower Bridge when the traffic came to a complete stop. I sat there without moving for at least half an hour. I could see a pub down on the river bank and there was a flight of steps leading down to it. I decided to go down and have a quick pint. I was sure the traffic wouldn't be moving for a while. One pint led to another and soon I didn't care about the van. I just decided not to bother climbing back up the steps and when I'd had enough beer I walked to the nearest tube station. I never found out what happened to the van and I never went back to C. Miles & Co.

I assumed I'd been sacked and I got a job as a delivery driver for a builder's merchant in Stratford. This was another hard job because as well as driving I had to load and unload bags of cement, sand by the ton, timber, boxes of nails, everything that was used on a building site. The name of the firm was Fowler and Son and I got friendly with the owner's son, Alan, and he took me and Sue to the Royal Festival Hall to see Dave Brubeck and Joe Harriet. My friendship with him didn't save me from the sack when I reversed the truck into a police car.

The Socialist Labor League had a group of members in the Electrical Trade Union and it was decided that I should become part of this group. The problem was that unless you were working in the industry you couldn't join the union and as most bigger firms had closed shops, you could not get a job without a union card. This was overcome by means of a letter to the union from a sympathizer of the SLL who was a small electrical contractor. This letter stated (falsely) that I had been working for him for a year as an electrician's mate. The letter did the trick and I was issued with a union card. I went for a job with Newham Council Direct Works Department where the SLL already had a couple of members working. I was hired and became one of over one hundred electricians and mates employed by the Council. There were thousands of council houses and flats and public buildings requiring maintenance, repairs and rewiring.

I was made the mate of Peter Price, the ETU shop steward. He was a Labor supporter but very right wing. It was obvious to him within hours of me starting that I had no idea about the job. He said he would teach me and he did. In return he put me in charge of fiddling our time sheets and expense claims. We would go to a house and spend an hour doing minor repairs then go back to the yard and book out all the materials needed to rewire the house. We would then have three days off and book the time down to rewiring the house. The materials would be used by Peter on a private job. There were inspectors who were supposed to make random checks to ensure that the work claimed had been done, but these inspectors knew better than to check up on a shop steward's work.

Although everybody who worked there had a car, van or truck the rules for expenses were governed by an archaic agreement that only provided for bus fares. How we were supposed to carry all our tools and materials on the bus was a mystery. Peter told me my job was to maximize the bus fares. I would pore over a street map of Newham and over the bus timetable and work out the most circuitous route by which we could get to the various addresses on our worksheet. We were making about £15 a week in expenses. Peter would take £5 to cover his car expenses and we split the remaining £10 between us.

One night a week I had to be at the party headquarters on Clapham High Street for guard duty. There were always two guards and we slept in bunk beds on the second floor. Quite what we were supposed to do if there was an intruder I don't know. No instructions were given for the guarding of the premises.

Before going to bed we would work for a few hours in the party's print shop. Plough Press, proof reading that week's edition of the Newsletter or books that were about to be published by the party's publishing company, New Park Publications. I worked with Peter Hendry and I remember he was proof reading a book written by Trotsky when Mike Banda, who ran the print shop, looked over his shoulder and asked him what on earth he was doing. Apparently Hendry thought Trotsky's command of English left something to be desired and he was "correcting" Trotsky's grammar, punctuation and syntax. It is fortunate that Mike Banda spotted this or as Healy put it:
"We would have been the laughing stock of the world movement."

In 1966 the National Union of Seamen launched a national strike. Unlike a strike in a factory where everyone walks out together a seamen's strike takes a few weeks to mature as strike action begins as each ship comes into a British port. We used to sell the Newsletter at the Royal Docks every Friday but now we were there every day at 6 a.m.. The party put out a series of leaflets written by Gerry Healy aimed not just at the seamen but also at the dockers. We wanted the dockers to come out on strike in support of the seamen. We held a public meeting at which Gerry Healy spoke and this was attended by hundreds of seamen.

In Liverpool the dockers, led by the Socialist Labor League's Peter Kerrigan, did strike and a bus load of them came to the Royal Docks to try to get the London dockers to come out. The Communist Party had leadership positions in the National Union of Seamen and they also had a lot of influence with the dockers. Jack Dash, a Communist Party member, and leading shop steward, worked at the Royal Docks and could easily have brought the dockers out on strike if the party had wanted him to. Harold Wilson started a red scare by revealing in parliament the names of seamen and dockers who had met with Bert Ramelson, by now the Communist Party's industrial organizer. This red scare was taken up by the tabloid press.

CHAPTER TWELVE

"supposing, supposing that my arse was closing and you had your nose in, supposing" Harold

At the beginning of June 1966 Susan told me she thought she was pregnant. I had been asking her to marry me almost since I met her and now I asked her again and she accepted. We went to the doctor's office together and he confirmed the pregnancy and calculated that the baby was due in January, 1967. This meant that Susan would have to leave college, she could not keep up with the strenuous program while pregnant. She accepted this gracefully, and she and I went to the college and saw Lisa Ullman, the principal, and explained the situation. Ms. Ullman told Susan she could return at any time she wished after the baby was born, as she had been an exceptional student.

I started looking around for a flat as we couldn't start a family in my one roomed bedsit. I was earning £18 a week and paying rent of £4 per week. When I started looking at two bedroom flats I got a shock. Even in low rent districts of the East End rents were between £10 and £15 per week. On Friday night Susan came up to London as usual and I told her about the high cost of renting a flat. We decided that the best course of action was to see if my father and mother would take us in and move to Bradford. I called them from a phone box and they said we could have my attic bedroom until we found a place of our own. We immediately packed a suitcase and hitch hiked to Bradford. We didn't tell Gerry Healy or anyone else in the SLL of our plans as we knew there would be a major scene and every effort would be made to keep us in London.

After settling into my parents house we returned to London in a rented car and picked up the rest of my possessions from Leytonstone. We telephoned Susan's sister, Carol, and asked her to tell Susan's parents she was pregnant and that we were getting married. Her father, Reuben was furious but her mother, Renee, was very philosophical about Susan being pregnant:
"It takes two to tango" she told Carol.
We arranged for both sets of parents to meet in the Woodthorpe Hotel, a pub in Manchester; we thought that in a public place they would behave themselves. It was a difficult meeting to say the least as both sets of parents thought that their offspring had been tricked into marriage!! They asked us when we were getting married and Susan said:
"Sometime in the next few months"
"Oh no, you will get married next week!" her father replied.
We went to the registry office in nearby Bury and obtained a marriage license. Because Susan was under twenty one we needed her parent's consent but we just forged the signatures as we didn't want to have to wait until the evening to obtain these. The wedding date was set for 9th of July, 1966.

Susan found a job as a buyer's assistant at Grattan Warehouse, a mail order catalogue company in Bradford. Naturally she did not tell them she was pregnant or they would not have hired her. I approached Arndale about getting my job back but was rebuffed. Until I could find something better I went to work with father. By this time he was working three days a week at a convent on Bradford Road and he somehow persuaded them to pay me to help him a for a few weeks.

Susan went to stay with her parents in Manchester a few days before the wedding. The day before the wedding I rented a car from Rent-a-Wreck at Odsal and that evening went over to Manchester to take flowers for Susan and her sister, Carol, to carry, a corsage for her mother and a buttonhole for her father. Carol was to be Susan's bridesmaid. My brothers Michael and

John went with me and a family friend, a Finn called Esa Pulsa came along. Esa was in the wool trade working for his father's firm in Finland. He had been sent to Bradford for a few month's training and was lodging with my parents at the time. He had a camera and was to take photographs of the wedding. My brother John was to be best man. On the way back we stopped at a pub in Ripponden and drank a few beers.

The wedding was scheduled for 11 a.m., and next morning father and mother, John and I set off in the rented car. We had only gone about five miles when the car started making a terrible noise and smoke began pouring from the exhaust pipe. Fortunately we were not too far from Rent-a-Wreck and we limped our way there. By the time we got another car and got on the road again it was past 10 am. We didn't arrive at the registry office in Bury until 11.30 a.m. Susan's father, Reuben, was out in the street looking for us. He thought I was going to jilt his daughter. He was very relieved to see us. The wedding ceremony only lasted about twenty minutes and Susan and her sister laughed all the way through it. There was no wedding reception, just a couple of drinks in a pub and then we went back to Bradford as man and wife. On Sunday we went to Whitby for the day, that was the extent of our honeymoon. When we asked Esa for the wedding photographs he said he was sorry but he had forgotten to put film in the camera.

A couple of weeks later I got a job as a van salesman with Home Products, a division of Great Universal Stores. There were about a dozen salesmen covering the Bradford area. Each salesman had an Austin A35 van provided and this was stocked from a central warehouse with everything from shoes to hearth rugs. The job involved door to door selling and collecting the weekly payments from established customers. My area was Buttershaw estate and it was a hard slog; it was difficult getting paid, people were out or pretended to be out or said:
"Sorry, I'll pay you next week".
Quite a few customers offered me sexual favors in return for marking their book as paid. This was all very well but it meant I would have to make the payment out of my wages. Some weeks I had very little money left from my pay packet.

Making Hen's Meat

A few weeks later I secured a job back in the property business. This was working as Bradford Manager for Newhost Holdings, a firm owned by a Mr. Neuwirth of Golders Green, London. He owned about a dozen large Victorian houses in the Manningham area of Bradford. Some were occupied with eight to ten bed sitters in each house. I had to collect the rents, empty the electric meters and organize any essential repairs and maintenance. The other houses were vacant and I had to organize their conversion into bedsitters. This meant finding contractors, agreeing a price and supervising the work. My wage was £20 a week and was to be increased by £1 a week for every additional house that the firm bought. This was the most I had ever earned and Susan and I were able to move out of my parents' house into a small cottage across the street from them, number 5 Ashwell Road. The landlord was Dennis Richardson, who I had known all my life, and he charged us the low rent of £1 per week, including rates.

Everyone rallied round to help us to furnish the house; Raymond Clegg gave us a leather sofa; Mr. & Mrs. Marsden, friends of my parents, gave us a double bed and Harold Dean, the milkman, transported it in his van; the Bishop of Bradford, for whom father was now working a couple of days a week, gave us an antique wrought iron child's bed and Susan's parents bought us a dining table and six chairs. The most generous were Jean and Peter Thornton who paid for us to have a fitted carpet in the living room and for a gas fire. Jean, who was pregnant herself at the time, laid the carpet. I was worried to death that she was going to give birth whilst in our living room laying carpet.

In October I received a message from Albert Ramsey at Arndale, to go and see him. He offered me a job as his assistant at a starting salary of £850 per annum, plus a small car, an Austin 1100. Although this was a pay cut from £20 a week to £17 a week it was a job with far better prospects and a car and all running expenses was worth more than the £3 a week difference. Needless to say I took the position.

I came home from work one day and Sue said look at all this money. She had £100 in cash. She had been stuck in a lift at Grattan Warehouse and when she was eventually rescued she asked to see the nurse because she wasn't feeling well. By this time her boss was aware she was pregnant but thought she was only five months when in fact she was nearly eight months pregnant. Her boss said they couldn't risk her having an accident in her condition so she was terminated; but he gave her three months wages to sweeten her termination. This enabled us to buy clothes, a crib, a pram, and all the other items we needed for the baby.

On New Year's Eve Jean and Peter Thornton always threw a party. This was a very boozy affair and all the New Left crowd from Bradford and Spenborough attended. By now Sue was eight months pregnant and didn't feel up to going so I said I would stay at home with her. At ten o'clock Sue said she was going to bed and suggested I go to the party for a couple of hours. At the party I had a few drinks and ended up giving Diana Batchelor a lift home. She only lived in the next street and I definitely had an ulterior motive in offering her a ride. Diana was in her late twenties and was tall and shapely. She had long dark hair and always dressed very attractively. I had been necking with her at the party and had ended up on the floor with her under a table. Diana's hobby was having sex with married men just to piss their wives off.

I awoke next morning at nine o'clock and when I opened my eyes I was looking at the sky through a sky light in the roof above me. For a moment I didn't know where I was and then I saw Diana sleeping next to me. I dressed hurriedly and drove home. Sue was standing outside the front door as I drove up and across the street was my mother with her arms akimbo. I didn't need this welcoming committee.
"Where have you been?" asked Sue
"I had a few drinks too many so I slept at the Thorntons" I replied
"You're a bloody liar Gary, I've already phoned Jean Thornton and she told me you left about midnight with Diana Batchelor."
   Then she hit me a resounding smack across the back of my head.

Making Hen's Meat

"Give it him, Susan, he deserves it!" shouted mother from across the street.

The baby was due on 12th January and was to be born at home. The visiting midwife would deliver the baby with help if needed from Dr. Liversedge. Provided you had hot running water and there were no complications all babies were born at home at this time. By 20th January the baby had still not arrived and we went to see the doctor:
"Take her on the swings and roundabout and rocking horse on Heaton Hill" was the medical advice we received.
Finally on 25th January Susan went into labor and I sent for the midwife. After ten hours the labor suddenly stopped. The doctor came and told the midwife to give Susan some medication and admit her to hospital. After the doctor had gone the midwife totally ignored him and said:
"Doctors! They don't know what they are talking about, I have been delivering babies for twenty years, and we'll deliver this one!"

Susan was having a very hard time and the midwife brought in gas and air for her; no other drugs were used at this time for the pain. I took a few good snorts of gas and air myself. Jean Thornton came to see if she could help and brought a bottle of Beefeater Gin with her. Between the gin and the gas and air I was in no condition to help, so Jean stayed with Sue and gave her advice and comfort. By this time Jean had five children of her own so she really could help Sue.

Finally after thirty six hours in labor the baby was born at 3 a.m. on 27th January, 1967. I was so overcome with joy when I saw this perfectly formed little boy pop out that I burst into tears. The baby was born blue and the midwife went out to her car and brought in oxygen which she administered to him in a hastily constructed oxygen tent. We called the baby Simon John Healy Spence. Healy was after Gerry Healy, John after my brother. As soon as the baby was quiet Sue and I fell asleep. Neither of us had slept for the duration of the labor and we were exhausted. Three hours later we were awakened by the baby crying. I went downstairs to make him a bottle of milk. When I came back Sue was trying to change his nappy without success. I had to fetch my mother from across the road to show us how it was done.

When Simon was a few weeks old we were visiting Sue's parents in Manchester and went to show Simon off to Sue's three maiden aunts, Esther, Rosie and Pearly. They gave Simon a £1 note and he gripped it firmly:
"Look at the way he's holding onto that £1 note" said Esther, "you can see the Yorkshire blood in him."
I thought this very funny; they were definitely Lancastrians first and Jews second.

Things at Arndale were not so rosy as they used to be. Sam Chippindale's strong point was certainly not finance. He just ploughed ahead with his development program and left the financing to others. In 1966 the company was unable to pay a dividend and its shares fell to fourteen shillings. The problem was they had too many schemes at the site assembly stage or under construction and not income producing. They were struggling to make payments on their loans. Inevitably Arndale became a takeover target and five companies were interested.

Arnold Hagenbach was a willing seller and Sam Chippindale realized that in this situation a takeover was inevitable. One of the bidders was Land Securities, the country's largest property company with issued capital of £40,000,000 compared to Arndale's £2,000,000. Hagenbach was in favor of their offer but Sam Chippindale opposed it. He knew that if Land Securities bought Arndale any prospect of maintaining the Bradford office was unlikely and that most of his loyal employees would lose their jobs. He favored Town & City Properties bid because their Chairman, Barry East, agreed that Arndale, if owned by Town & City, could continue to run as an autonomous entity from Bradford and continue to build its Arndale Centers. Sam Chippindale got his way and the company was sold to Town & City. All the employees were retained.

Making Hen's Meat

Jean and Peter Thornton had five children by this time, and another on the way. Although Peter's plumbing business had expanded into electrical work and fire alarms he was barely making enough money to keep Jean and the children in the style to which they had become accustomed. Peter and Jean, sometimes alone, sometimes in partnership with Peter's sister Alma and her husband Bert, began buying houses in Manningham, where they lived and converting them into bedsitters. The arithmetic was fairly simple. You could buy a large Victorian house in run down condition for £2,000 and to convert it to ten bedsitters, furnished and with appliances cost another £2,000 so the total investment was £4,000. The ten bedsitters could be let at £4 a week each to produce an annual income of £ 2,000. This was a 50% return on capital. The house could be paid for and the bank loans repaid in two years. It is not surprising that Neuwirth was investing in the same kind of deal from his base in Golders Green, London. In London he would be lucky to make much more than 10% per annum, just enough to pay the bank interest.

The Thorntons had just bought a house and before they could start work on it they needed all the rubbish clearing out and the linoleum covering the floors taking up. They offered me the job and said they would pay me £5 a day. One Saturday I started on this job and was pulling up the lino which was old and brittle and tended to break into small pieces. I was throwing it out of the windows into the yard for later removal by Peter. Under the lino in one room were a lot of old newspapers and as I threw one of these out of the window I saw an envelope drop out of the paper and land in the yard.

I went down to investigate and inside the envelope was £40 in cash. I couldn't believe it, this was more than two weeks wages. I headed straight for a nearby pub on Lumb Lane. After a couple of pints there I went to the White Swan further down the road and stayed there until closing time at 3 p.m.. Then I went to Bibby's, a West Indian owned club in a back-to-back house near Bradford City Football Ground, Valley Parade. Licensing hours did not matter to Bibby, the owner, because this club or shebeen was totally illegal; it had no license. It was open twenty four hours a day, seven days a week and was always packed with alcoholics, small time criminals and plain clothes policemen. The police obviously turned a blind eye to the breaches of the licensing law because it suited them to have a place that was a resort of criminals. They probably hoped to pick up information at Bibby's.

I got very drunk indeed, drinking beer, rum and peppermint and cheap red wine. That night about nine o'clock there was a knock on the door of 5, Ashwell Road and Sue opened it to be greeted by David Green, who garaged his car in a lock-up garage he rented next to our house. He told Sue he had been driving home when he had seen someone lying in the road on a pedestrian crossing on Manningham Lane. It proved to be me fast asleep. I must have blacked out walking home from Bibby's and fallen asleep where I fell. Sue and David got me out of the car and into the house and Sue started bollocking me. I gave her the £30 I had left and this quietened her. She helped me upstairs and into the bathroom. I was soon taking a shit and vomiting simultaneously and Sue wrapped me in a blanket and left me to sleep on the bathroom floor.

Life was getting interesting at Arndale. I was helping Albert Ramsey lease up a completed scheme at Walkden in Lancashire and also helping with the supervision of construction and letting of a covered Arndale Center at Stretford in Manchester. We were negotiating with town councils throughout the north of England to try to be appointed as developers for town center schemes and one such council was at Droylsden in Lancashire. The labor councilors had agreed to come, at Arndale's expense, to look at some completed schemes and Albert Ramsey gave me the job of showing them round. I first met them in Shipley where I showed them the developments we had just completed around a new market square. We had hired a coach to transport them and they had loaded crates of beer on board.

I took them for lunch at the Bankfield Hotel and then to Arndale's office to meet Sam Chippindale. He offered them a cup of tea. I knew this was not what they had in mind and I opened up the cocktail cabinet and began handing out glasses of whisky and gin and tonic. They then headed off in their motor coach to the north east where I planned to show them the new Jarrow town center. They stayed the night at the Roker Park Hotel and I took them out to a night club in Sunderland. They all had a few too many to drink and when I met them next morning they were much the worse for wear, especially the Mayor who seemed to be still drunk. After meeting the Jarrow officials and councilors at the town hall we went to inspect the new town center and then to look at a new swimming pool the council had just built and of which they were very proud. Unfortunately the Mayor of Droylsden missed his footing and fell into the deep end of the swimming pool. He couldn't swim and there was a hilarious situation with the Mayor of Jarrow removing his chain of office and stripping off his clothes and diving in to save him. That was the end of Arndale's hope of being appointed to redevelop Droylsden town center.

For the first seven months of his life Simon gave us no peace. He cried and cried every night. If we rocked his crib he was quiet but as soon as we stopped rocking he cried again. In desperation we took him out in the car and drove around until he fell asleep. As soon as we got home and I turned off the car engine he was awake and started crying again. We were both exhausted and in no condition to be looking after a baby. Inevitably this led to pointless arguments and after one such row, Sue packed up and went back to her mother in Manchester. I drove her and the baby to the railway station and her mother and father met her in Manchester. After a couple of days she came back home. One day Simon was crawling around and he grabbed a towelling nappy off the newly washed pile, stuck it in his mouth and started sucking. From that day he was inseparable from his "loving blanket" and he started sleeping through the night and our lives returned to normal.

At weekends we often drove to Manchester to see Sue's parents. We would take them shopping at Kwik Save down Cheetham Hill Road and then call at a Jewish deli, Lapidus' and buy chopped liver and pickle meat. We went to the baker's round the corner from, their house and bought fresh hot bagels. We ate the pickle meat for lunch with chips and peas and slices of crusty Jewish bread. The bagels and chopped liver we took home to Bradford. There was no Jewish shop in Bradford, the nearest was twelve miles away in Leeds.

In the summer we went to Whitby on the east coast of Yorkshire for a week's holiday. We stayed in a small boarding house on the sea front. We had very little money left after paying for the accommodation and spent the week on the beach or walking around the harbor or the old town on the east side of the river. A real treat for Sue was being able to stay in bed late while I went for a walk with Simon in his push chair. I loved these early morning walks and usually went down to the harbor and watched the fishing boats preparing to set sail. The gulls were wheeling overhead and although Simon was only seven months old he seemed to respond to them. I used to stop at a little café and buy a cup of hot chocolate and put half of this into Simon's bottle and he guzzled on it contentedly.

When we returned to Bradford we were flat broke and decided Sue should try to get a part time job to supplement my meager income. A local private school on Wilmer Road, called Tinakori Towers was advertising for a part time teacher. Sue applied and to her surprise got the job. She would not have been able to teach in the public school system without a Teacher Training Certificate but it seemed that this private school did not care. Sue worked three mornings a week teaching art and dance(or as they called it music and movement) to six to eleven year olds. My mother looked after Simon while Sue was working. Fortunately Sue and mother got on very well together and mother taught Sue how to cook and I think Sue really appreciated my mother's help. I was very pleased when she mastered the art of cooking Yorkshire puddings.

Tony Milnes and his girl friend, Rosemary, (who I met in Jeumont, France) came home to Bradford to get married. It was the custom to have a 'bachelor's night out' the night before the wedding but for some reason Tony's bachelor night included women. Rosemary was there and as my mother was babysitting

Sue came along. Tony's brother Johnny was there with his good friend Brian Bloggs. Johnny had a broken arm and it was in a plaster cast.

After a couple of hours in a pub we went to a late night discotheque in Shipley and were having a great time drinking and dancing when trouble broke out on the dance floor between Tony and another guy when they collided. This soon calmed down and we thought no more of it but as Tony was leaving the disco the guy he'd had the trouble with and a couple of his friends attacked him. I ran back into the disco to get Brian Bloggs who had a reputation as a ferocious fighter. I hid behind a car and watched Bloggs and the Milnes brothers fight off the three guys and send them running. It was very funny to watch Johnny fighting with his broken arm.

Sue and I took Simon for a walk in Heaton Woods one Saturday morning. We parked the car on Shay Lane, got the push chair out of the boot of the car and spent a happy hour strolling beside the stream. The next morning we were going to walk in the park and I opened the car boot to get out the push chair. It wasn't there. We realized we must have forgotten to load it when we had been in Heaton Woods so we drove back to Shay Lane to see if we could find it. The push chair wasn't there but there were half a dozen police cars and policemen were combing the woods. We told a policeman we had lost a push chair and he explained that they had a report of the empty push chair and had collected it and taken it to the police station. They were searching the woods looking for the mother and child they assumed must be missing. They were very good about the whole situation and seemed relieved to learn that it was a false alarm.

Life settled into a familiar routine. Work from 9 a.m. to 6 p.m., then home to help Sue put Simon to bed. Then we would watch TV or read. On Friday night mother would baby sit for a couple of hours and we would go to the Delvers and play dominoes and drink beer. On the way home we would collect fish and chips from Joe Parson's shop. At the weekend we would often drive to Manchester to see Sue's parents. If the weather was good we would go into Heaton Park with them and go for a drink and lunch at the Heaton Park Hotel.

In the summer of 1968 we went to Abersoch in North Wales for our holiday. We stayed in a small hotel and had a wonderful week. The weather was good and we spent a lot of time on the beach with Simon. We let him run around naked which he loved and he had a great time paddling in the sea and building sand castles. One day Joe and Dorothy Greenald, who were staying in Edward Thompson's holiday cottage in the North Wales mountains, came to visit us and later in the week we visited them in the mountains. Joe and Dorothy lived in Spen Valley and we had met them through the Thorntons.

Dorothy had been a labor councilor and a magistrate and was active in CND. In her role as a magistrate she occasionally had no option but to send someone to jail. She realized how much the families suffered and became an active member of the Prisoners Aid Society. Single handedly Dorothy has helped hundreds, if not thousands, of families in need providing them with furniture and food when it was most needed. She was a one woman social services department and only passed away in 2000 at the age of ninety six.

In May, 1968, there was a revolutionary upheaval in France. Hundreds of thousands of students went on strike in defense of education rights. Pitched street battles between students and the police were common place. Inspired by the students ten million workers struck and seized the factories evicting the owners and management. The ruling class began to flee the country. The army did not intervene; the officer class were afraid to send a conscript army against the workers. What was needed was a party to take the lead and take the power which was well within the grasp of the workers. The powerful Communist Party settled for a promise of elections and a referendum and strengthened DeGaulle's weakened position. In Czechoslovakia Premier Dubcek's "Prague Spring" liberalization process was brought to an end by Soviet and Warsaw Pact tanks. In London on 27th October, 1968 the biggest oppositional demonstration of the 20th century took place in protest against the Vietnam War. Media commentators speculated on the dangers of insurrection.

In these circumstances it is not surprising that I decided to become politically active again. I contacted Trevor Holdsworth and said I wanted to rejoin the Bradford branch of the SLL. Trevor checked with party headquarters and they said I was welcome; as far as the party was concerned I had never resigned or been expelled so there was no need for a probationary period, they regarded me as having been on a leave of absence. I attended branch meetings and one Young Socialist meeting a week and sold Newsletters in the pubs on Saturday nights, but not much more.

Sue had quit the job at Tinakori Towers and was working in the evenings as a bartender at the Queens Hotel in Daisy Hill. Later she worked as a bartender at West Bradford Golf Club at Chellow Grange. This meant I had to baby sit two or three evenings a week so my political activities were restricted.

Early in 1969 Sue discovered she was pregnant again and on 14th August another boy, James Benjamin, was born. Because of the difficulty Sue had had delivering Simon she was admitted to the Bradford Royal Infirmary to give birth to James. He was due at the end of July and when he was two weeks late she was taken into hospital. Eventually Sue was induced and we were then told the baby was premature. Something was screwed up about the dates, how could he be three weeks late and premature? He weighed 6 lbs 8 ozs and was covered in black hair, not just on his head but all down his back. James was a very contented baby and we did not have the sleeping problems with him that we had with Simon, probably because the very first thing we purchased for him was a dummy! As long as he was not wet or hungry he was fine.

On 27th September, 1969 the SLL's daily newspaper, The Workers Press, was launched. To coincide with this a demonstration was held in Brighton, on the south coast of England, where the Labor Party was holding its annual conference. Sue and I went on this demonstration and took Simon with us. We traveled down by car with Trevor Holdsworth and Janet Crawford.

The house we lived in at 5 Ashwell Road had only one full sized bedroom. The second 'bedroom' was only like an oversized closet and had room for only a crib or a small bed. Simon had this room and James slept in his crib in the main bedroom with us. It was time to move and the obvious thing to do was to buy a house. The problem was we had no money for a deposit and would only be able to afford a mortgage on a low priced house. Eventually we found a small development of new houses in Cullingworth, a small village about seven miles from Bradford on the way to Haworth. There were about a dozen three bedroomed semi-detached houses on a new cul-de-sac called Manor Gardens. A lot of development was taking place in Cullingworth mainly of four bedroomed detached houses. The developer of Manor Gardens had misjudged the market and the houses were completed without any sales. He then offered them to rent with an option to purchase at the low price of £2,750. If and when the option was exercised the rent paid would count towards the purchase price.

This was a deal that even we could afford and in November we moved into our new home. Once again friends had rallied round to help us equip the new house. Father and brother Michael did a lot of the painting and Albert Ramsey gave us enough wall mounted oil filled electric radiators to heat every room. Living in Cullingworth was fine for me. I had a company car and could be home in fifteen minutes. I often came home for lunch. Sue had no car and had two young children to care for. Unlike Heaton, where the shops and village center were a hundred yards from our house, the center of Cullingworth was almost a mile away. Come rain or shine Sue had to walk there with James in his pram and Simon toddling along beside her. Sue had picked up my mother's habit of shopping every day and although we went to a supermarket together at the weekend to buy the basics she still bought meat, vegetables and bread daily.

On Saturday mornings I would take Simon for a ride in the car, usually to Haworth, home of the Bronte family, which was only three miles away. On the way we would stop and explore the countryside. Simon had his wellington boots on and loved to paddle in what he called his secret streams. Sue's mother and father had by this time acquired a car, a Triumph Herald, so they often visited us at weekends. Sue's mother was the driver but she had no license. She had taken driving lessons and had failed the test three times. After the third failure she simply removed the L plates and drove unlicensed for the rest of her life.

My day started very early. As the only Bradford member of the SLL with a car I had to be at Exchange Station at 6 a.m. to pick up that day's edition of the Workers Press. It was not sold at newsagents and was distributed entirely by party members and sympathizers. I would meet the other members at 6.30 a.m. and hand them each a bundle of papers and they dispersed to factories and mills throughout the city to sell the paper to workers arriving for the day shift. I would criss-cross Bradford and the surrounding area delivering the paper to the houses of people who had subscribed to the paper. There were about twenty of these subscribers and I would drive about a hundred miles to deliver to them. Then I would go to Arndale, to work at my day job.

In May we had been in the house for six months and could exercise the option to purchase. We had paid £100 in rent and this became the deposit for the house. We borrowed the remaining £2,650 from a building society and finally could say we owned our own house.

My brother Michael had by this time left Dallas & Co and was working for A. W. Bain and Sons, a large insurance broker with offices throughout Britain and Ireland. He had been offered a transfer to Dublin and was making plans to move his family over there. He had three children, Mark, Richard and Heather. Shortly after Mike told me that he was moving to Dublin I was thumbing through the Estates Gazette when I read an advert for a development executive for a Dublin Company, Hardwicke, Ltd. The advert said 'expected to be of interest to those already earning £3,000 per annum or more'. I was only earning £1,000 per annum but, what the hell, I'd had a few drinks and the idea of a move to Dublin, where Mike and Liz and the kids were going to be sounded appealing.

I wrote a letter of application and prepared a curriculum vitae. On Monday I mailed the letter and CV and promptly forgot all about it.

Sue's sister, Carol, came to stay with us for a few days and after we had been to Haworth to eat at the Black Bull we returned home and found a telegram waiting for me. The telegram read:
"Please telephone Paul Byrne at Hardwicke, Ltd, to set up an appointment for an interview"
I was very excited at the prospect of moving to Dublin. I had been there two or three times for Albert Ramsey who was trying to negotiate the purchase of sites in Ballyfermot, Finglas and Kilbarrack from Dublin Corporation. From what I had seen, Dublin looked like both a beautiful city and a fun place to live. I phoned Paul Byrne and it was agreed I would fly over the following Saturday morning and take a taxi to their offices for an 11 am interview.

I was interviewed by a committee of four people, Mont Kavanagh the managing director, Charles Judd, a director who was Mont's brother-in-law, or nephew or some class of relation, Neil Smith, their accountant and also somehow related and Paul Byrne, the company secretary and financial controller. I really didn't care whether I got the job or not so I was totally relaxed at the interview and gave a good account of myself. At the conclusion of the interview, Mont Kavanagh asked me what salary I would require if they offered me the position. I said £3,500 per annum, a fortune by my standards. £70 a week, the same salary as a British cabinet minister received. Mont said the salary was fine. I could also have a company car of my choice up to two thousand:
"Pounds or c.c.'s?" I asked.
"Pounds" said Mont, with a twinkle in his eye.
They would pay my removal expenses and give me a flat rent free until I found a house. They would loan me the deposit for a house and this could be repaid by deduction from my salary.

We all had drinks; I remember Charles Judd and I had a gin and tonic and the others had scotch. Mont and his colleagues withdrew to his office and left me alone in the boardroom. The

offices were in a large Georgian house on Wellington Road in the fashionable inner city neighborhood of Ballsbridge and the boardroom and Mont's office were located in a semi-basement. From the boardroom I looked across a small garden and car park to the mews which had once been stabling but was now disused. Mont Kavanagh and his colleagues returned and Mont poured us all another drink. Mont said that before they formally offered me the job they would like to meet my wife. They wanted to make certain that she was happy about moving to Dublin. They didn't want me taking the job and then quitting because my wife wanted to return to England, as had happened to them with a previous employee.
The following Saturday Sue and I flew to Dublin for the weekend. We had a rental car and a room at the Intercontinental Hotel in Ballsbridge all courtesy of Hardwicke, Ltd. Sue had her hair done and bought herself a new coat at C&A Stores in Bradford. The coat was of red PVC and made Sue look very sexy. The meeting with the Hardwicke directors went swimmingly and once more we all had drinks while we settled the details of my employment. It was arranged that I would start work in a month's time in July 1970 and would stay in a hotel at Hardwicke's expense until our furniture arrived from England and we could move into the flat. They agreed to buy me a Ford Capri and I chose a deep purple color called aubergine.

Sue and I had lunch at the Intercontinental Hotel and went for a drive around Dublin. We visited Howth, a small town on the north side of Dublin Bay. Howth has a picturesque little harbor and we walked along the harbor wall looking out to the small island called Ireland's Eye which legend has it was once visited by Robin Hood. Susan and I had a blazing row while walking along the harbor wall. We ended up pushing and shoving and jabbing each other. Susan's glasses fell off and broke. The rest of the weekend was a blur as far as Susan was concerned.

1. Gary's maternal great grandfather, Joseph Atkinson, a railwayman at Dacre Banks, North Yorkshire, 1905.

2. Gary's paternal forebears at a wedding. Back row, left to right, John Sutcliffe Spence, great grandfather, Victor Hedley Spence, great uncle, Victor's wife, Gladys, Alfred Brighty Spence, great uncle in the uniform of the Bradford Pals Battalion, great uncle, Gilbert Spence, the bridegroom and his wife, Mabel, rest unknown. Front row, left to right, Harriet Spence, great grandmother, Bertha Harriet Spence, grandmother, rest unknown.

3. Gary's maternal grandfather Ashbel Atkinson in the uniform of the Durham Light Infantry, 1915.

4. Gary's maternal grandmother. Ethel Atkinson (nee Moister) in 1915.

5. Gary's father, Harold Spence in 1919.

6. Susan Spence's maternal grandparents. Samuel and Yetta Lader. Left to right their children Irene (Susan's mother), Sydney and Sydney's wife Hesse.

7. Susan's parents Reuben and Irene Salkey (nee Lader) on their wedding day in 1940.

8. Gary's paternal grandfather Mark Newbold with Gary's brother, Michael Spence, in 1942.

9. Harold and Mary Spence with their three children Gary, John and Michael at Bridlington, East Yorkshire in 1950.

10. The group of Carlton Grammar School boys who were to visit France in the summer of 1957 pictured with the group leader, Dr. Singer. Gary is in the middle of the front row.

11. Thirteen year old Gary discovers the opposite sex; he is pictured here with Stephanie and Monique at La Plage Blanc, Hossegor, France in August, 1957.

12. Sunday School drama group in 1958 at Heaton Baptist Church, Bradford. Gary is on the extreme left.

13. Gary's future wife Susan and her sister, Carol, in 1959.

14. Janne Lee, Gary Spence and Pam Bergin in fancy dress for the student's Rag Day on Broadway, Bradford in 1960. The black building in the background is Swan Arcade which was demolished to make way for Arndale House.

15. Gary's father and brother, Harold and John Spence, enjoy a pint of beer together in 1961.

16. Harold, Mary and John Spence pictured outside St. Barnabas Church, Heaton, Bradford with Michael and Liz Spence's three children, Heather, Richard and Mark. The occasion was the Christening of Heather in 1969.

17. Gary and Susan Spence pictured outside 12, Ashwell Road, Heaton, Bradford on their wedding day, July 9th, 1966.

18. Gary and Susan's first child, Simon John Healy Spence, aged four months pictured in Lister Park, Bradford with Susan and her mother and father, Reuben and Renee Salkey in 1967.

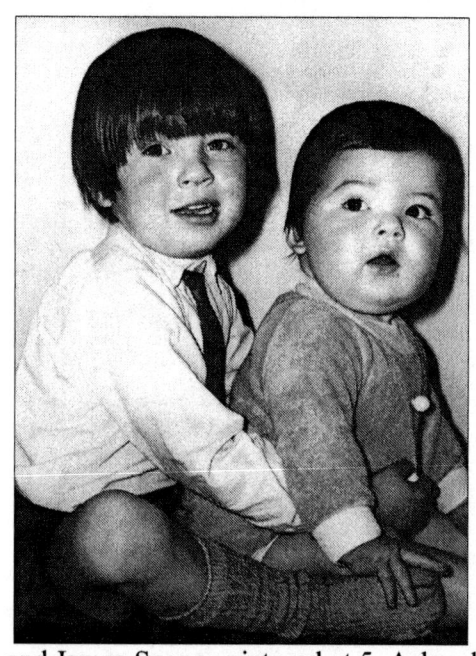

19. Simon and James Spence pictured at 5, Ashwell Road, Heaton, Bradford at Christmas, 1969.

20. Simon and James Spence pictured in the back garden at 15, St. Canice's Road, Glasnevin, Dublin in 1971.

21. Gary with his father, Harold and sons, Simon and James, on the strand at the Dingle Peninsula, County Kerry, Ireland, in 1972.

22. Susan Spence with Simon about to attend his first day of school at Sacred Heart Boys National School, St. Canice's Road, Glasnevin, Dublin in 1971.

23. Gary and Susan with their three children, Dominic (in Susan's arms) and Simon and James on the camel's back at Golden Sands on the Black Sea coast of Bulgaria in 1976.

24. Susan Spence with Simon, James and Dominic, in the Botanic Gardens, Dublin in 1976.

25. Gary Spence looks on as Ken Rohan and John McConnell sign the contract for the sale of McConnell's headquarters office building on Pearse Street, Dublin to Rohan Commercial Properties in 1973.

26. Gary Spence (standing) assisted by his secretary, Norma Lynch, at the signing of a contract to build a new factory in Tallaght, County Dublin for Gempak.

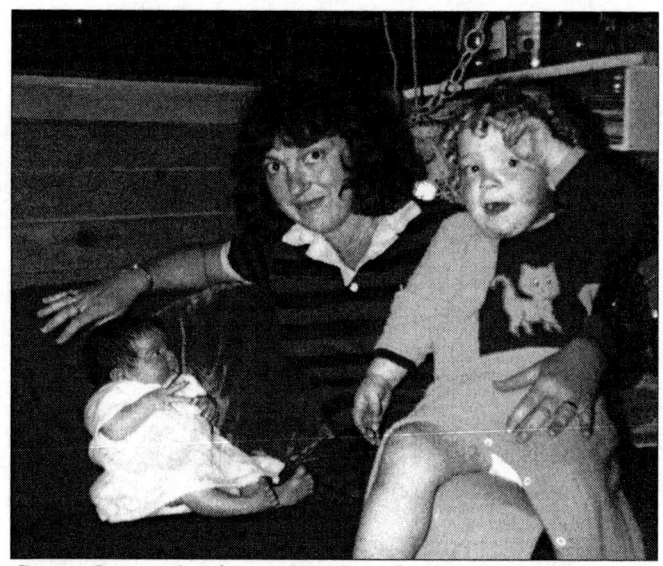

27. Susan Spence's sister, Carol Oxford, with her two children, Tanya and Lorna.

28. Johnny Milnes, Gary's lifelong friend, gets acquainted with Simon and Carol Oxford's python, Monty.

29. Building the offices and warehouse for 3 Guys in Tallaght, County Dublin in 1976. Left to right, Tom McGeogh, sales director, Sitecast, Arthur Lyons, quantity surveyor, Gary Spence, property director of 3 Guys, Albert Gubay, Chairman of 3 Guys, John Ward, site foreman, Sitecast and Ambrose Kelly, architect.

30. Harold Spence pictured with (left to right) Richard Spence, Richard's father, Michael and John Spence in 1980.

31. James Spence (standing) with Simon and Dominic in America in 1980.

32. Gary with Mike Johnson eating dinner at 810 Edgehill Road, Charlotte, North Carolina in 1981.

33. Gary with Deane Brunson at 810 Edgehill Road, Charlotte in 1982.

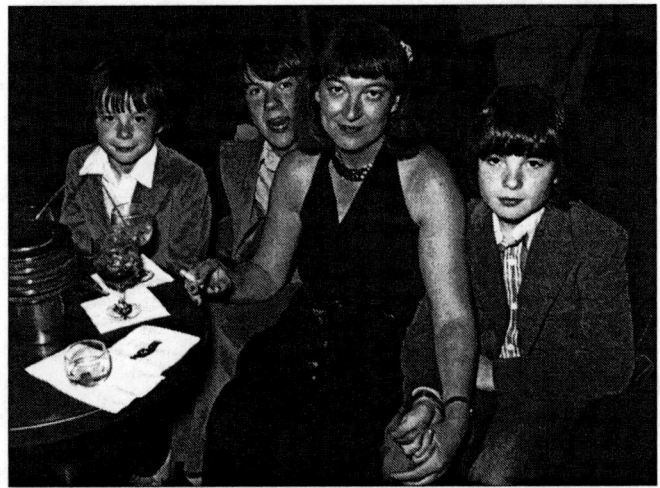

34. Susan Spence on a Caribbean cruise with (left to right) Dominic, Simon and James in 1982.

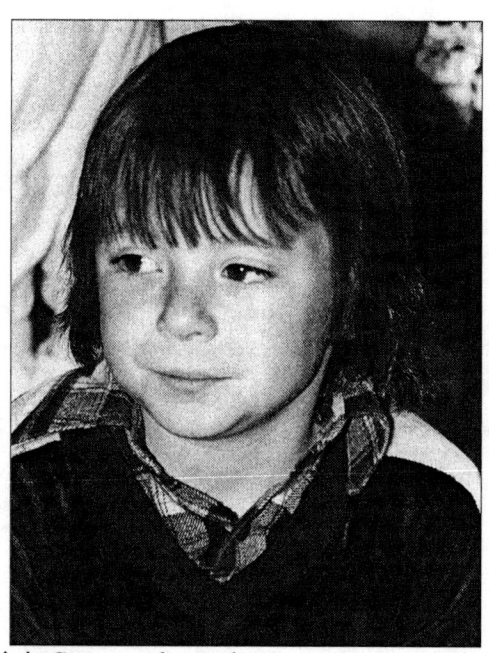
35. Dominic Spence, the author's youngest son in 1983.

36. Gary and Dominic Spence with the Carolina Lightning's coach, English soccer star, Rodney Marsh.

37. Gary and Susan celebrate Susan's birthday in 1983.

38. Becky Sippe and Deidre Mistri, in the screened porch at 810 Edgehill Road in 1983.

39. At a fancy dress party in 1983 (left to right) James, Gary, Dominic, Susan and Simon.

40. Gary and secretary, 3 Guys, Salisbury, North Carolina in 1984.

41. In the 3 Guys boardroom the decision is made to put the company into Chapter X1 (left to right) Ron Jones, Len Clarke, Jim Ward and Gary Spence in 1985.

42. Susan, Gary and Dominic with limo outside Ballymaloe House, County Cork, Ireland, 1985.

43. Gary with his mother, Mary, and son, Simon, at St. Barnabas Church, Heaton, Bradford, for the wedding of Mark and Janet Spence in 1985.

44. In Edinburgh in 1995, Chuck Sullivan, James, Susan, Dominic and Gary.

45. Peter Thorton, Chuck Sullivan and James Spence at the rehearsal dinner for Simon and Ellen Spence's wedding in Charlotte in 1994.

46. The union of the Spence and Barnett families, 23rd April, 1994 (left to right) Susan, James, Kim Barnett, Simon, Ellen, Bobby Barnett, Gina Barnett, Gary and Dominic.

47. Pictured at Simon and Ellen's wedding are Darryl Poovey, James and the late Wade Yarborough.

48. Simon, Susan and Dominic with Susan's father, Reuben Salkey outside his home, 24 Dovedale Avenue, Prestwich in 1995.

49. Dinner at the Tucker's house, Riverhills, Lake Wylie, South Carolina in July 1997. Pictured (left to right) Gary, Marion Tucker, Tracy Tucker, Susan.

50. James and Michele Spence on their wedding day, October 14, 2000, at the River House, Grassy Creek, North Carolina with Michele's children, Tyler and Lauren.

51. Jacob with his English cousin, Holly at Disneyworld in 2002.

52. At Fripp Island, South Carolina, 2002, (left to right) Ellen, Susan, Simon, Jacob, Kim Barnett, Ethan, Bobby Barnett, Gina Barnett and Gary.

53. Susan, Dominic and Gary on Dominic and Anne's wedding day, September 28, 2003 in Charleston, South Carolina.

54. Jacob gives his new cousin, Megan Kelly Spence, a bottle in 2004.

55. Simon, Ethan and Jacob at Fripp Island in 2004.

56. Gary, Jacob, Susan and Ethan celebrating Susan's birthday in 2004.

57. Gary and Susan's grandsons, Ethan and Jacob in 2004.

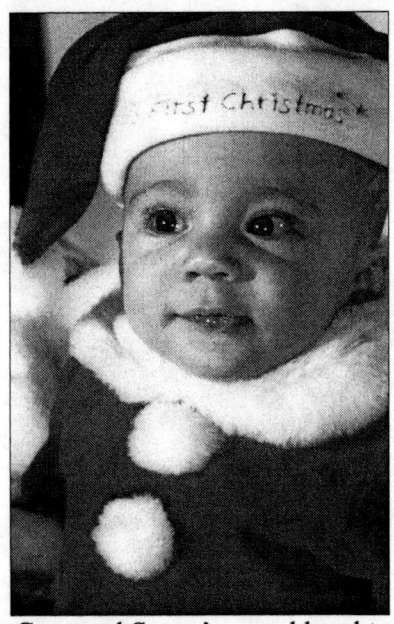

58. Megan, Gary and Susan's granddaughter, ready for Christmas in 2004.

59. The English Spences, in 2004. (Back row, left to right) Mark, Janet, Michael, Richard, John, Sue. (Front row, left to right) Holly, Clare, Matthew.

60 The American Spences, in 2004. (From left to Right) Dominic, Anne, Megan, Michele, James, Susan, Gary, Ethan, Ellen, Simon and Jacob.

CHAPTER THIRTEEN

"I have no pain dear mother now but oh! I am so dry connect me to a brewery and leave me there to die"
Harold

When we returned to Bradford we put the house up for sale through an estate agent called David Spence at an asking price of £3,000 and got a quotation from Pickfords for moving our few sticks of furniture to Dublin. I gave in my notice at Arndale for the second time. Sam Chippindale was very understanding when I told him what my salary was going to be. I met my brother, Michael, and asked him when he was moving to Dublin. He told me his transfer had been cancelled – c'est la vie.

We took the two boys to my mother's house the day Pickfords came for the furniture. As the truck was being loaded we had a succession of visitors, the local tradesmen, the butcher, the baker and the candlestick maker coming to have their accounts settled. The next day Sue and I flew to Dublin with ten month old James; we left Simon with my mother; brother John was to fly to Dublin with him a few days after our furniture had arrived and we had moved into the flat.

We stayed at the Lansdowne Hotel on Baggot Street and drank every night in the hotel's basement bar, the Pirate's Den. A few days later our furniture arrived and we moved into the first and second floor of 37 Belmont Avenue, Donnybrook, another fashionable inner city suburb of Dublin. The accommodation was rather down at heel and there were rats in the overgrown backyard and mice in the kitchen. We were made to feel at home by Mrs. Hogan, an old lady who occupied the ground floor and basement flat. She used to invite Sue in for a cup of tea most mornings and one day Sue told her how much she liked her tea and asked what brand it was. It transpired that the reason the tea gave Sue such a lift was that Mrs. Hogan always added a big splash of Paddy Whiskey to the teapot.

The job was a dream. I arrived at work about 9 a.m., Paul Byrne came in about 10 am and Mont Kavanagh about 11 am. About 12.30 p.m. we would meet in the boardroom and have drinks followed by an excellent lunch, cooked by an Italian chef, Felice. We would return to our offices about 2.30 p.m. and I would leave between 5 p.m. and 5.30 p.m.. Paul would stay behind talking to Mont Kavanagh until about 7 p.m..

Hardwicke was an old family firm and owned a considerable number of rental houses in Dublin. They had become the leading developers of office property thanks to an association with Jones Lang Wootton, a London firm of chartered surveyors. They had built new office buildings on Lansdowne Road and Burlington Road in Ballsbridge and owned sites where development was imminent on Mount Street and St. Stephen's Green. In addition they were piecing together a very large site close to the Dail (Parliament) on Kildare Street and Molesworth Street. Jones Lang Wootton had opened a Dublin office under the management of an Englishman, David Bailey, and Norman Bowie, a senior partner, came over from London to supervise a few days each month. He always spent a day at our offices and we would stay late and eat dinner prepared by the incomparable Felice.

Paul Byrne had worked in London for many years before returning to Dublin and his years working in property in London made him a vital part of the Hardwicke management. Paul Byrne's department did all the rent collection and they had a clerk of works called Michael Aherne who oversaw maintenance and repairs and all new construction. Leasing and site acquisition was done by Jones Lang Wootton and Lisney & Co. This left very little for me to do apart from looking for new sites and liaising with the agents in connection with leasing and management issues. I would go out 'looking for sites' and spend my time exploring Dublin. I quickly became a Hibernophile and as well as exploring Dublin I read voraciously on the history of Ireland, the struggle for independence, the civil war, and the civil rights movement which was campaigning for equal rights for Catholics in Northern Ireland.

Paul Byrne and I became very close friends and he and his wife Audrey socialized a lot with Sue and I. Paul introduced us to his circle of friends and to a very busy social life. Through a Hardwicke employee, Mr. Young, we were shown a house on Dublin's northside, 15 St. Canices Road, Glasnevin. The house belonged to a relation of his, Mrs. Greene. We went to see the house with him and when Mrs. Greene, who was a very old woman, let us in, we thought she must have an advanced system of radar. Every room was crowded with small tables that were full of knick-knacks. She was able to negotiate a route through and around them with great speed, while we took a long time following her as we were scared of leaving a path of destruction in our wake. We bought the house for £3,500. Our house in England had been sold to our own agent for the price we had paid for it, and after agents and solicitors fees the amount due to us was precisely zero. We borrowed the deposit for the Dublin house from Hardwicke and got a mortgage for the balance of the purchase price.

I got into the habit of going to one of the pubs near the office after work, usually Searson's, Mooney's or the Club House all in nearby Baggot Street. The traffic to the northside was impossible at 5.30 p.m. and it made sense to wait an hour before heading home. Paul Byrne would join me at 6.30 p.m. or 7 p.m. and I would say:
"I'll just have one with you and then I'll be off home to the wife and kids". Inevitably one led to two and two to three. By 8 p.m. a big crowd of us would be assembled round a table in Searson's,

Harry McCormick, who was with Hill Samuel, Sean Dillon, an estate agent, Brendan Flynn and Finbar Holland, both property developers, Lorcan Burke, Jr., an impresarrio, Tony Ryan, who owned a small hotel, to name but a few. By this time I knew I would be in trouble with Sue so I would call her and tell her to get a babysitter, call a cab, and come and join us. Very often she would and, after a few drinks, I would take her out for a meal. We were beginning to eat out a lot and I was getting used to having enough money in my pocket to do this.

On Christmas eve, Ove Arup, consulting engineers, with an office at 10, Wellington Road, just two doors away from Hardwicke, had a Christmas Party. All the Hardwicke staff went to this party and there were big pitchers of Guinness to which I helped myself. After two or three pints I remarked to Paul Byrne that the Guinness seemed more potent than usual and also tasted rather sweet:
"That's not Guinness" said Paul "it's Black Velvet, a 50/50 mix of Guinness and Champagne. You will get very drunk very quickly drinking that."
Paul and I were amongst the last to leave the party at about 10 p.m. and walked, or rather staggered, back to Hardwicke's parking lot to collect our cars and drive home. We hugged each other and wished each other a Merry Christmas and both walked to our cars and started the engines and put our cars into reverse. Then we reversed into each other. We got out of the cars, looked at the damage, laughed and said Merry Christmas again and headed home.

One Saturday night Paul and Audrey Byrne invited us to go to the Irish Cabaret at Jury's Hotel (formerly the Intercontinental). They had a crowd of friends there, in particular Lorcan Burke, Jr, who was married to Paul's very beautiful sister, Madeline, and Lorcan's two brothers and their wives. Drinking and talking before the show I happened to mention that there was one mealy mouthed Irishman I couldn't stand and that was Eamon Andrews, a talk show host on BBC TV. There was a dead silence broken by Paul saying:

"Eamon Andrews is married to Grainne Burke, sister to these three"
I tried to pass it off as a joke saying I knew of the relationship and just wanted to see how they reacted.

At a party at Lorcan Burke Jr's house Paul took me aside and said he was going to make a little speech welcoming me to Dublin and introducing me to those present. He would then propose a toast and wanted me to respond to it by saying a few words in Irish, which he taught me. I stood on a chair and Paul gave his little speech introducing Gary and Sue Spence from England and proposing a toast to our health. Right on cue I raised my glass and said phonetically:
"Pogue na hone" There was an uproar. I asked Lorcan what was wrong:
"They don't like a fecking Englishman telling them to kiss his arse" said Lorcan.

Lorcan's father, Lorcan Burke Sr. owned two of Dublin's principal theatres, the Gaiety and the Olympia. We started going to the Olympia with Paul and Audrey, who could get in free due to their family connections. For some reason Eileen, who ran the box office, got it into her head that I was Gary Burke, son of the owner, so I could get in free whenever I wanted. When there was a show on that we particularly liked Sue and I would go several times. We became regulars at Joseph and the Amazing Technicolor Dreamcoat, Jesus Christ Superstar and Evita.

On one occasion we went to the Olympia Theater with Paul and Audrey to see the Halle Orchestra, a famous symphony orchestra from Manchester, being conducted by Sir John Barbarolli, in a performance for charity. At the interval we went to the Green Room and had a couple of drinks with Lorcan Sr. He drank large quantities of whiskey and seemed to be already a little the worse for wear. As the show ended Lorcan, Sr. took the stage and said:
"On behalf of you all I would like to thank our visitors from England for the wonderful performance which enabled us to raise £3,000 for the St. Vincent de Paul Society. So would you please

join me in a special round of applause for Mr. John Barboli and his band"

After the show we went to Buswell's Hotel across from Dail Eireann, the Irish Parliament. This was one of our favorite hang outs and I took a seat at the bar. "You can't sit there, that's Brian Lenehan's seat" said the bartender.

"Well where is he?" I said

"He isn't here but he might come in" said the bartender.

"Well" said I "this is a public bar and I don't think you can reserve seats".

A few minutes later Brian Lenehan, the Minister for Finance, came in and said: "You're in my place".

"It's just as much my place as yours" said I.

He just scowled at me and took another seat. We started talking and ended up becoming, if not friends, at least drinking companions.

A crowd of us started to have a party every Saturday night at one of the group's houses. The first week was to be our turn and we bought a load of booze and cooked up a big pot of spaghetti sauce, got the kids to bed and at the appointed time, 8.30 p.m. were ready and waiting. 9 p.m. came, then 9.30 p.m. with no arrivals. When it got to be 10.30 p.m. we went to bed. At 11.15 p.m. the door bell rang and there they were, the whole crowd. We soon got used to the idea that in Dublin no matter what time you invited people for they wouldn't come until the pubs closed.

We had a wide choice of babysitters in Glasnevin and they were often very experienced because they came from large families and had grown up looking after their younger brothers and sisters. One of our regular babysitters was Bernadette, a stunning redhead, with green eyes and classic Irish looks. One night after we came home Sue went straight to bed and I put my arms round Bernadette and tried to kiss her. She hit me a stinging blow across the face and I was careful never to touch her again.

One day I was going to look at a centre city property that was for sale and as I walked down Middle Abbey Street I saw Lorcan, Jr.

parked at a parking meter, just sitting there having a smoke. I tapped on the window and when he opened it I said:
"What are you doing, Lorcan, do you want to come and have a drink"
"I can't go anywhere" he said "not until my money runs out on this parking meter".

At one of our weekly lunch meetings at Hardwicke the discussion turned to the possibility of buying a site for development in Tallaght. Tallaght was then a small town to the immediate south west of the city of Dublin and was slated by Dublin County Coucil for development into a new town. They were predicting 1,000,000 sq. ft. of retail space and 3,000,000 sq. ft. of offices in addition to tens of thousands of new houses. Charles Judd, who lived in a large house in a secluded valley in the foothills of the Wicklow Hills south of Tallaght said he had a shepherd, Paddy Flynn, who knew all the farmers who owned land in Tallaght.

It was agreed that on Wednesday I would meet Paddy at Charles' house and he and I would drive around and he would introduce me to these landowners. I met him as planned and by 2 p.m. our work was done and I took him for a drink to Bridget Burke's Pub. I never drank whiskey but after a couple of pints of Guinness, of which I had grown enormously fond, I agreed to try a glass of Jameson 12 year old. I liked it so much I had another and another. I left the pub about 4 p.m. and drove Paddy home and set off for Dublin. By this time I was feeling drunk and an all consuming tiredness enveloped me. I had to open the window and put my head out in order to get the wind in my face to stop myself from falling asleep. Foolishly, instead of going home, I went back to the office. I parked the car and went in the back door past the boardroom and Mont Kavanagh's office and up the stairs. I had just reached the top of the stairs when Mont Kavanagh's door opened:
"Good afternoon Gary" he said "come down and tell me how you got on in Tallaght".
I misjudged the position of the first step and tumbled head over heels down the stairs, landing at his feet. He helped me to my feet and reeled from the smell of whiskey on my breath.

Making Hen's Meat

"Gary, I do believe you're drunk" he said in his most urbane manner "go on home, and I'll see you tomorrow"
Tomorrow came and went and nothing was said about Tallaght. At our weekly management meeting on Thursday item five was Tallaght.
"Now we come to item five, Tallaght" said Mont Kavanagh "which I propose we delete from the agenda" and that was the end of Tallaght as far as Hardwicke was concerned.

Shortly after I had joined Hardwicke we had a visit to the office from a girl called Sheila Hurley. She was a Canadian who had recently married a Dubliner, Mick Hurley. She had previously worked at Hardwicke and had stopped to visit her old friends. I was immediately struck by both her looks and personality and asked her to meet me for a drink after work and to my surprise she agreed. We went to the roof top bar at Jury's Hotel and drank Bloody Marys. She and I started seeing each other almost every evening as her husband, who was a recently qualified doctor, worked at the hospital until 10 p.m. It seemed strange that someone who had only been married four months would start spending a lot of time with another guy but that's what happened. She and I used to hug and kiss but it never went any further than that. When I met her husband I really liked him and I invited him and Sheila home for dinner. We all got a bit drunk and Mick insisted on showing us his penile frenulum. I didn't even know a penis had a frenulum but you live and learn. The situation looked like it was going to get messy and I was rather relieved when Mick and Sheila moved to her home country, Canada.

Through Paul Byrne I had met Paddy and Collette Little, who lived around the corner from them with their three young children. Paddy was a wild and crazy guy and was always getting into scrapes. We used to drink in a cabaret club called the Old Sheiling owned by an Irish American by the name of Bill Fuller. Bill was as tough as nails and stood for no nonsense. One night Paddy asked Bill's girlfriend, Kitty McMahon, to dance with him. All the time they were dancing Paddy was hitting on her, telling her how he had a hard on for her. Kitty told Bill and he dragged Paddy from his seat and threw him down a flight of steps on to the parking lot. Then he took a flying leap and landed with both feet on Paddy's leg which broke in three places. Paddy sued and won a substantial settlement.

One Sunday afternoon Sue and I were at Paddy and Collete's when Paddy said: "Lets watch a movie."
He sent the kids outside to play and put a tape in the VCR. It was the most horrendous porno movie I'd ever seen. It was obviously designed for the Irish market because the participants were dressed up as priests and nuns and choirboys. After about ten minutes Sue said we had to leave and Paddy took the hint and turned it off.

Paddy had spent five years in the British Royal Air Force and claimed that that had turned him bisexual. He said that homosexuality was rife in the RAF and it might have been true because when he took me to the RAF club in Dublin it was like being in a gay bar. In retrospect it's amazing that there was an RAF club in Dublin. But there was and, for all I know, there still is.

In September, 1971 Simon started school at the age of four and a half. He was enrolled in Sacred Heart Boys National School which was on the street where we lived about a five minute walk from our house. Although we weren't Christians we agreed that Simon could participate in prayers and religious education. We figured he had a big enough handicap speaking with a Bradford accent and didn't need to draw attention to the differences between him and the Irish boys. Irish was compulsory and the school teacher even gave Simon an Irish name, Simone McSpellan.

By this time drinking was becoming a dominant part of my life. In England I used to have a pint or two most evenings and maybe three or four at the weekends but I almost never drank liquor and rarely drank at lunch time. In Ireland drinking had become a way of life. We drank in the office between 12.30 p.m. and 2p.m. and we often drank again between 4.30 p.m. and 5 p.m.. I was in the pub by 5.30 p.m. and either stayed there until closing time or went home and ate dinner and then went to one of the local pubs, The Slipper Bar or the Addison Lodge or to Glasnevin Tennis Club of which I had become a social member. This meant I had joined the club so I could drink there and had no intention of playing tennis. Still, I reassured myself, I was doing my job and being well paid for it and neither Sue or the kids were going short of anything so I'd only really worry about my drinking if things got worse.

Babysitters were so easy to get that Sue went out with me two or three times a week and the only time I really spent with James and Simon was at the weekend when we would go to the beach at Portmarnock, north of Dublin, or sometimes down to Sandycove or Bray on the South side. We liked going to Portmarnock because right by the sand dunes was Portmarnock Country Club owned by the Burke family. Donal Burke was the manager. While the kids were on the beach I would go and have a drink and then rejoin them.

Sue and I often went out at night to the Country Club where they had a resident band the leader and singer being Joe Cahill. Sue took a job working there as a bartender for a while but quit when I got jealous because Joe Cahill was bringing her home at 2 a.m. after the Club closed. Sue's sister, Carol, came to stay with us and after a great day on the strand at Portmarnock we were on our way home when it suddenly started raining after several days of hot sunny weather. I touched my brakes on a bend and the car ended up in a ditch. We got out and could see that the ditch was maybe ten feet deep but two feet from the top a metal pipe crossed the ditch and the car was straddling this pipe from which water was pouring.

We walked to the nearest house to use a phone to call a tow truck to pull the car out of the ditch. The owner of the house offered us a cup of tea. When he went to fill the kettle he had no water and I had to confess that I thought I had burst the water main leading to his house. When I finally got home I felt guilty about it and filled two five gallon cans with water and took it out to the guy's house. He appeared very grateful for the gesture.

We had a succession of visitors. Jean Thornton came and spent a few days with us and I paid for mother and father to come over to stay for a week. I told father I wanted him to prune the apple trees in my back garden. He brought his pruning saw and long handled pruners and made a great job of it; the trees probably hadn't been pruned for thirty years. We took mother and father to a variety show at the Clontarf Castle with Paul and Audrey Byrne. The headliner was Chris Casey, a comedian who father found hilarious. Father had always been anti Irish, a typical prejudice amongst Englishmen. One week in Dublin put paid to that. He loved Dublin and he loved the Irish and for the rest of his life would not hear a bad word said about them.

One night I got a call from the police to say the burglar alarm was ringing at Hardwicke's office, 14 Wellington Road. Would I come over and silence the alarm and let the police check the building for signs of a break in. I took father with me and we let the guards into the building and silenced the alarm. There was no sign of a break in. I asked the guards if they would have a drink and naturally they said they would. We went into the boardroom and the four of us were sitting there drinking bottles of Guinness when there was a sharp rap on the window. It was the Garda Superintendent come to check on his men. He stayed and had a few glasses of whiskey and it was about 2 a.m., when they were preparing to leave, that I asked them if there was anything they could do so I would not be arrested for drunk driving on the way home. The superintendent took out a pad and wrote me a safe conduct. It said 'The bearer of this note, Mr. Gary Spence, has been assisting the police and is to be permitted to proceed to his home at 15 St. Canices Road without let or hindrance. Signed, Superintendent Seamus O'Connor.'

We also had a visit from Sue's parents, Reuben and Renee. They came over on the ferry with Renee driving. There was something about Reuben that really aggravated me. I think it was his total honesty. He would never consider anyone's feelings and would say whatever came into his head without dressing it up. He'd been annoying me for a couple of days and when he criticized Sue's cooking I completely blew my top and told him to leave. He and Renee packed their bags and went to stay in the Skylon Hotel on Airport Road for the rest of the week.

Making Hen's Meat

At Hardwicke we had decided to make an offer on a site in central Dublin. The property concerned was a closed down hardware store called Dockrells. It was located on Pearse Street and backed onto Trinity College. The property was being sold by David Bailey of Jones Lang Wootton and it was to be sold by sealed bid. I valued the property at £300,000 and recommended a bid at or around that level. Mont Kavanagh was very keen to buy the site and decided he wanted a second opinion on value. He phoned Norman Bowie at Jones Lang Wootton's London office and asked if he could advise on value without causing any ethical problems as their Dublin office was the selling agent. Norman said it was no problem for one office to act for the seller and another for the buyer.

It was arranged that I would fly to London and I had an appointment with Norman Bowie for 6 p.m., the following day. On arrival at his office he told me it was his wedding anniversary and he wanted to be home soon as he and his wife were going out to celebrate. I gave him the facts and figures on the site and he proceeded to prepare a residual valuation. When he had finished, in about fifteen minutes, he handed me his handwritten single sheet valuation. He valued the site at £350,000. Now Mont Kavanagh had a dilemma, should he offer £300,000 or £350,000 or somewhere in between. He asked David Bailey what the procedure for bidding was to be. David said bids were to be in by 6 p.m. the following Friday and he proposed to pick up the bids personally between 4 p.m. and 6 p.m.. Mont asked him to pick up the Hardwicke bid last at 6 p.m.. Two offers were then prepared one at £300,000 and one at £350,000 and placed in the top drawer of Mont Kavanagh's desk with a notation on the sealed envelopes as to which bid was which.

On the appointed day David Bailey arrived at 6 p.m. as arranged. We all fixed ourselves drinks and Mont said:
"Well, David, our bid is in this drawer but before I give it to you why not open the other bids and let's see what has been offered".
David thought about it for a few moments and said:

"Why not?" and took eight sealed envelopes from his briefcase. He opened the bids and the highest one was £295,000:
"Well" said Mont "we've just beaten that" and handed David the envelope containing the £300,000 bid. This little piece of subterfuge had saved Mont Kavanagh £50,000. He was very annoyed when Norman Bowie sent him a bill for £3,500 for his fifteen minute valuation.

In July we took a weeks holiday on the Dingle Peninsula in County Kerry in south west Ireland. We stayed in a small hotel overlooking Inch Strand. This is a marvelous piece of coastline warmed by the Gulf Stream with fuschia hedges ten feet tall and palm trees growing profusely. We visited Dingle, a charming little town with a harbor and a small fishing fleet. Beyond Dingle we stopped for refreshment in Ballyferriter and then had a few drinks in Kruger's Pub in Dunquin. This is as far west as you can go in Europe. The next parish after Dunquin is New York. We visited the Gallarus Oratory, a thousand year old Christian church, built of stone with a corbelled roof.

We had noticed signs outside many of the small farms on the way to Dunquin. The signs read 'Beehive Huts 5/- per family'. We asked someone in Kruger's Pub what a beehive hut was and they told us they were old habitations built of stone but shaped like an igloo. They were over one thousand years old. We stopped at a farm with one of the signs, paid our five shillings, and the farmer's wife showed us a group of three beehive huts. I was amazed at how perfectly preserved they were considering their great age and remarked on this to the farmer's wife:
"Arragh feck" she says " my husband, Seamus, only built these last year for the tourist trade!"

So enchanted were we with this part of Ireland that we rented a cottage in Dingle for a week in July 1972 and invited my parents to join us.

On Good Friday I was mowing the grass with a motor mower in the back garden. I didn't know James, who was two and a half years old, was walking behind me and when I turned the mower round he fell over the grass box. His hand went into the rotating cylinder. The motor cut out. I bent down and looked at his hand which seemed to be okay. Then I saw blood running from under the cuff of a thick sweater he was wearing. I rolled back the sleeve of the sweater to reveal a cut on his wrist that had gone down to the bone. The sweater had probably saved him from having his hand cut completely off. I panicked. I rushed into the house screaming for Sue to come and look. Fortunately she remained calm and said we needed to get him to hospital. I turned on the head lights and flashers and drove as fast as I could to the emergency room at the Mater Hospital. They told us they couldn't stitch him up because they didn't have a needle small enough and told us to take him to the Children's Hospital. At the Children's Hospital I was bollocked by one of the nuns who ran the place for letting James bleed on the terrazzo floor. While Sue waited for a doctor to stitch him up I went in search of a pub. I badly needed a shot of liquor. When I found a pub it was closed. I had forgotten that the pubs didn't open in Ireland on Good Friday.

Early in May, 1972 we had a call from Peter Thornton. His marriage to Jean was over and they were separated. He was very depressed and needed a break so we invited him over. He flew to Dublin next day and I picked him up at the airport. Jean had opened a letter addressed to him from a young girl telling him she was pregnant with his baby and asking for his help. Peter told us he had sex with the girl when she couldn't afford the rent for one of his bedsitters. He marked her rent book "Paid" in much the same way as I had done when someone couldn't pay Home Products. Peter was so distraught about Jean kicking him out that he had attempted suicide by connecting a hose to his van's exhaust pipe and putting the other end into the van and closing the windows. He was saved from certain death by the van running out of petrol.

On May 17, 1972 Peter again narrowly escaped death or injury when a car bomb went off in Central Dublin. He was only fifty yards away from the explosion at the time. Peter hired a car and went on a tour of Ireland on his own. He picked up a young hitch hiker who it turned out was in the Provisional IRA and was wanted by the Garda Siochana, and after being stopped at a road block he was arrested. Peter was also taken into custody and it took him several hours to prove his identity and innocence. Finally he was released. Peter stayed with us for a couple of weeks and seemed to be much more his old self when he left us to go back to England.

At Whitsuntide we took the car ferry over to England for five days to stay with my parents in Bradford The boys got to know big grandmother who was now living at 12 Ashwell Road. My mother and father had taken pity on her and after little grandma died had taken her in. She lived with them until 1978 when she moved into a nursing home. She died in 1980. They also got to know my brothers John and Mike, his wife Liz and their children, Mark, Richard and Heather. In subsequent years they all made trips to England and stayed either with my parents or with Mike and Liz.

In July we went for a week to a farmhouse, Desert House in Clonakilty, County Cork, then we went to Dingle and were joined there by my mother and father. We had a house in the center of town that was very old fashioned. There were no carpets just lino on the floor and it reminded me of growing up in England in the fifties. In the rural areas around Dingle you would see more donkey carts than cars. The farmers would bring their milk to a central dairy operated under the auspices of An Bord Bainne, The Irish Dairy Board. It was not uncommon to see twenty or thirty donkeys and carts outside a creamery with just a handful of tractors and land rovers.

Father and mother loved Dingle. Mother liked going to a butcher's shop and having a joint cut out of a whole side of beef. There was a butchers shop right across the street from where we were staying in what is now Doyle's Seafood Restaurant. We would see sheep being driven into the back of the shop for slaughtering. Father liked the many opportunities for drinking. Dingle had a population of only about three thousand but had over one hundred licensed premises. This dated back to the days when Dingle had been a major port, and a center for smuggling, and the town had a much bigger population. Some of the 'pubs' were no more than a room in someone's house with a few bottles of beer for sale. They stayed open in order to retain their license which could have considerable value, particularly for transferring to Dublin where no more licenses were being issued other than where there was a proven increase in population. You could go to the barber shop and drink a pint of Guinness while having your haircut because the barber had a license.

We made our H.Q. Thomas Ashe's pub on John Street. He was the local Guinness bottler and had a very prosperous business. His wife, Kate Ashe, would see me and dad come in, then mother would join us. Then mother would go home and Sue would join us. We were never all in the pub together. Kate asked why and we explained someone had to be back at the house to mind the kids:
"Sure if you all want to drink here, I'll send one of my girls to baby-sit" she said. And she did. We could all go out together for the rest of the week. Pub closing time was officially 11 p.m. but the local guard would come in around that time. for a few pints and I've seen the parish priest come in after midnight. One night at about 1 a.m. I asked Kate Ashe when she closed:
"Ah now" she said "usually about the middle of October".
While we were in Dingle Sue discovered she was pregnant again, with an expected date of March 10, 1973.

Meanwhile, back at Hardwicke, things were going swimmingly. I'd got into a routine and was having a great time looking for sites and looking for tenants. A Northern Irishman, John Ballance had joined the company as project manager and he brought a lot of humor into our day to day work. He had a knack of getting Mont Kavanagh and Charles Judd to relax and our weekly dinner meetings began to turn into joke telling sessions with John always able to top anyone else's joke.

We had a scheme under development in St. Stephen's Green. This was a forty thousand square foot office building and Jones Lang Wootton and Lisney & Co were the letting agents. One day I got a call from Charles Spence, the real estate director of the Bank of

Nova Scotia, a Canadian bank. He was planning to be in Dublin the following week and wanted to meet me at the St. Stephen's Green site.

When we met he told me he needed 5,000 sq. ft. of ground floor space for the bank but also had the Canadian Embassy lined up to take the top floor. I suggested he lease the whole building and sub-let to the Embassy and sub-let the other three floors. He liked the idea and asked, if he agreed to this proposal, could they name the building Canada House. I told him there would be no problem so he asked for a three month option on the building. I agreed he could have this for a fee of £10,000. We walked across the street to the Shelbourne Hotel for a drink in the Horseshoe Bar and from there I called Mont Kavanagh to get approval for the deal. He said he would get Paul Byrne to draw up an Option Agreement so that Spence could sign it before flying out. He did sign it and he did exercise the option so I was very popular at Hardwicke. Mont Kavanagh gave me a £1,000 pay rise bringing my salary to £4,500 per annum.

Sue had become good friends with Eileen Fitzpatrick who lived with her husband Joe and two children Paul and Rebecca at 39, St. Canice's Road. Their kids were the same age as ours so Simon and Paul went to school together. Joe was a typical Dubliner. Very well read and with a wonderful use of language and a died in the wool republican. He and I got on well together because we shared the same political views. He always took Eileen out twice a year on her birthday and on their wedding anniversary 'whether she deserved it or not'. Eileen seemed quite happy with this and neither Joe or Eileen could understand Sue going out three or four nights a week.

Sue and I had started going to traditional music pubs such as O'Donahue's on Baggot Street, the Bark Tavern on the Quays and Portobello Harbor on the Grand Canal. We loved to listen to the Dubliners and the Wolfe Tones. We often used to see Luke Kelly and Ronnie Drew of the Dublineers in Neary's Bar or Davy Byrne's off Grafton Street. We also went to pubs where there was entertainment such as the Baggot Inn, The Addison Lodge, The

Clontarf Castle, the Old Sheiling and the Country Club at Pormarnock. One night a week we usually went to the Chariot Inn in Phibsborough where we danced to the music of an Irish Showband. On one occasion we were asked to stop dancing so close together. Sue was wearing suede hotpants, which were all the rage, and we weren't so much dancing as moving round the dance floor in a clinch.

On March 8th 1973 Sue was admitted to the Rotunda Hospital on Parnell Street, Ireland's foremost maternity hospital. I was left to look after Simon and James. Simon was six and James was three years old. I got them to bed by 9 p.m. and called the hospital to be told Sue had started in labor. About 1 am there was a loud banging at the door. I asked who it was and a loud voice shouted: "It's me, Big John, open the fecking door".
Big John was a fearsome character. He was a tinker who lived with his extended family in a group of caravans and tents on St. Canice's Road opposite Simon's school. Sue had befriended John's wife and mother and as well as giving them money, food and clothing, would let them come in the house to bathe their children and themselves. Big John constantly beat his wife and was forever in trouble with the police for assault and public drunkenness. I could tell by his manner that he was very drunk and no way was I going to open the door. I told him to go away, it was the middle of the night and he would wake up the children. His response was to shatter the stained glass window in the door with an axe or hammer.

I was afraid for my life and I called 999 and asked for police assistance. Big John heard me make the call and staggered off. Ten minutes later the police arrived. I asked them to go after Big John and arrest him. They said they'd already taken care of him. I asked if they'd arrested him and one of them replied:
" Indeed we have not t'would be a waste of time. But we've beaten the bejasus out of him. He won't bother you again this night"

Next morning the phone rang at 8 a.m. It was the Rotunda hospital to say a baby boy had just been born. I took Simon and

James to Eileen Fitztpatrick's and drove to the Rotunda Hospital. As I was walking into the hospital I saw a van delivering meat to the kitchens. The name on the van was Dominic Fitzpatrick of Moore Street. I went in to the hospital and gave Sue a big hug. She was looking very well and was enjoying the luxury of a private room and excellent food. A nurse brought the baby for me to see and as I held him I said to Sue:

"I've just seen a butcher's van with the name Dominic Fitzpatrick of Moore Street, what do you think to calling this little fellow Dominic".

Sue liked the idea and we named our third and final boy Dominic Gary Gerard Spence. The Gary was after me and the Gerard was after Gerry Healy whose full name was Thomas Gerard Healy.

In April Sue's sister, Carol, and her husband came to stay with us. Simon was just as big a drinker as me so I introduced him to the local pubs and while I was at work he would be drinking a few pints and having a few shots of vodka. Simon was very much the stiff upper lipped Englishman and was an arch conservative. For this reason he and I had a tacit agreement to stay off the subject of politics but in Dublin it is hard to avoid. One night we went to Portobello Harbor to hear the Wolfe Tones. They were singing a song, the chorus of which is:
"Wack folla diddle folla deedieday
So we say, hip hurray
Come and listen while we play
Wack folla diddle folla deedieday"

Instead of singing 'Come and listen while we play' the Wolfe Tones belted out 'Come and Join the IRA' to wild applause. Simon was outraged and I only calmed him down by pointing out that he was effectively a guest in someone's country and should behave accordingly. Then the Wolfe Tones sang "Kevin Barry". When they came to the line 'British Soldiers tortured Barry' I thought Simon would have an apoplectic fit. I told him it was an old song about events of long ago and under the influence of a shot of whiskey and another pint he calmed down. But the worst was yet to come. At the end of the performance the Wolfe Tones began to sing the Irish National Anthem, and as is customary everyone rose and joined in the singing. Everyone that is except Simon Oxford. People were staring at him and I bent down and said:

"For fuck's sake, Simon, stand up and sing God Save the Queen"

Thank God that when Simon Oxford had been drinking he lowered his voice so no one was any the wiser that he was singing God Save the Queen while they sang A Soldiers Song. We set off to take the Oxfords to Dun Laoghaire for the ferry home to England and stopped for a few drinks. They missed the ferry. Next morning from my office I telexed Simon Oxford's employer:

"Unavoidably detained in Ireland"

That night we missed the ferry again and again the next night. Only on the fourth attempt did we get them on board before sailing time.

CHAPTER FOURTEEN

"there they go, three strides and a rub and backards and forwards" Harold

In May 1973 I received a message to call Ken Rohan of the Rohan Group. I knew they were builders of prefabricated concrete bungalows and industrial buildings. I assumed he wanted to talk about doing building work for Hardwicke and so didn't return the call. He persisted and on the third attempt was put through to me. He asked me to come see him:
"What for?" I said.
"It's a private and personal matter" he replied.
Intrigued I went to see him at 5.30 p.m. that evening. He explained to me that the Rohan Group had been a small family business for years based in County Cork and that he and his brother, John, the company chairman, had recently taken the company public. They now wanted to expand the company's horizons by moving into commercial property and they wanted me to join them to run a company to be called Rohan Commercial Properties.

I asked him how he knew he wanted me for the job when he had never met me previously. He said I came highly recommended and I subsequently discovered that the recommendation was from Tommy Lombard of Jones Lang Wootton. I told Ken that I was very happy at Hardwicke and he said:
"You might be happier with us; tell me what it would take to get you to join us and I'll see if we can agree something."

Making Hen's Meat

That night I talked it over with Sue and we reflected that three years previously I had been earning £1,000 per annum, now I was on £4,500 plus a car and other benefits. We agreed I should stay at Hardwicke and that I would ask Ken Rohan for a deal he would never agree to. Next evening I met Ken and told him I wanted £6,500 per annum an Audi 100LS car and a 2.5% share of the profits of Rohan Commercial Properties. Ken stuck out his hand and said:
"That's a deal".
I shook his hand and we retired to the Shelbourne Hotel to celebrate and so that, to quote Ken, he "could find out what makes you tick."

The next day I gave one month's notice to Hardwicke but they asked me to leave that day, paying me in full for the month and letting me keep the company car until the Rohan Group provided me with one. I packed up my personal items and went straight round to the Rohan Group's office at 6, Mount Street Crescent and told Ken Rohan I could start work right away. He was delighted and showed me to the empty second floor room which was to be my office. This was a new experience for me, starting a company from scratch. I busied myself ordering furniture and hired a secretary, Norma Lynch, who was strikingly beautiful.

I began looking for a site for an office building in earnest and as well as talking to all the major agents in Dublin I made direct approaches to many property owners. Finally, I got into serious negotiations with John McConnell of McConnell Advertising who owned a building, which was their former headquarters, on Pearse Street across from Hardwicke's development in progress on the Dockrell's site. John McConnell appointed Tommy Lombard of Jones Lang Wootten to act for him and we finally agreed a price of £113,000. John McConnell began to show signs he might renege on the deal before contracts were exchanged so Ken Rohan phoned Tommy Lombard and said that as a professional he should tell John McConnell he could no longer act for him if he reneged on the deal. This did the trick and I had my first site under my belt.

The next few months were spent negotiating with three or four tenants in the building to get them to vacate and preparing plans for a planning application. Finally, the tenants were gone, at a cost of £17,000 making the total investment £130,000. Austin Murray was the appointed architect and on our behalf he obtained planning permission for ground floor showrooms with three floors of offices over and a penthouse flat.

Ken Rohan and his brother, John, and financial controller, Jack Casey had difficulty grasping my proposal that we should borrow the money, build the building, lease it and retain it as a long term investment. I prepared a thirty year projection and presented this at a board meeting in Cork. In the early years the rental income only just covered the interest on the loan and this made no sense to John Rohan. He seemed incapable of grasping the principle of investing for long term capital growth. Unbeknown to me Rohan's two main operating divisions, Roh-fab, which built pre-fab bungalows and Sitecast, the industrial builder and developer, were both having a bad year. The Rohan brothers badly needed a cash injection from somewhere because, as a public company, a year with next to zero profit would send the share price tumbling.

They asked me what I though the Pearse Street site could be sold for and I prepared a residual valuation using the most optimistic parameters and came up with a figure of £365,000. . This was almost a £250,000 profit and Ken Rohan's eyes lit up at the prospect. Ken mentioned to his bankers, Allied Irish Investment Bank, that he was thinking of selling the site and they asked to be given first the first option to purchase. They appointed Paddy Spain of Lisney & Co to act for them and he came to 6, Mount Street Crescent and went through my figures. To Ken's surprise and relief Paddy appeared to agree with all the figures in my valuation. And so it came about that Allied Irish Investment Bank bought the site and Rohan Group made a life saving profit of nearly £250,000. Jack Casey, the financial controller, phoned to congratulate me and said:
"Which fecking bank are you going to rob for us next year, Gary?"

Making Hen's Meat

In the summer, Sue, the three children and I went to Mulraney in County Mayo for our annual holiday. We loaded our luggage into the car and had gone about ten miles when I said:
"Sue, we've forgotten something"
"I'm sure we have" she said "what is it"
"We've forgotten the baby" I said as I did a u-turn and headed back to St. Canice's Road where we found Dominic fast asleep in his carry cot on the dining room table where we had left him.

We stayed in a small hotel owned by a barrister. The food was slim pickings but the price was so cheap we could afford to eat out to supplement the hotel fare. The view from the hotel was of the ocean and Achill Island and to the south of a mountain, Croagh Patrick, which is the scene of an annual barefoot pilgrimage. We spent most of the time on the beach, but one day took a trip south through Connemara to the city of Galway. We though Galway was wonderful and after a few drinks in the bar vowed that we would return and stay in the Great Southern Hotel in Eyre Square.

Later in the summer Simon who was six and a half went to England to stay with my parents for a week and then went to Blackpool for a week's holiday with Sue's parents. We sent him on the Aer Lingus plane under the care of one of the stewardesses and my mother and father collected him at the airport in Bradford. He became a regular visitor to England as did James and Dominic and we liked the idea of keeping them in touch with their roots. Many years later for my 40th birthday Simon wrote a poem about growing up in Bradford and re-visiting it – here it is:

<u>A CHILD WENT FORTH</u>

A child went forth every day
All he saw was reflected in his eyes
The cobbled streets he walked upon
The sky with the huge chimneys ever present
Grandpa and Granny by the fire

But then a move across the sea
To a different world, a different country

Gary Spence

School starts with sandboxes, playpens,
And crayons galore
New friends to meet, new things to learn
Walking home with the lads
Fighting and playing, but most of all
Making sure not to step on the cracks in the floor

Summer comes, bikes to ride, trees to climb
Visits to England to granny and grandpa's
Pushing the trolley in the grocery store
A big boy now, at least he thinks
But the chimneys are still there
And granny and grandpa still wait by the fire

In September, after a holiday in Donegal, James started school at Sacred Heart. His name became Seamus McSpellan. Sue would walk down to Eileen's at 39 St. Canice's Road and they would walk to school together and always have tea or coffee after dropping the kids off at school. One day after school Sue had to go to the shops. Simon was playing at Eileen's so she had Dominic in the push chair and James walking along beside her. At 5, St. Canice's Road lived an old lady called Mrs. Dwyer and Sue stopped to chat to her. Mrs. Dwyer patted James on the head and said.
"What a nice big boy, going to school as well"
James immediately gave her the V sign.
"I bet you don't know what that means" said Mrs. Dwyer
"I do" said James "it means fuck off and it means fuck off to you"
"The things they pick up at school" said Mrs. Dwyer
"I didn't hear it at school" said James "I got it from my Dad, he says fuck off all the time".

Late in 1974 I began to feel ill. It was nothing specific just a general feeling of acute depression and malaise coupled with some bizarre symptoms. I became afraid of riding in lifts, I would have a tightening of the chest, get dry mouth and begin hyperventilating; I used to wake up thinking there were insects or animals crawling over the bed; I would wake up thinking there were people in the back garden and would be in and out of bed looking out of the window all night long; I became dizzy whenever I went into a business meeting. This would last a few minutes and then pass away but was very disconcerting while it lasted. I went to see Dr. McKeever, the family doctor and he put me on a course of tranquilizers. He attributed the symptoms to stress.

On 14 December the Rohan Group's Christmas party was held at the Green Isle Hotel on the Naas Road. Sue and I left at about 11 p.m. and as soon as we made the turn onto the South Circular Road a guard on a motor cycle came alongside and signaled me to stop. He told me he had followed me for three miles and I had been driving at 60 m.p.h. in a 30 m.p.h. zone and had gone through a red traffic light. He droned on and on and I was getting slightly bored so I decided to test his reactions and said:
"Do me a favor, charge me or let me go on home."
"I'll charge you alright" he said and wrote me a ticket for six separate offences. It took a lot of string pulling and a threat to send the guard to border duty to get the charges dropped.

Just a few days later I was out with Sue at the Old Sheiling in Raheny and as I was driving home on Collins Avenue I noticed a Garda car behind us. Sure enough he pulled us over and he breathalysed me and naturally I tested positive. I decided to plead with the guard:
"Look" I said "If I lose my license, I'll lose my job and then I'll have no income. I've got a wife and young children. I'm almost home and I've not been in an accident, can't you, please, give me a break".
"We can't let you drive," said the guard "so sit in the back and my partner will drive you home with me following."
When we got home I got out of the car and the guard said:
"Let me see you open your front door."
I did so:
"I was just checking you hadn't lied to me about where you lived," he said "here you can keep this as a souvenir." and he threw me the breathalyser. I believed that there truly was a God.

I was drinking very heavily at this time. My couple of pints a day in England had been transformed into a major problem. I would often slip out of the office at about 11 am and go to the local bar and have a couple of pints of Guinness. At lunch time I would have another three pints and I would be back in the pub at 5.30 p.m. or 6 p.m.. I would drink for a couple of hours then head towards home. I would usually stop at a bar on the Airport Road and have one or two more drinks and then go home, eat some dinner and go to bed. As well as beer and Guinness I was drinking gin & tonic, bacardi and coke and sometimes whiskey or cognac.

I got into the habit of meeting Ken Rohan's secretary, Monica Daly, in the pub after work and after a few drinks would drive her home to Dunboyne in County Meath. We often stopped at the Grasshopper in Clonee and had a few drinks and maybe dinner. She and I were having a little fling and this probably added to my stress because I didn't particularly want Ken Rohan or Sue to know about me and Monica.

One day I had to go to Cork to a monthly board meeting. I got the train to Cork and had to rent a car to drive the few miles to Ballinacurra. I got to the door of the Hertz office and had a dizzy spell and simply couldn't go in. I thought maybe a couple of pints would calm my nerves but I had no money. I went to the office of an estate agent I knew, Spike O'Sullivan, and borrowed £5. I went to the Imperial Hotel on South Mall and drank a couple of pints of Guinness. This made me feel worse not better so I phoned Ken Rohan and told him I had been taken ill and was returning to Dublin for medical assistance. I got Spike O'Sullivan to drive me to the station and got the next train to Dublin.

I went straight to Dr. McKeever's house and he phoned the Mater Hospital and arranged for me to be admitted that evening. Before going to the hospital I went for a final drink at the Slipper Bar and after a few pints of Guinness I started drinking stingers, a lethal cocktail of crème de menthe and cognac. I arrived at the hospital drunk. I was put in a ward with five or six other men, most of them having had heart attacks and in a much worse condition than me. I was there for three weeks and three of my room mates shuffled off this mortal coil before my very eyes. This did not inspire confidence in the medical staff. The nursing sisters were wonderful and I have only happy memories of them. The psychiatrist assigned to my case put me on a very heavy dose of Valium, 250 miligrams daily by injection, and forbade me to drink. I was allowed to dress and leave the hospital for a walk (or rather a shuffle) round the neighborhood in the mornings and I became a regular in two or three pubs in Drumcondra where my nickname was "The Orange Juice Kid", on account of me drinking it by the pint. The only specific treatment I can recall, apart from the heavy sedation, was an attempt at aversion therapy to cure my fear of lifts. I was put into the hospital lift and surrounded by half a dozen medical students who would ride me up and down, down and up for half an hour. This was half an hour of sheer terror as far as I was concerned and confirmed in me my fear of lifts, which I have to this day.

Ken Rohan and Monica both visited me in hospital and Monica took me home to see the kids on one occasion. Sue came to visit me every day without fail. After three weeks I was discharged and given a letter to my doctor with details of the medication that was recommended.

When I returned to work I felt a little better but was unable to stay off the booze. I now developed a habit of taking Valium with a pint of Guinness. This seemed to double the effect of both so that before long I was drunk but very, very tranquil. By Spring of 1976 I was in a worse condition than I had been before I was hospitalized and I was finding the routine of daily life to be almost more than I could handle. I was very depressed and I honestly don't know how Sue put up with me.

Finally, in desperation, I went to see a hypnotist. He hypnotized me and I was 'under' for two hours. I felt totally at peace when I 'awoke' and found myself smiling for the first time in a year. I went straight home to share the good news with Sue. Unfortunately by next morning I felt as bad as ever. I couldn't afford the time or the money to spend two hours a day with a hypnotist so there had to be a better solution.

I went and talked to Ken Rohan openly and frankly about what was happening. I asked if he could recommend a good doctor. He made an appointment for me to see a psychiatrist friend of his in Fitzwilliam Square. It was a long session and there was a lot of Freudian stuff about father figures in the shape of Sam Chippindale, Gerry Healy, Mont Kavanagh and Ken Rohan. I think Ken was about 29 and I was 31 so I hardly saw him as a father figure. Finally I said:
"What about medication, isn't there something other than Valium, Ativan and Librium?"

He thought for a while and said there was a new drug that might do the trick. It had not yet been approved for sale in the US although it was of US manufacture but it could be prescribed in Ireland. He told me it was still in the experimental stage and there were special dietary requirements associated with it. It was forbidden to eat cheese or legumes or to drink any alcohol. I asked him what the effect would be if I took the drug and consumed the forbidden foods or drink: "Death" he replied.

The drug was called Parstelin and it truly was like a magic bullet. It cured me of all my problems overnight. No longer befuddled by alcohol I began spending more time with the family and we started taking the boys out to restaurants in the early evening because I was now getting home for 6 or 6.30 p.m.. I found I had boundless energy and was getting up at 5 am and working in the garden for a couple of hours before going to work.

In October we went for a two week holiday to Bulgaria. We had seen this advertised in the Irish Times at an incredibly cheap price. The Bulgarians were desperately in need of foreign currency. We could have two weeks in Bulgaria for the price that we would have paid for a weekend in London. We flew direct from Dublin to Varna on a Russian jet liner. When we arrived at Varna airport we had to change our pounds into levs at the government bureau de change. We were told that any levs we had left would not be changed back so we may as well spend it all. We were also given meal vouchers, three vouchers per person per day. These were each exchangeable for a meal in any restaurant in Bulgaria. Finally we were issued with identity cards which we were told to carry with us at all times.

We went by coach to the resort where we were to stay, about twenty miles from Varna on the Black Sea coast. The resort had an English name, Golden Sands. We were taken to our hotel which was occupied entirely by Irish and English people. We soon discovered that all the hotels were occupied by a single nationality. There were several hotels for Russians and several for the Germans who made up the bulk of visitors to Bulgaria. The staff at each hotel spoke the language of the guests. Bulgarian was not a language many foreigners knew and it was doubly impossible for us because of the use of the Cyrillic alphabet. German was the lingua franca and as I could speak a little school boy German we were generally able to communicate.

The beach was wonderful and we spent a lot of time there with the children. We were used to donkey rides on the beach in England; here they had camel rides which the children loved. There was a wide variety of restaurants spread throughout the resort and we visited many of them; we found the meal ticket system to be a great idea. Our favorite restaurant was built of stone resembling an old mill. It had a functioning water wheel, which turned a spit on which beautiful little chickens were roasted. We became friendly with a waiter who spoke some English and he explained to us that every Bulgarian had the use of a plot of land for growing fruit and vegetables, similar to the allotment system in England. On his day off we walked a mile to his garden where we met his aged mother. They gave us bunches of grapes and a water melon. We got fed up of carrying the water melon and I tipped it off the top of the cliff into the Black Sea.

One day we went for a cruise and another day we took the bus to Varna. Varna was a fairly bleak city but the most surprising thing was the lack of traffic other than public transport. What few cars we saw were parked up with a waterproof cover over them looking as if they were rarely used. We surmised that there was a fuel shortage. We saw a bride and groom emerging from a public building and as we watched another bride and groom appeared and another. They were carrying out marriages at about five minute intervals. In the main city square there was a large crowd. On closer examination there were hundreds of family groups. In each group was a boy of about sixteen with his head shaved, a weeping mother and a solemn looking father. This was a mustering point for conscripted soldiers. As we watched a fleet of army trucks appeared and there were tearful farewells as the sixteen year old boys boarded the trucks.

During the second week of our stay the woman who cleaned our room started pointing at Dominic's pushchair and then started pushing it around the room. We thought she wanted to take Dominic for a walk, but no – that wasn't it. Finally we got the hotel receptionist to come up and act as interpreter. The cleaner wanted to buy the pushchair. It had cost us about £8 so we quoted a price in levs equivalent to £30 and she agreed to pay it. The next morning she brought us the money and we promised to hand over the push chair on our final day. Now she pointed to my denim jeans, these cost about £4 so I quoted £20 and she bought both my jeans and Sue's. Next she pointed to Sue's nylon tights, these had cost 20p in Dunne's Stores so Sue said £2 and sold five pairs. With the money we made we could now go on an excursion to Sofia, the capital of Bulgaria. A bus picked us up at the hotel next morning and then went around to the other hotels picking up Russians, Germans, French, Italians and Spaniards.

When we were about half way to Varna Airport the bus driver reminded everybody that they would need their identity cards to board the airplane to Sofia. We had forgotten our cards so I walked to the front of the bus and told the driver of our problem. I asked him to take us back to the hotel to collect the identity cards he said "No" so I handed him 50 levs and he said "Yes". He did a U-turn and headed back to Golden Sands. Our fellow passengers went crazy, especially the Germans. Finally, we boarded the plane an hour late. They had held the plane for us because we belonged to that rare breed, foreign tourists, with pounds and marks and francs to spend.

Obviously the Bulgarian government did not subscribe to the Warsaw Convention on air travel. The plane was already full but hanging from the roof of the plane for the full length of the aisle were straps for standing passengers to hang onto just like you see on the buses and tubes in London. We all refused to stand so to our embarrassment Bulgarians were ordered to vacate their seats and make room for the tourists to sit down. Simon traveled to Sofia sitting on the knee of a uniformed four star general.

We visited a museum and art gallery and then watched the changing of the guard in the main square in front of the Presidential Palace. We were surprised to see the guards goose stepping, we had always thought that to be a specifically Nazi march. There was a very big crowd standing behind a barrier all around the square. Just as the guards were marching and counter marching Dominic ran into the middle of the square, pulled down his pants and had a pee. We expected to be arrested but nothing happened. We also visited the memorial to Edward Thompson's brother who was killed fighting with the partisans in the Second World War.

CHAPTER FIFTEEN

"he ought to be shot with shit out of a rubber gun" Harold

For some reason Ken Rohan had not shown any enthusiasm for more commercial deals and had moved me sideways to sell land and buildings for Rohan Industrial Estates and win building contracts for Sitecast. I proved quite adept at this and as well as selling several factories in Tallaght I helped him with site acquisition.

One day in February, 1976 I received a phone call that was to shape my life for the next twenty years. The phone call was from Geoff Mason and he was calling to set up a breakfast meeting with him and a client at the Burlington Hotel at 9 am the following day. Geoff Mason was a partner in Mason Owen and Partners, Chartered Surveyors of Liverpool and specialized in retail property. He and Barry Owen had been in business together since they were young men in the 1960's and they were the pre-eminent retail agents in the North of England. I had met Geoff several times when I worked for Arndale Developments.

When I walked into the restaurant at the Burlington Hotel Geoff greeted me and introduced me to his client, Albert Morris, who he said was an agent for an American client who wanted to build a 250,000 sq. ft. warehouse in Dublin. He asked if my company could build this and I said we could offer a full design and build service and would be delighted to work with him. He sketched out what he had in mind on a napkin and asked me to prepare a drawing and give him a cost estimate. I said I would get back to him in two to three weeks. He laughed out loud at this and said he was returning to the States the next day and needed the drawing and price by 4 p.m. that day. I returned to the office and when I told Ken Rohan of the inquiry he was very excited. This would be the largest building Sitecast had ever built and he was very keen to secure the contract. In fact it would be the largest single storey structure in Ireland.

We instructed the in-house design department to prepare a drawing using Sitecast's pre-cast concrete portal frame as the main structural element. The walls were to be in block work with a concrete floor slab and a profiled asbestos roof with 10% roof lights. Very simple and straightforward and very economical. At 4 p.m. I met Geoff and Albert again and presented them with the drawing and told them that our ball park estimate without any site works and assuming a level site with normal ground bearing capacity was £2,000,000. Albert said he wanted it building for half that and I said it couldn't be done. He said he would work with me to prune the specification and find cost savings.

That night over dinner Albert and Geoff told me they were also looking for sites for shopping centers and needed to buy a fifteen acre site for the warehouse. We agreed to meet again in two weeks time and I promised to have a revised price and drawing for them based upon further information provided by Albert during our dinner meeting. The next time we met I had further drawings for Albert and a revised price showing a reduction of £200,000. Albert said we were moving in the right direction but needed to find more savings.

We were meeting in Albert's hotel room at Jury's Hotel and Geoff said they had decided to take me into their confidence, because they trusted me, but the information they were going to give me was for my ears only. Geoff then told me Albert's real name was Gubay not Morris and he was the client not the agent of an American company. He was operating under an assumed name because he did not want to forewarn his competitors that he was moving into Ireland.

Gary Spence

"Albert is a very, very wealthy man" said Geoff

Over dinner A.G., as Albert Gubay asked me to call him, told his life story and as far as I can remember this is what he said:

"I was born in Rhyl, North Wales in 1928. My father was an Iraqi Jew and my mother was Irish. I served two years in the navy and was demobbed with £80 in 1952. I bought a truck and started selling sweets off the back of it. Sweets were rationed and so was sugar but I made my own sweets without sugar in a factory I set up in an old cinema. Because they did not contain sugar they were not subject to rationing. Then I expanded into wholesaling and this included wholesaling groceries. I started retailing through market stalls and then opened a grocery store in Rhyl. By 1962 I had three grocery stores in Rhyl, Chester and Wrexham and that year I opened Britain's first drive in supermarket in a 7,000 sq. ft. building in Prestatyn. In late 1964 I visited the USA and saw discount drug stores retailing a limited range of nationally branded lines at low prices and doing high volumes. I also visited Germany and saw the Aldi Stores doing the same thing for groceries. We tested the concept in 1965 at a store in Colwyn Bay and it was much more successful than my other stores. The other stores were converted to the new concept. We changed the name to Kwik Save Discount and by 1967 we had thirteen stores. By 1970 we had twenty four stores and made a profit of over £500,000 on sales of over £10,000,000. In 1970 I took the company public but I kept 45 % of the shares and my partner Ken Nicholson kept 15%.

A 130,000 sq.ft. central warehouse was opened in Prestatyn and we operated our own delivery trucks, shop fitting workshop, garage and waste paper baling facility. All stock operations were computerized using an IBM computer and software developed in-house. More stores were opened and profitability increased. I became bored once the warehouse was up and completed, the computer systems installed and everything was running like clockwork. I had hired and trained executives and the systems were so good that I was no longer needed . I decided to sell my shares and open another business elsewhere.

In May 1972 I sold nearly 30% of the company's shares for £7,400,000 and in the next few months sold the remaining 15%. At the end of 1972 I resigned as Chairman and moved to New Zealand which I had visited regularly in the preceding eighteen months. I had already acquired sites for a warehouse and several shopping centers there. Construction of the warehouse was under way. My sister, Yvonne, and her husband, Gerry Senior, had settled in New Zealand to assist with the business. In all I cleared £14,000,000 from the sale of my shares in Kwik Save. The share price dropped sharply after my departure but there was no justification for this and the company has since gone from strength to strength and the share price has recovered. There was a suspicion of skeletons in the cupboard, but those suspicions were soon seen to be unfounded. There was a Department of Trade investigation into the sale of my shares to see if I had contravened the Companies Act. When the inspector's report was published in 1974 I was exonerated and no contravention of the act was found.

With the experience of developing Kwik Save and the availability of cash I was able to quickly establish a presence in Auckland, New Zealand. I named the company 3 Guys after an American Discount retailer, 2 Guys from Harrison. We opened stores of 21,600 sq. ft. and I now have 10 stores operating and have captured 30% of the Auckland grocery market. Unfortunately, my marriage broke down while I was living in New Zealand and as the company was in good hands I moved to Connecticut for a year to be with my sister, Irene and her husband. I lost a lot of weight working out at a gym.

I came back to live in the Isle of Man in 1974 and needed another challenge. It had to be an English speaking country which meant either Ireland, Australia, South Africa or America. I decided on Ireland because it's near to home and my mother is Irish. With Geoff's help I'm close to buying four shopping center sites from Dublin Corporation and we are negotiating on five or six others. We need to buy a fifteen to twenty acre site for a warehouse and the intention is to have stores throughout Ireland. We are thinking in terms of thirty stores."

Gary Spence

From then on I was to spend one or two days a week with A.G. as Ken Rohan had agreed I could help him to find sites with the understanding that the Rohan Group would be given the opportunity to negotiate the building contracts

Just before Easter I was in a meeting with A.G.'s solicitor, Tony Twomey, and a sandwich lunch was served. I helped myself to three or four sandwiches and suddenly realized I had eaten cheese which was not permitted while I was taking Parstelin. I left the meeting and drove to the nearest hospital. They pumped my stomach and put me in bed for observation. A psychiatrist came to see me and asked why I had tried to commit suicide. I told him I hadn't, that eating the cheese was a genuine mistake, but he was unconvinced. I spent most of Easter in hospital but Sue and the children visited me each day.

In the summer we went, at A.G.'s invitation, for a week's holiday on the Isle of Man. We stayed at his house, Greeba Towers and toured all the sights. We traveled on horse drawn trams and steam trains and a railway up Snaefell, the island's highest mountain. A.G. went to London on business for a few days while we were there. I honestly think the noise the children made may have aggravated him and that the trip to London was to escape from them.

By July A.G. (with my help) had bought a fifteen acre site for the warehouse in Tallaght from the Irish Land Company and finalized deals with Dublin Corporation to buy sites in Kilbarrack, Finglas, Ballyfermot and Rathfarnham. We had also bought a half completed shopping center at Firhouse in Tallaght, a site from Dublin County Council in Ballybrack and a site in Bray. In August I signed the building contract with A.G.'s company, 3 Guys Ltd, for Sitecast to build the 250,000 sq. ft. warehouse. This included a joiner's shop, a garage and truck maintenance facility, an area for frozen foods and a baling station. Under a separate contract Roh-Fab was to build an adjacent 5,000 sq. ft. office building.

Making Hen's Meat

As soon as the contract was signed A.G. asked me if I would come to work for him. I asked what the deal would be and he said he would pay me the same as Ken Rohan was paying me (by this time £8,500 per annum) provide me with the same car (an Audi 100LS) and give me 2.5% of the shares in the company. I would be on the Board of 3 Guys with the title of Property Director. I accepted the offer and gave my notice to the Rohan Group.

By this time it was public knowledge that A.G. was going to start a discount grocery store chain and the newspapers and magazines, TV and radio were constantly running stories about him, some true, some mere speculation and rumor. With his large head and shock of curly hair, his distinctive walk, and his bizarre sense of humor A.G. was an easily recognizable character and a media man's delight. The cartoonists loved him and so did the reporters; he was always ready for an interview and came out with some memorable lines. Everywhere he went he was recognized and all the publicity undoubtedly helped in staff recruiting and in purchasing. The existing supermarket chains, Dunnes Stores, Quinsworth, H. Williams, Superquin and 5 Star were in a state of panic and were calling for Government action to prevent the entry of so formidable a competitor to their market-place. Ben Dunne, Chairman of Dunnes Stores was quoted as saying:

> "This man should be investigated before he be let into Ireland by the Departments of Finance and Industry and Commerce. The government should know if he intends to pay his taxes and if he intends to adopt fair trade practices".

The grocery store owners got together to lobby Dublin City Council to refuse planning permission for A.G.'s supermarkets. In this they were successful. There developed a strange situation; A.G. had bought sites for supermarkets in Finglas and Kilbarrack from Dublin Corporation subject to planning permission. He was then refused permission but exercised his right to appeal to the government and eventually was successful. The one location that could not be blocked was Firhouse in Tallaght as it was an existing half built supermarket and shopping center and no new planning permission was needed. A.G. believed that once he got this store open the tide of public opinion would turn in his favor. He was quoted in the Irish Independent of November 6, 1976 as saying :

> "Up to now, the Councilors have been pressurized by worried supermarket bosses to 'keep Gubay out' but next June when the housewives come to my stores Councilors will be pressurized by residents to 'let Gubay in'"

In another memorable quote in the Irish Press of February 10, 1977 he said:

> "I love to see a green empty field, and then six months later, see one of my markets there, with housewives flocking in and out. In New Zealand the housewives used to kiss me in the shops; imagine, they kissed me. It was quite something, I can tell you."

Working for A.G. was a challenge every day. He set an example that I could not match. Not only was he the hardest worker I had ever met, his singleness of purpose was extraordinary. He went against the conventional wisdom and in this period of establishing the business knew every detail of every aspect of his fledgling organization. He was a great simplifier; where the tendency in other businesses was to complicate. He cut right to the heart of matters and made quick and certain decisions. His concept was simple, but its very simplicity was difficult to emulate. Others tried to copy his concept in England, New Zealand and Ireland, but all failed. The major problem was that they had too much overhead in what A.G. called their 'palaces', overhead which they could not get rid of. He accused his competitors of building palaces which meant they had to charge palace prices. He was quoted in the Irish Press of March 18, 1977 as saying;

> "I do not spend money on interiors....my places are functional - just that, and no more."

A.G.'s concept embraced a series of simple policies which taken together enabled him to operate with the lowest gross margin in the industry and yet produce the highest net margin. In the year he sold Kwik Save the net margin was almost 8% compared to an industry average of 2%. Conventional supermarkets carried eight to ten thousand lines. A.G. carried four hundred and fifty. The lines he carried were the items housewives bought each week; tea, coffee, butter, sugar, cereals, canned goods and so on. Where other stores might carry three brands of baked beans in three sizes making a total of nine lines, A.G. would carry only the national brand leader in its most popular size. A.G. carried only national brands at a time when his competitors were increasingly introducing unknown brands and house brands in an effort to remain competitive. The theory behind A.G's. policy was that the only way the housewife knew she was getting a bargain was when she could compare prices of like items. It was impossible to compare a house brand price to a national brand price due to the difference in quality. A.G. used to make the point by saying:

> "I don't sell cheap groceries, I sell groceries cheap"

Selling only national brands, in only one size, enabled A.G. to rack up enormous volumes in the items which he carried, and with a central warehouse he was able to buy these lines in volumes that manufacturers loved thus giving him a negotiating advantage when it came to price. Kwik Save was the first supermarket company in Britain with a central warehouse as was 3 Guys in New Zealand and Ireland.

A.G. would place orders by the truckload and no item was bought in less than pallet quantities. If there was a special deal or discount on an item he would think nothing of buying in six months' stock; with double digit inflation this was better than money in the bank. The warehouse gave him control over his stock. He was rarely out of stock in the stores because he controlled the deliveries. He was able to buy at significant discounts compared to his competitors, due to the volume of his purchases and the reduction in delivery costs created by having a single drop to one point instead of multiple drops to individual supermarkets. He guaranteed to turn a delivery truck round in an hour and often it was close to thirty minutes.

At the store level there were wide aisles so that the shelves could be restocked while the store was open without inconveniencing the shoppers. Conventional supermarkets had to stock their shelves at night or hinder the customers from purchasing. Goods were shelved in their original cartons with the front cut off and were not price marked, thus eliminating two expensive and time consuming elements. The price was simply displayed on a card above the item. The check out operators had memorized all four hundred and fifty prices. This was possible by having a limited number of price points and teaching the operators to mentally associate products with the same price. There were no free bags and no bag boys. The check out operator moved the items from one shopping cart to another and on completion of the transaction the customers wheeled the cart to a packing out shelf or direct to their cars.

A.G. had a fully computerized stock control system enabling the stores to be accurately replenished in a timely fashion and ensuring that the grocery buyer did not let the warehouse run out of stock of any item. Apart from a weekly stock take the store manager had very few duties other than ensuring that the shelves were filled, the price cards were accurate, and the store was kept clean. The check out operation was run by a female supervisor and the manager had little involvement in this aspect of the business. Additionally the managers were not involved with the sale of meat, greengrocery or in store bakery items. This de-skilling of the management operation meant that virtually anyone could be trained very quickly to manage a store.

The meat, greengrocery and bakery departments were operated by concessionaires. They were rented a basic shell space and paid for their own fitting out. They operated as a shop within a shop, even taking their own money. Their rent was a percentage of 3 Guys' sales, not their own; A.G.'s theory here was that if he produced the foot traffic they should be able to produce the sales. If A.G. only broke even on his sales of dry groceries he still ended up with 3%

in rental from the concessionaires. Additionally, by building a small shopping center, A.G. had a further rental income and in Ireland rents achieved were comparable to High Street rents.

Although I was called the Property Director my role was multi-faceted and as the only employee I was, in effect, A.G.'s personal assistant. Until the offices were ready I ran things from my house and employed a neighbor as a part time secretary. As well as assisting in site finding I was also responsible for obtaining planning permissions. We hired Ambrose Kelly as the company's architect and Arthur Lyons as quantity surveyor. We also had a planning specialist, Kieran O'Malley and took advice from a Senior Counsel, Eamon Walsh. I soon learned that A.G. liked to surround himself with a team of experts and did not mind paying for first class expertise.

Shortly after I joined him he asked me who was the best building contract lawyer in Ireland and I told him Max Abrahamson.

"Put him on a retainer" said A.G.

"Why?" I asked "We have no building contract dispute"

"No" said A.G. "But if we ever do we want to have the best advice"

Max Abrahamson was put on a £1000 per annum retainer and in the end we did need his services.

In addition to the work being done by Rohan on the warehouse and offices we did much of the fitting out work by direct labor. This included the floor finish in the warehouse, the tarmac areas around the warehouse and all the finishing trades in the offices. While the warehouse was spartan and functional the offices were finished to a very high standard with wood paneled offices and fitted carpets. There was an impressive foyer with a terrazzo floor and a well appointed boardroom.

I was also involved in putting together the team who would run 3 Guys. We advertised for an accountant/company secretary and for a computer specialist, both board level appointments with equity participation. We received hundreds of applications and interviewed dozens of people before hiring Dermot Gogarty as the accountant and John Halpin as the computer specialist. Both were sent to 3 Guys in New Zealand for six months training. Mike Johnson, a friend of Geoff Mason's, who lived in London, was hired as grocery buyer. Although he had no background in grocery buying he was very personable and adept at figures. He also went to New Zealand for training but not before he had me drinking again.

Mike Johnson loved his food and wine and cigars and was something of an epicure. We nicknamed him 'fine wine and big cigars". The first time I met him was in A.G.'s room in Jury's Hotel and we all went out to dinner to a wonderful French restaurant called Le Coq Hardi. Mike chose the wines and he persuaded me that one glass of Puligny Montrachet would do me no harm. Taking Parstelin and drinking was akin to playing Russian roulette but for some reason I tried a glass and waited thirty minutes to see if there was any adverse reaction. There was not so I had a couple more glasses of wine without any problem. The next day I felt like a drink, but decided to stick to wine. Within a couple of weeks I was drinking two bottles of wine a day and I thought this was crazy – I might as well go back on the Guinness and gin and tonics. So I did.

John Powell, who had worked with AG at Kwik Save and was with 3 Guys in New Zealand was to come to Ireland as stores director and Ted Gaskell was hired from Kwik Save as his deputy. A friend of A.G.'s from England, Roy Wolfe, whose background was in building, was hired as warehouse director and Martin Foley was hired to run the garage.

I first realized that to A.G. money was power when I went with him to the Audi Volkswagen dealer to buy me an Audi. He negotiated endlessly until he had obtained a discount of 12.5%. then came the move I was to see over and over again:
"I'm going to need at least six of these cars, maybe more and I'll be paying cash. I need two Audis and one Volkswagen Scirocco today [this was for himself] " he said

The discount went up to 15% and I had learned a lesson in negotiating. All three cars were kept at my modest house on St.

Canice's Road. There was my orange Audi, a white Audi, which was to be Dermot Gogarty's and A.G.'s green Scirocco. Joe Fitzpatrick saw the three cars lined up on my front lawn and said: "Jasus, Gary, they look like the flag of Ireland".

The next task was house buying. First we bought a large house in the south eastern suburbs of Dublin intended for occupation by A.G. However, he loaned this house to Roger Hartley, a regional manager from America, who A.G. had met when staying with his sister Irene. We bought a mews house for A.G. in Rathgar, only a ten minute drive from the warehouse and offices in Tallaght. So there would be a smooth transition and people could begin to work right away without the usual settling in problems A.G. told me to buy houses for use by John Powell, Ted Gaskell, Roy Wolfe, Mike Johnson, John Halpin and John Moore.

We decided to buy in a new subdivision in Tallaght called Kingswood Heights. I went there and picked out six houses of different sizes and styles dependent on whether the proposed occupiers were single or married, with or without children and so on. When the salesman realized I planned to buy six houses and pay cash for them he thought all his dreams had come true. We obtained a substantial discount for this bulk purchase and it paid off for A.G. in two ways. First, it made his employees happy, second, when he came to sell the houses, one at a time, he made a substantial profit. We even furnished the houses, down to buying curtains and basic crockery and cutlery.

My other function was to assist in all the purchasing, except for the groceries. The kind of things this involved were buying a cardboard baling machine, garage equipment, joinery machines and equipment, emergency generators, Mercedes trucks and Fruehauf trailers, fork lifts and pallet jacks, shopping carts, combitainers, hydraulic lifting platforms, refrigeration equipment, sweeping and scrubbing machines and so on. The amazing thing to me was that A.G. was sufficiently expert in all these disparate fields to be able to more than hold his own with the salesmen we dealt with. He went into enormous detail with every item.

To buy the shopping carts he and I went to Germany and visited the Fischer factory. This visit led to some modifications, not least buying bigger carts than A.G. had used before. It was his experience that people stopped shopping when the cart was full so if you provided a bigger cart the average spend per customer should increase. For the purchase of the glass doors to go on the refrigerated display cases A.G. and I visited Sweden. Much of the joinery equipment was bought at an auction of equipment owned by a Dublin company that had gone bankrupt. We talked to one of the workers there and offered him a job if he would mark our cards as to which machines were in good condition and which we should not buy. He gave us the advice we needed and both he and his son were put on A.G.'s payroll.

For the regional managers and store supervisors we decided to buy Ford cars and after scouring the country for the best deal we finally decided on a Ford dealer in Mullingar. So tight was the dealer's profit margin that when he delivered the cars to us the salesman had to hitchhike back to Mullingar.

As the warehouse and offices neared completion I moved to a bungalow on Main Road, Tallaght so I would not have to commute from the northside of Dublin. This cost £12,000 and A.G. loaned me the money. Simon and James started attending Templeogue Boy's School and when he was five in 1978, Dominic also went there. Sue started a nursery school for a church in Firhouse. This was a 9 a.m. to 12 noon three day a week job and she took Dominic with her. She got this job without reference to me and took out a bank loan and bought herself a car, a second hand mini. This enabled her to take the children to school and then go to the nursery school in Firhouse.

Once we moved to Tallaght we were very close to County Wicklow and started spending time in the Wicklow hills. We often took the children to Powerscourt House and Gardens and the nearby waterfall. We started eating regularly at the Roundwood Inn and the Enniscree Lodge. The Enniscree Lodge became our regular haunt on Sunday lunch times and we would often sit outside in the grounds before lunch drinking champagne. On

Making Hen's Meat

Saturday mornings we usually went to a little market in Blessington and bought duck eggs and potato cakes. If we weren't heading for the hills or the coast we would often go to Phoenix Park which occupies about 10% of Dublin's land area and is the biggest enclosed park in Europe. We would watch the herd of deer, which has been in the park since the eighteenth century, and then we usually went to Dublin Zoo, which is located in the park. On Sunday afternoons we would often watch the polo as a friend of ours, Arthur Lyons (the quantity surveyor), was an avid polo player.

There was so much media interest in A.G. that he hired a public relations consultant to organize his interviews, control press releases and generally manage 3 Guys' image. The consultant's name was Don Hall; his father, Frank Hall, had a weekly satirical program on RTE, Irish Television. A.G. was invited to appear on the Late, Late Show, Ireland's highest rated TV program, which was aired at 9.30 p.m. on Saturday nights and was hosted by Gay Byrne. A.G. and I had dinner with Gay Byrne and his wife in the King Sitric restaurant in Howth a few days before the show. This enabled Gay Byrne to prepare his format for the program.

Also on the program was Pat Quinn of Quinsworth supermarkets. Quinn had sold his own small supermarket company to Galen Weston and become an employee of his. He had someone planted in the audience who asked him what the badge was that we was wearing. Quinn said it was the badge of RGDATA, the Irish grocery organization, who spent a lot of their funds on helping out people who had been in the grocery business and had fallen on hard times. He said A.G. was not a member and had not made any financial contribution. A.G. was astonished. He said he hadn't yet got one grocery store open. At the appropriate time he would join and contribute.

The overall program went very much in A.G.'s favor as we were to discover the next night. A.G. and his girlfriend, Carmel, Sue and I went to a pub in Howth called the Abbey Tavern which featured Irish traditional music. When we walked in the crowd recognized A.G. from the previous night's television appearance.

There was a spontaneous round of applause and for the rest of the evening A.G. was kept busy shaking hands and signing autographs. Many years later Pat Quinn was to say that the thing he regretted most in his life was the way he had attacked A.G. on the Late, Late Show.

We bought Mercedes trucks from the Irish dealer but could not get a satisfactory price on trailers, so we bought six trailers in England. These had to come into Dublin docks and be cleared through customs. There would be a VAT payment due because Irish VAT was charged at a higher rate than in England. Martin Foley, the garage manager, went to England to get the first trailer and as we had someone moving from England to Ireland to work for the company he loaded the trailer with their furniture. I met him at the docks at 11 p.m. and the customs men asked to look in the trailer. They found a few things that were not allowed into Ireland, such as house plants, and seized these.

Then they told us we were clear to go. They had been so busy checking the contents they hadn't realized we were importing the trailer. A.G. was very amused by this and the next four trailers came in the same way. The final trailer was spotted by the customs men and they accused me of trying to smuggle it in. They threatened to seize the trailer and hold it until the VAT account was paid. I had the invoice for the trailer and persuaded them to seize the invoice and let the trailer in. The next day the VAT was paid.

Most days A.G. and I would visit the building sites and then look at possible new locations. We had some great laughs travelling around together. I remember meeting the owner of a site in Dun Laoghaire and we asked him what price he wanted for the site:
"The price is £200,000, and this is a firm price and not negotiable, so make me an offer" he replied.

One day we were going to the site at Vevay Road, Bray and we got lost and stopped to ask the way. A.G. was driving and I had my window open and was being given directions by a big guy who

was trying hard to be helpful. It was obvious he didn't know the way and A.G. was impatient to be off so he whispered to me:
"Tell the guy to fuck off and I'll drive away real quick"
so I said:
"You've no idea what you're talking about. Why don't you fuck off"
A.G. started to pull away, then stamped on the brakes leaving me face to face with a very angry man who was about to choke me. A.G. was doubled up laughing. It took me a while to see the funny side of this incident.

On another occasion we were stopped at O'Connell Bridge at the junction of D'Olier Street, the Quays and O'Connell street. There was a guard on point duty and eventually he waved for us to proceed. A.G., who was driving, did not move. The guard waved again and A.G. stuck his hand out of the window and beckoned for the guard to come to him. As a very angry red-faced guard approached. A.G. said:
"Hand me a pad and a pen, Gary"
I handed them to him and when the guard finally got to the car, A.G. looked him in the eye and said:
"Name, rank and number please"
"Never mind that, why didn't you move when I signaled you, you're holding up all the traffic in Dublin!" said the guard
"I have traveled around the world" said A.G. "And never have I seen a policeman direct traffic as well as you"
The guard had by now recognized A.G.
"Well thank you Mr. Gubay" he said, his chest swelling with pride.
"The reason I want your name, rank and number is so I can write to your superintendent and tell him what a fine job you're doing"
The guard gave the requested information
"The name of your police station" said A.G.
"Pearse Street"
"And the name of your superintendent?"
"Superintendent Dan Murphy"
"Well I think that's all, you can go back to directing traffic now" said A.G. dismissively.

A.G. and I laughed about this all day. I was amazed at the lengths to which he would go to satisfy both his and my sense of humor. Sometimes he brought the humor directly into the business. On one occasion we were buying pallet jacks: we required six for the warehouse and two per store, so buying in advance for thirty stores, we needed sixty six. Having negotiated a very low price for the pallet jacks A.G. inquired, dead pan:
"How much for one thousand?"
The price came tumbling down. A.G. said:
"We'll take sixty now and notify you when we need the others. Gary write up a purchase order"
I went to my office and a minute later A.G. walked in
"A fucking thousand pallet jacks and the guy stood for it. You know how to write the purchase order?" he asked
"Of course I know how to write a purchase order" I said
"Don't forget to put on the order 'if and when required'" said A.G. I laughed so much A.G. thought I was going to have a heart attack. That little word "if" made all the difference.

By Spring of 1977 the offices were ready for occupation. As the furniture was being delivered and the IBM system was being installed A.G. and I moved in and were soon joined by Dermot Gogarty, John Halpin and Mike Johnson who had finished their training in New Zealand. Not long after John Powell and Ted Gaskell arrived from New Zealand and England respectively; Roy Wolfe and Martin Foley were already installed in the still incomplete warehouse and garage facility. A joiner arrived from New Zealand with a sample of every item of store fitting that would be needed and another joiner, Phil Jones, who had worked for Kwik Save, came from Wales. A plumber, John Moore, who A.G. had met in the Isle of Man, came over and went to live in one of the houses in Kingswood Heights.

It soon became apparent to A.G. that while Mike Johnson was a wizard with figures he was not a tough enough negotiator to be the Buying Director. An Englishman who already lived in Dublin, Trevor Wilson, was hired to do the buying. Mike Johnson was made responsible for buying items that were delivered direct to the stores, such as milk and bread and for price checking the competition and working with A.G. to establish 3 Guys retail prices for every item to be sold. The pricing policy was simple. On every item we were 10% to 30% cheaper than the lowest priced competitor. 3 Guys prices were determined solely by the market place and never by adding a mark-up to the purchase price.

A.G. knew that his company was so lean and efficient that he could price anywhere between 10% and 30% below the competition and still make money. Some items would be sold at or below cost because the competitors' prices forced this situation. The profit on other items would vary – all that mattered to A.G. was the final average gross margin. His competitors needed a gross margin of 20 to 25% to survive – he could make a good profit at 10% because his overhead was much lower.

One of A.G.'s favorite ploys at this time was to keep announcing an opening date for the Firhouse store, although he knew it was still several months away. The competition would lower their prices in anticipation of the opening then put them up again. A.G. felt sure this was not lost on the Irish consumers; even without opening he was able to dictate industry wide prices and please the consumer.

In the first year with A.G. I went out to eat with him a lot at a wide variety of restaurants. A.G.'s favorite restaurant was the Mirabeau in Dun Laogohaire run by Sean Kinsella. The prices were so outrageously high that many Irish companies forbade their staff from eating there on their expense accounts. A.G. always ate the same thing; a plate of Dublin Bay Prawns swimming in garlic butter, followed by Chicken Maryland, fried chicken and fried banana. A.G. bet me I couldn't get someone different to buy us dinner there once a week for a year. I won the bet.

One of the few occasions when A.G. was picking up the tab at the Mirabeau was when we took Frank Cairns and Karl Jones for dinner. They were the Property Editors of the Irish Independent and Irish Times respectively and they had given us some very positive publicity. They both arrived a little late and a little drunk and by the time we had drunk pre dinner cocktails and wine with

the first course they were positively flying. Karl Jones suddenly leaned across and picked up A.G.'s fried banana and threw it over his shoulder and across the restaurant where it landed in the lap of a very surprised customer. A few minutes later Sean Kinsella came to the table carrying the fried banana on a platter and went to A.G. and said:
"You are the only person in here eating Chicken Maryland. This banana has landed on the Spanish Ambassador and ruined his suit. What is the big idea?"
A.G. denied all knowledge. Karl Jones owned up and said:
"Give him a bottle of Dom Perignon Champagne with my apologies and compliments"
A.G. had to pick up the £100 price of the champagne and Sean Kinsella barred Karl Jones from the Mirabeau. He relented when Karl wrote a letter of apology.

In June A.G. took a trip to New Zealand and took the architect, Ambrose Kelly, with him. He was away for ten days and Sue and I took the opportunity to have a long weekend away. We went with Mike Johnson to Ballymaloe House in East Cork. What can I tell you about Ballymaloe except to say it is the most wonderful place on earth. It is a large house which incorporates the remains of a Geraldine castle and it is set in the midst of a four hundred acre working farm. Here Myrtle Allen cooks in an incomparable way. There is no set menu although the same dishes are often prepared. Each day's menu is determined by what fish has been brought into nearby Ballycotton Harbor, what vegetables are available from the farm, what fruit is in season; has the butcher, Mr. Cuddigan from Cloyne, slaughtered some particularly fine fat lambs. The finest local produce, cooked to exacting standards is the secret of Ballymaloe's success. The rooms are warm and welcoming with fresh flowers. There are no TV's or radios and no locks on the doors. But the center of everything is the kitchen. You start the day with fresh squeezed orange juice and coffee made from Myrtle's own selection of coffee beans. The bread is freshly baked, the butter rich and creamy, the oatmeal locally stoneground, the bacon, sausage, black and white puddings and mushrooms are all locally produced. The eggs are fresh that day. Myrtle Allen had created a gem which was almost unknown except to a privileged few, like Mike Johnson, when we first went there.

It is now world famous and has spawned several other businesses run by the children and grandchildren of the Allens. There is the Ballymaloe Cookery School, a clothing and gift shop, a coffee shop, a furniture manufacturer and much much more. Ballymaloe was to become our home away from home and remains our favorite place in the world. Whenever we get the opportunity we go there not just for the food and the ambience, but to turn the clock back to a time when time did not matter, when life was led at a different pace, when we were at one with the world.

On the fifteen acre site of the warehouse and offices there was one tree, a majestic elm, that must have been a hundred years old. It was situated where the offices were to be built. A.G. moved the offices back twenty feet to save the tree. While he was in New Zealand I noticed the tree was dropping a few leaves, something it should not be doing in June. I mentioned this to A.G. on his return and he immediately called an arborologist who diagnosed the early stages of Dutch elm disease. The treatment was expensive and consisted of drilling a circle of holes in the trunk of the tree and injecting some specialized product. The treatment worked. A.G. was enormously proud of having saved that tree, and I saw a different side to this ruthless entrepreneurial capitalist.

We had a lot to do to be ready for the opening of the first store at Firhouse. We finalized deals with the concessionaires; a very old established Dublin butcher F.X. Buckley took the meat concession, John Archer of Kinsealy Farms was the greengrocer and Dominic Fusco the baker. Work was underway on the stores at Bray and Lucan and planning permission had been obtained for the stores at Ballybrack and Finglas. In Ballyfermot the local residents had lodged an appeal against the planning permission but a donation of £500 led to this being withdrawn. We were all set for our first six stores. Only Kilbarrack was still awaiting permission and A.G. told me that if I got permission granted before Christmas then he would take me on his next trip to New Zealand.

When A.G. had signed the building contract for the warehouse Ken Rohan had insisted on an irrevocable letter of credit for the full contract price which could be drawn against in installments as the work progressed. This cost A.G. £2,000 and he was outraged. He said to Ken Rohan:
"You will regret having done this. The gloves are off and I will get that £2,000 back a hundred fold."

At the end of June, 1977 a building in course of construction close to our warehouse collapsed during a strong wind. The builder was Sitecast and the system was the same as for our warehouse, a pre-cast concrete portal frame. As our contract with Sitecast was a design and build contract we had no engineer on our team to whom we could turn for assurances about the structural stability of our warehouse. We called in Morgan Sheehy of Ove Arup & Partners, the world's leading firm of Structural Engineers. When we received his report we were horrified. He concluded that in certain circumstances with a wind of high velocity the warehouse could collapse! We presented the report to Sitecast and asked for their proposals. In the meantime we told them they must continue building in accordance with the contract but we would cease paying them. Eventually Ove Arup came up with some remedial proposals and Sitecast carried these out. Ken Rohan rued the day he had asked A.G. for that irrevocable letter of credit.

Finally, the first 3 Guys Store in Ireland opened at Firhouse on September 27, 1977 and was an immediate success. Sales were £200,000 a week which was more than Kwik Save's best store in Coventry. This figure did not include the sales of meat, greengrocery and bakery items. By February of 1978 we had store number two open in Bray and opened four mores stores that year at Lucan, Ballybrack, Ballyfermot and Finglas. We now looked further afield and by the end of 1978 had acquired sites in Dundalk, Mullingar, Portlaoise, Carlow, Newbridge, Navan and Athlone and still had two undeveloped sites in Dublin at Rathfarnam and Kilbarrack. The Navan store was the first store to open outside Dublin in December, 1978 and construction was underway in Kilbarrack, Mullingar, Athlone, Newbridge and Portlaoise.

In spring of 1978 A.G. honored his promise and took me to New Zealand. We were accompanied by his in house solicitor, Jim Scowcroft, who ran A.G.'s world wide affairs from the Isle of Man. Scowcroft's wife, Joan also went on the trip. We flew to London and then to Los Angeles where we had a two day lay-over. We visited Disneyland, which A.G. found enthralling. He had been there several times before and was full of admiration for the Disney operation. He was particularly impressed with the way they kept the lines moving and by the perfect cleanliness.

The Air New Zealand flight from Los Angeles to Auckland took seventeen hours with a re-fueling stop at Tahiti. As we approached Auckland the pilot invited A.G. and I to the flight deck and A.G. asked him about the planned approach to Auckland International Airport. The pilot pointed out the proposed route. A.G. said he wished they could change the route and come in low over Papatoetoe where his warehouse was located so he could show it me from the air. The pilot spoke to the control tower and to my astonishment they changed the approach to that requested by A.G. As we neared the airport A.G. pretended to make an announcement to the passengers:
"We shall be landing at Auckland International Airport as soon as they get the sheep off the runway. Please set your watches back forty years."

At the airport A.G.'s New Zealand directors met us and we all went to Gerry and Yvonne Senior's apartment. Yvonne was A.G.'s sister. After A.G. was brought up to date on the affairs of his New Zealand operation he said he wanted to go eat at his favorite Chinese restaurant. It was pointed out that it was 11 am on Sunday morning and the restaurant didn't open on Sunday:
"Give the owner a ring at home and see if he'll open up for me" said A.G.
An hour later we were tucking into the finest Chinese food I had ever eaten. I did not get to see much of Auckland; the week was spent either working in the stores or attending a complex court

case in which Ivor Moseley was accused of producing a forged document entitling him to a commission if he found a buyer for 3 Guys.

Back in Dublin A.G. was having fun and games with grocery suppliers. One or two of the main manufacturers had succumbed to pressure from the other supermarkets and refused to supply 3 Guys. One of these was Batchelors whose canned peas were far and away the market leader in Ireland. Finally they agreed to supply A.G. and he ordered a month's stock and repeated this for the next five months. But he did not put the peas on sale, instead he stockpiled them in the warehouse. It seemed Batchelors were unaware of the fact that their peas were not on sale in 3 Guys. These peas cost 10 pence a can and everybody retailed them at 15 pence to 17 pence. When, after six months, A.G. put then on sale he did so at a price of 8 pence. The other supermarkets were furious at Bachelors, who they were sure had sold to 3 Guys for 7 pence or less, and demanded action. Batchelors marketing director came to see A.G. and said unless 3 Guys put up the price to at least 11 pence they would stop supplying them again.
"You'd better come down to the warehouse" said A.G.
One whole aisle of the warehouse was stacked floor to ceiling with every can of peas A.G. had bought in the preceding six months.
"Stop supplying me if you like" said A.G. "I've enough stock to last six months"
Batchelors begged A.G. to put up the price and he finally relented on condition that they give him a rebate of 3 pence for every can of peas he had bought from them. They agreed and he put the price up. They were paying him to sell at a profit!

CHAPTER SIXTEEN

"he needs a balloon full of hot shit throwing at him" Harold

In late 1978 A.G. was approached by Tesco, the leading British supermarket operator, who wanted to buy 3 Guys. After much heart searching A.G. agreed to sell 50% provided he was left in control of the management of 3 Guys. A.G. had invested, by means of a loan to the company, £5,500,000 but a revaluation showed the fixed assets (mainly property) to be worth £12,600,000, thus the chain was worth £7,100,000 with no allowance for goodwill. Tesco agreed to pay £4,200,000 for half the company. Peat Marwick Mitchell and Healy and Baker carried out due diligence for Tesco but shortly before the deal was set to close Tesco advised A.G. they had to have 51% not the agreed 50%. The reason they gave was that unless they had control they could not bring the profits onto their parent company balance sheet. A.G. was annoyed but agreed on condition that he be given a management contract giving him total authority and control over every aspect of the 3 Guys business. This was agreed to and the deal closed in December 1978 at the offices of Berwin Leighton, Tesco's solicitors. In that morning's Irish Times was an interview with Ralph Temple, Finance Director of Tesco in which he said that Tesco would import their own brand groceries into Ireland on a massive scale. A.G. was furious about this interview which had the Irish trade unions up in arms as massive imports could lead to lay offs in food manufacturing plants in Ireland.

After the deal was concluded and A.G.'s solicitor, Jim Scowcroft, had the check for £4,200,000 A.G. confronted Temple in front of a room full of solicitors and other advisers. He read out the interview, spelled out how foolish and ill advised it was and pointed out that it was a breach of his management contract for Temple to speak to the press about the affairs of 3 Guys, and forbade him from doing so in the future:
"You, Mr. Temple, are a prize cunt." he concluded.
Temple went white, then red, he shook so furiously that his wig slid halfway off his head. Victor Benjamin, senior partner of Berwin Leighton cleared the room and led Ralph Temple off to his office leaving, A.G., Scowcroft and I alone. Finally Benjamin returned and said an apology would be in order. A.G. and Scowcroft conferred and A.G. said:
"Bring him in, I'll apologize"
This was A.G.'s apology:
"I wish to apologize for the intemperate language I used, however, my sentiments remain unchanged"

Ralph Temple's actions were a warning of what was to come. Tesco tried to interfere in every aspect of the running of the business. A.G. the entrepreneur and Tesco the corporate giant were unhappy bedfellows. I 'found' a memo from Francis Krejsa, the Property Director of Tesco, to one of his staff instructing him to inspect, with a view to purchase, specific sites in Cork and Dublin and stating that under no circumstances were A.G. or any of his staff to know that Tesco were looking for sites in Ireland on their own account. This was a clear breach of A.G.'s management contract.

Finally, in desparation A.G. offered to buy back Tesco's 51% shareholding for £5,000,000. Tesco refused but said they would buy A.G. out and paid £5,500,000 in March 1979 with A.G. reserving the right to sue for more. The day after A.G. was bought out Sir John (Jack) Cohen, founder of Tesco, died. I phoned Leslie Porter, the chairman of Tesco and Sir John's son-in-law, and asked if we should close the stores for the day as a mark of

respect, a custom in Ireland. He said Sir John wouldn't want that, just fly the flags at half mast. I said
"We have no flags, shall I buy some"
"No" he replied.

CHAPTER SEVENTEEN

"he went with a right fullock" Harold

A.G. went straight to America to start up yet another 3 Guys chain and over the next few months he was joined by Trevor Wilson, Mike Johnson, John Halpin, Martin Foley, John Powell, Ted Gaskell, Roy Wolfe and Phil Jones. He did not offer to take me as he had already appointed a real estate agent in America and felt he could manage without me. Although I had no share certificate he honored his word on my 2.5% share holding and paid me accordingly.

I agreed to work for Tesco and, with Ed Lyons, Geoff Mason's partner in the Dublin firm of Mason Owen and Lyons, started looking for sites in all the major cities in the Irish Republic. Initial targets were Cork, Limerick, Waterford, Galway and Sligo. Ed Lyons had potential sites lined up in all these towns and lots of others when I received a message one Friday from Tesco's Managing Director, Ian McLaurin, to say that he and several colleagues were flying to Ireland on Monday in the corporate jet and wanted to tour Ireland looking at available sites. I told him the corporate jet couldn't land at Galway or Sligo and suggested I charter an Islander for a couple of days and he agreed.

The problem I had was that Ed Lyons knew the sites and I didn't and this was Friday and they were coming on Monday. Ed and I discussed this and agreed the only way I could see all the sites was by helicopter. I hired a helicopter from Irish Helicopters at Dublin

Making Hen's Meat

Airport and at 8 a.m. Saturday morning Ed, Sue, Simon, James, Dominic and I boarded the helicopter and headed first for Ballymaloe House. The only directions I gave to the pilot was to tell him it was near the village of Shanagarry and handed him a menu which had a drawing of Ballymaloe House on it. We arrived two hours later and the pilot put the helicopter down on the first tee of the golf course.

Mike Johnson was staying at Ballymaloe prior to moving to the States and came out to see who was arriving by helicopter. He was very pleased it was me but when I told him the firm were paying for the helicopter not me, he was disappointed. He was spending his money as fast as he could and he wanted me to do the same. Myrtle Allen said:
"I don't think much of your pilot, Gary, when the Pilkingtons come from St. Helens their pilot lands on the croquet lawn, between the hoops."

We all had breakfast together and then Ed and I set off for an eight hour trip around Ireland. Let me tell you this helicopter was cold and so noisy that conversation was virtually impossible. The only light relief was the couple of times we put down in the middle of nowhere to take a piss.

The two day trip with the Tesco executives was a great success and they instructed me to make offers on several sites. We ate a magnificent lunch at the Arbutus Lodge in Cork, probably one of the finest French restaurants outside of France. We stayed the night at Ashford Castle landing the Islander plane on the nearby racecourse. Next morning we flew to Sligo where the landing strip was on the beach. I had hired a limousine and we could see this waiting on a road about a quarter of a mile from where we had landed. We walked while the plane taxied along the beach behind us with our luggage.

After looking at the site we drove back to Dublin through Northern Ireland. The Tesco people were shocked to see the reality of Northern Ireland with British troops with automatic weapons patrolling the streets and the police stations surrounded by barricades. I found Francis Krejsa, Tesco's Property Director, who was now my boss, to be a right royal pain in the arse and at the end of May I quit the job.

We went to Ballymaloe House for a couple of weeks and had a wonderfully relaxing holiday. The children had by now befriended the Allen grandchildren and they pretty much looked after themselves. On one occasion we were horrified to see them on the roof pretending to shoot at us; they had climbed out through an attic window. Sue's sister Carol came to stay at Ballymaloe and one day we went down to Valencia Island in West Cork and then to Kinsale for lunch at Actons Hotel. Sue and Carol went off to find a chemist's shop and then secreted themselves in the bathroom for a long time. When they emerged Carol was in a sate of considerable stress, she had been carrying out a pregnancy test and sure enough she was pregnant.

We decided we might move back to England and would look at houses around Kingston on Thames in Surrey to be near to Carol and Simon and the expected baby. Carol and Simon lived on a house boat on the Thames so we stayed in an hotel as there wasn't room for all of us on the boat. We were a little surprised by house prices which at this time were much higher than in Dublin. We were sufficiently serious about moving to start looking for schools for the children. We arranged an interview at Kingston on Thames Grammar School for Simon, who was twelve years old, and he was accepted.

When we returned to Dublin there was a message for me to call Ambrose McInerney of McInerney Properties, Ireland's largest housebuilder. He offered me a job to set up a Commercial Property Division at a salary of £20,000 per annum plus 5% of the equity in the new company. I talked this over with Sue and we decided we were so happy in Dublin we should stay and I therefore accepted the offer with a starting date of September 1, 1979.

In July I received a call from A.G. Everything in the garden was far from rosy on the real estate front in the USA. He had bought four sites in Charlotte, North Carolina and had construction under way on two of these. He was building 42,000 sq. ft. stores (twice as big as in New Zealand and Ireland) plus shops for lease and out parcels for sale or lease. He had also bought twenty acres in Salisbury, North Carolina and was building a 300,000 sq. ft. warehouse plus a separate building for a joiners shop and garage, and a 10,000 sq. ft. office building. He was having problems with real estate agents, architects and builders. He had already changed architects and builders once on all the schemes and was finding it difficult to control everything that was going on. Would I come and join him – the same deal as in Ireland. I said I'd think about it.

I talked it over with Sue and we decided that the McInerney offer was probably as good as A.G.'s offer and was bound to be less stressful. Anything would be less stressful than working for A.G. I called him and told him my decision but two days later he was on the phone again. He asked if I'd do him one favor – would I go to New Zealand for a week at his expense and look at his real estate portfolio, evaluate it and give him recommendations for each property. How could I refuse as good as he'd been to me?

In Mid July I flew from Dublin to London and then to Los Angeles where I had a layover. I visited the sights and had a look at the shops down Rodeo Drive. Then I took the ferry to Catalina Island, but beautiful as it was, I found it no fun on my own. I am one of those people who needs company to be truly happy. I came back from Catalina Island by flying boat and returned to the Hyatt Hotel where I went to the bar and got drunk.

The next day I flew to New Zealand and was met at the airport by Ron Jones, the stores director. I stayed with Gerry Senior's brother and his wife who made me very welcome. I saw more of Auckland on this visit than I had with A.G. . It is a very beautiful city with what must be one of the most attractive harbors in the world. You can't get over that feeling that it's the 1950's. Many of the cars are twenty to thirty years old; cars are very expensive in New Zealand as they have to be imported and its thirteen thousand miles – half way round the world – from Britain, the main source of supply. And as for the fashions, well let me tell you that when you buy a suit you get two pairs of trousers, a pair of long trousers and a pair of short ones. Can you imagine seeing office workers heading for work in pin stripe suits and bowler hats with pin stripe shorts and knee high socks. It is quite a sight.

A.G. called me when I was in New Zealand and said that as I was going home via America why not make a small detour and spend a few days with him. It seemed like a good idea at the time. My flight was changed so that I would fly Auckland-Los Angeles-New York-Charlotte. When I arrived in New York who was there to meet my flight but Sue and the kids. A.G. had arranged for them to join me for my stay in Charlotte. We arrived in Charlotte on July 29, at about 9.30 p.m. and were met by A.G.'s brother in law, Gerry Senior.

When we walked out of the airport we could not believe the heat and humidity. It was like walking into a steam bath and we were relieved to get into the air conditioned comfort of Gerry's Mercedes. He took us to the Sheraton Hotel on McDowell Street where rooms had been reserved for us and said A.G. would be round in the morning at 9 a.m. to meet us. We showered and changed and went down for something to eat. The restaurant was closed so we asked if we could have a sandwich only to be told that no food was available until breakfast. There was only one other hotel in uptown Charlotte, the Radisson and this had no food after 10 p.m.. There were only two restaurants in uptown Charlotte at this time and both had stopped serving. We finally took a taxi to The Athens Restaurant on Independence Boulevard, a greasy spoon serving breakfast 24 hours a day. It seemed that despite Charlotte's size it was under-provided with restaurants and other amenities.

The next morning A.G. picked me up at 9 am and arranged for Sue and the boys to be picked up by his sister to be shown the sights. A.G. took me to a site on North Tryon Street where a 42,000 sq. ft. store and about fifteen shops were under construction. He was hoping to get his first store open before Christmas. In adjacent shopping centers were a Kroger supermarket (a national chain) and a Food Town supermarket (a regional chain) Food Town had the lowest prices in the area and used the acronym in its advertising LFPINC – Lowest Food Prices in North Carolina. We then drove thirty five miles to Salisbury where the 300,000 sq.ft. warehouse was under construction. The steel frame was up, the roofing in progress and the floor slab was being poured. It was a very impressive structure and well located for Interstate 85. A.G. envisaged a chain of fifty stores with the bulk of them in the towns which were adjacent to Interstates 85, 77 and 40 all of which were close at hand. He then took me to a mill town, Kannapolis, where work had just commenced on a scheme that was almost a replica of the one on North Tryon Street.

When we came back to Charlotte he took me to see his other three sites: Albermarle Road, where construction had commenced, Wendover Road, where initial site works were in progress, and Tyvola Road next to Interstate 77, where the heavily wooded site was being cleared. It was obvious he needed help. Shortly, he was going to have to turn his mind to establishing the grocery business and would not have the time available to oversee all this building work. A.G. loaned us a car and suggested we take the children to Disney World in Florida. I felt very unsafe driving a large American car on the right hand side of the road and couldn't face the ten to twelve hour drive so, without telling A.G., I chartered a small plane and we flew down to Orlando and took a taxi to our hotel in Disney World. The children had a wonderful time but I began to feel disoriented and dizzy and had to seek assistance at the emergency room of the local hospital. They prescribed some stronger tranquilizers than the ones I was taking and I soon felt okay again.

When we returned to Charlotte we met A.G. for lunch at the Saucy Crepe Restaurant in Villa Square on Providence Road. We sat outside on the patio overlooking an ornamental pool and ate lunch and drank wine and felt on top of the world. A.G. said :
"Do you believe in democracy Gary"
"Yes, I do" said I.

"Good because I want your family to vote on something and if you believe in democracy you'll agree to be bound by the family's decision"
"Yes, that sounds fair enough"
"How would you like to come and live here, and have Gary work for me again? All those in favor raise your right hand"

Simon, James and Dominic's hands shot in the air, Sue also raised her hand. The die was cast, we were coming to America. This is a fine example of how A.G. usually gets his own way. We agreed we would try to move from Ireland to America by mid-September and we went with Helen Adams, a local realtor, to look at houses. After some hesitation we took the plunge and bought a 4 bedroomed house on Edgehill Road, Charlotte, in fashionable Myers Park. We paid $126,000 which seemed reasonable for this large house with a swimming pool in the back garden. We decided we would bring very little furniture from Ireland, so we met with a decorator, Juanita, and described the type of furniture we had in mind. We gave her $30,000 and left the furnishing of the house to her. We needed to get the boys into a school and after conflicting reports about the quality of the public schools in Charlotte, we opted for a private school, Charlotte Country Day and enrolled all three boys.

We arrived back in Ireland on August 10, 1979 and put the house in Tallaght up for sale. We hired a removal company and sent our dining table and chairs and a few other items to Charlotte. With the assistance of A.G.'s solicitor, Jim Scowcroft, we applied for E-2 Investor Visas at the American Embassy in Dublin. These were issued on September 12, 1979 and were valid for four years and gave us the right to both live and work in the States.

CHAPTER EIGHTEEN

"honi soit qui mal y pense – bugger you Jack, I'm alright" Harold

On September 15, 1979 we flew out of Dublin Airport for New York. We stayed for a few days in New York and went to see the sights. We stayed at the Algonquin Hotel which we liked very much. We hired a taxi for the day and went to see all the famous landmarks. We went for lunch to the Windows on the World restaurant at the top of the World Trade Center and when we returned to our taxi were amazed to see our Russian taxi driver sitting by his cab playing a trumpet.

When we arrived in Charlotte the house was not quite ready but Mike Johnson had rented a flat for us nearby. We had asked A.G. to buy us a car (at our expense) and there in the driveway of 810 Edgehill Road was a brand new white Mercedes. It was virtually impossible to live in Charlotte without a car so we went and bought a Volkswagen Rabbit for Sue.

I started work right away and A.G. introduced me to the firm's attorney, Deane Brunson, architect Thomas "Rick" Rickenbaker, and real estate agent, Arnold Benton, of Carter & Associates. I became very close friends with both Deane and Rick and they often called at my house. In fact Rick Rickenbaker usually stopped by on his way home from the office and drank a few glasses of scotch, of which he was very fond, while I drank gin and tonic.

Making Hen's Meat

A few days after we moved into our new house a neighbor, Becky Sippe, who lived on Hermitage Road, came calling to bring us a little house warming gift. We were to become close friends of Becky, her husband, Larry, and their three children, Laura, David and Mark who were about the same age as our three children. We continued our friendship with Mike Johnson who also lived in Charlotte on nearby Queens Road. The rest of the management team who had arrived from England, Ireland and New Zealand opted to live in or near Salisbury. Mike Johnson and I could never understand this. Limited as the opportunities were for social and cultural events in Charlotte, it was, from our viewpoint, infinitely preferable to Salisbury. Over time we found Charlotte's hidden secrets and as the city grew we came to love it and the people who lived there.

After work Mike and I would usually go for a few drinks to either the Saucy Crepe or Frank Redd's Wine Shop on Park Road. We both developed a taste for champagne and usually drank a couple of bottles every evening. We often made an Irish drink called black velvet which is 50% champagne and 50% Guinness. We found a few decent restaurants to frequent. We liked the Epicurean and Mangiones Italian Restaurant, both on East Boulevard, and a little French restaurant, Chez Daniel, was particularly good. We became friends with the owner, Daniel, and he and his wife, Danielle, would come to our house and cooked on one occasion. We often ate at the Silver Cricket, owned by Charles and Marion Tucker. Marion was English and her husband, Charles, a Virginian, was an Anglophile and had adopted an English voice and manners. They opened another restaurant, The Lamplighter, on Morehead Street, and then sold the Silver Cricket and opened Nicklebys' in Villa Square where the Saucy Crepe had been. Finally they opened a rotisserie restaurant at Cotswold Mall but it was not a success so they changed the format to Mexican. We also went to Casablaca, a middle eastern restaurant on Independence Boulevard and to the Tandoori House, a very good little Indian restaurant. There were one or two good chinese restaurants and a particular favorite was the Great Wall on Montford Drive. There was also a very good Mexican restaurant, La Paz.

Sue's cooking became more adventurous under Mike's influence and we had lots of dinner Parties. Mike and I would go to Redd's Wine Store on South Boulevard and Mike would select the wines. When we were not working life pretty much revolved around eating and drinking and our favorite watering holes were Nickleby's, Dowdy's Brown Derby restaurant, Redd's wineshop, Picassos, La Paz and Five Steps Down.

In January, 1980, we opened the first 3 Guys' Store in America on NorthTryon Street, Charlotte, We had a banner on the storefront that read "Lower Prices than LFPINC". This infuriated Ralph Ketner, President of Food Town, because he had spent years promoting his company as the low price leader and had even registered the acronym LFPINC (meaning Lowest Food Prices in North Carolina). He and A.G. were interviewed together on the radio and Ketner admitted that 3 Guys' prices were lower on the lines we carried but said he had lower prices than us on the lines we didn't carry. I'm still trying to work that out. We launched a law suit against Food Town for false and misleading advertising and ultimately they dropped LFPINC and advertised "Over 6800 Low Prices".

Kroger, who had a store next door to 3 Guys on North Tryon Street, launched a campaign called "3 Times the Difference" - if you could buy your groceries elsewhere cheaper than at Kroger then if you presented the two receipts for identical items they would pay you in cash three times the difference. Obviously no member of the public would take up this challenge because it would mean shopping at two stores and buying identical items. A.G., however, did take up the challenge. He ran thirty or forty items through a scanner at 3 Guys and got an itemized receipt and with the press accompanying him went to the Kroger Store next door and bought the identical items. 3 Guys won hands down so he collected his three times the difference in cash and this was reported in the press. This incensed Kroger and when, in February, 1980, we opened another store right next to them on Albermarle Road they cut their prices, but only in these two stores, to the same price or lower than 3 Guys. We had no alternative but to cut our prices because we had to have the lowest prices. Deane Brunson, our attorney, drew our attention to a North Carolina Statute which prevents predatory pricing. This law is intended to inhibit a large corporation from preventing a small competitor from gaining a foothold in the market place by a pricing policy aimed specifically at putting that competitor out of business.

That is precisely what Kroger were doing. They had thousands of stores nationwide but they had cut their prices to below cost in only two stores, the ones adjacent to 3 Guys. We went to see the North Carolina Attorney General, Rufus Edmiston, at his office in Raleigh and asked him to take action against Kroger for their predatory pricing. His response was
"Bring me the body and the smoking gun, and then I'll act"
It other words if Kroger put you out of business I'll do something, until then you're on your own. In the end Kroger closed their stores in Charlotte and withdrew from the market.

The North Tryon Street store had good sales approaching $200,000 per week but when the store in Albermarle Road opened with sales of $120,000 per week a considerable percentage of these sales came at the expense of the North Tryon Street store. Clearly the catchment areas were overlapping and we had to give careful thought to the stores under construction at Tyvola Road and Wendover Road. Our third store opened in May in Kannapolis; a small mill town thirty miles north of Charlotte. The majority of people in Kannopolis were employed at a textile factory, Cannon Mills. This store was an immediate success with sales of over $150,000 per week.

We began to study the American consumer in depth and realized that whilst 90% of the population in England, Ireland and New Zealand were working class and therefore likely to shop for price, in America it was different. We had to consider demographics when choosing store locations. The success of Kannapolis told us to aim for smaller towns where the majority of the inhabitants worked in blue collar jobs in manufacturing industry. We Americanized the stores by taking checks for the first time and by taking the money for the meat and produce sales at our check outs.

This was made possible because we had scanning and did not have to rely on memory pricing. Our original concessionaires, who were small companies, could not keep pace with our scheduled openings so we brought in a new operator for the meat and produce, Bobby Fogle, who had a small chain of supermarkets in Columbia, South Carolina. We also took the decision to make our future stores the size of the stores in Ireland and New Zealand, about 20,000 sq. ft. We therefore reduced the size of the Charlotte stores under construction at Wendover Road and Tyvola Road and leased out the balance of the space.

The introduction of scanning not only made it possible to take the concessionaires money it also made re-ordering an entirely automatic process and eliminated the need for the weekly stock take. This is commonplace now but 3 Guys was the pioneer. There were two other benefits, first a bigger range of products could be sold if desired because the check out operators no longer had to memorize the prices, second, and for the same reason more price changes could be implemented each week enabling us to react quickly to changed market conditions.

While Arnold Benton had found the sites in Charlotte, Kanappolis and Salisbury he was not the man to travel to small towns all over North and South Carolina; that would be too much like hard work for Arnold. A.G. used to refer to Arnold as Crime, because whenever they went to a restaurant Arnold would disappear when the check appeared; he called him Crime because:
"Crime does not pay"
We made a deal with a real estate agent in Salisbury called Bud Johnson of Realty World. He agreed to work for a flat fee of $5,000 for every site which he introduced and we purchased or leased.

Not only were the two stores in Charlotte not performing quite as well as anticipated the shop leasing was also below expectations. In Ireland we had been signing twenty year leases with tenants at £10 (about $20) per sq. ft., with reviews every five years. In Charlotte a typical deal was for a three year lease with five 3 year options at a rent of between $5 and $8 per sq. ft. Even at those low rents we could only lease about half of the shops. As we drove around North and South Carolina we noticed lots of empty buildings. There were dozens of old A&P Supermarkets empty and also former Food Towns, Harris Teeters and Winn Dixies. These stores were in the 17,000 sq.ft. to 25,000 sq. ft. range and had been vacated because competition had forced them out of the market (in A&P's case), or because they had relocated to bigger stores. We asked Bud Johnson to check on some of these stores and found they could be rented for between $1.50 and $3 per sq. ft. It was obvious that this was a tenants' market and it was pointless to go on building shopping centers at $2,000,000 a time when we could rent stores for next to nothing. We found an English architect in Salisbury, Doug Tennant, and we hired him at a flat fee for the remodeling of the 'old stores'.

The first store we rented was in Albermarle, North Carolina, about thirty miles east of Charlotte, and we paid $1.50 per sq. ft. for 17,000 sq. ft. The landlord, Buck Nance, made all the modifications we required at his expense including a truck unloading ramp and a hydraulic lifting platform. A.G. was in New Zealand when we opened this store in June 1981 and it is a good thing he was. The first day was a nightmare. Something was wrong with the scanning system. When the first customer got to the checkout the operator scanned a can of beans and it came up as Kellogs cornflakes, a tin of corned beef came up as three pairs of ladies panties and so on. The items weren't price marked and the girls knew none of the prices so we had to have the manager and area manager stand behind the checkouts looking up every price on a computer spread sheet. People were amazingly patient and that night the whole system was re-programmed and everything was fine the next day. The store was a great success and we knew we now had the winning formula. To quote A.G.:

> "We have now solved the problem of the Americanization of 3 Guys . Now it is just a matter of how many stores, how fast"

The next stores to open were in Gastonia and Winston-Salem and they achieved volumes higher than any store A.G. had owned in the three countries in which he had previously operated. The two remaining Charlotte stores were then opened and it was full speed ahead. I was running three direct labor crews to get the stores open as fast as possible. By the end of 1981 we had twelve stores open and we opened ten more in 1982 and by the time A.G. returned to the Isle of Man in early 1983 we had twenty eight stores open.

CHAPTER NINETEEN

*"if a hen and a half
laid an egg and a half
in a day and a half
how many apples
in a barrel of plums"*
Harold

We had a baby sitter in Ireland called Anne Colfer and we invited her to come over to the States for six months to help look after the boys. We had no spare bedroom so Rick Rickenbaker loaned us his thirty foot recreational vehicle and we parked it in our driveway and Anne stayed there.

Through Becky Sippe we were introduced to Deirdre Mistri and her husband, Adi. Adi was an architect and he and Deirdre had met at the University of Virginia. They had a son, Alex, who was the same age as Dominic and they became close friends. Sue and Deirdre used to go shopping for clothes together and they loved to find designer clothes for cents on the dollar. Deirdre taught Sue the art of scanning a store:
"You walk in and just look around for a few seconds, it takes a practiced eye but it is something you can learn" Deirdre told Sue "You know immediately where the bargains are located and if it is worthwhile staying to shop".
Sue and Deirdre soon became best friends and used to spend lots of time together.

Making Hen's Meat

Adi taught the boys to play soccer in our backyard and they became very enthusiastic soccer players. They joined teams in the Charlotte Junior Soccer League and were soon playing in select teams. Simon transferred to Myers Park High School and won a place in the varsity team and James played for Charlotte Country Day. Between practice and games there was one of them needing a lift somewhere every night of the week and during the day on Saturday and Sundays. Charlotte got a professional soccer team, the Carolina Lightning, coached by Rodney Marsh, a famous English player. We never missed a match and on one memorable occasion Adi Mistri won a new car in a competition to kick a football through its open sun-roof.

Sue would go to Providence Frames whenever she wanted a painting or photograph framed and we became friendly with Debbie, the owner, and her boyfriend, Jack Bass. Sue also made friends with Wade Yarborough, who worked for Debbie, and one evening told me she had arranged to play tennis with him the next morning at Edgehill Park right across from our house. I was suspicious of this blossoming friendship and decided to take a peek at Wade Yarborough. I came back from work and parked the car on Edgehill Road beside the park. Sue and Wade were playing tennis. Wade was skipping and flouncing around the court, screaming and laughing outrageously; he was the most obviously gay guy I had ever seen. Satisfied I went back to work. I soon got to know Wade and his partner Darryl and they were the most civilized couple I had ever met. Wade was an opera buff and had a great record collection; my middle son, James, came to love opera as a direct result of our friendship with Wade and Darryl.

We had Wade and Darryl and Deirdre and Adi round for dinner and they got on like a house on fire. Wade and Darryl invited the four of us round to their house for dinner the following Saturday. We arrived at their house on Queens Road about 7 p.m. and had a few cocktails. We then sat at the dining table and Wade and Darryl went into the kitchen to fetch the soup. I don't remember whose idea it was but the four of us stripped completely naked and then resumed our seats at the table. I know we'd been drinking but I think we must also have been smoking some pot. Wade and

Darryl came in with a tureen of soup and while Darryl held the tureen Wade ladled the soup into our soup bowls. Nothing was said about our nakedness until Wade said to Deirdre:
"Kindly remove your mammary gland from the soup!"

After the soup was finished Wade and Darryl again went into the kitchen and came back with the main course. Now they were completely naked. There was an embarrassed silence until I said:
"It was supposed to be funny, but nobody laughed, lets all get dressed"

We found an inn in Ashe County near the Blue Ridge Parkway about a hundred miles from Charlotte that was to become our home away from home for the next few years.

Although on a much smaller scale than Ballymaloe House it had many of the same attributes. The kitchen was at the heart of Glendale Springs Inn and here Gayle Winston, the innkeeper, cooked with a style reminiscent of a fine French restaurant. As well as the more traditional offerings Gayle cooked a wonderful deep fried herbed crepe filled with gruyere cheese, an asparagus omelet and veal with bacon, herbs and red wine in puff pastry. For dessert not only were souffles offered but also homemade grapefruit and kir sorbets.

The bedrooms were simply furnished but the little touches made it special: the fresh flowers, the carafe of dry sherry and the absence of T.V., radio or telephone. We quickly fell in love with Glendale Springs Inn and with the innkeeper, Gayle Winston. Later she sold the inn and opened the River House, a country inn and restaurant a few miles north of Glendale Springs in Grassy Creek. Here the Glendale Springs atmosphere has been re-created on a somewhat larger scale.

We needed a family doctor and after asking around chose Dr. Phillip Naumoff, an old Jewish doctor, whose surgery was in the Doctor's Building on Kings Drive, very close to our house. I went to see him to get a prescription for Parstelin but he said he wouldn't prescribe that drug. Instead he prescribed Ativan which

I found to be very good. I had been having dizzy spells and feelings of deep foreboding again but the Ativan seemed to work very well. If I was feeling bad an Ativan would calm me in a matter of minutes. I often took Ativan with alcohol which seemed to double the effect.

I developed a serious pain in the arse and went to see Dr. Naumoff about it. He had me strip off and lay face down on a couch. He examined me and said it was piles. He called in his 75 year old nurse and seemed to be examining me again when I felt the most excruciating pain.

"What the fuck are you doing" I said.
"I was just cutting off your piles" he said, brandishing a blood stained scalpel.
"Shouldn't I have gone to the hospital and had a proper operation?" I asked
"Nonsense," said Naumoff "Why waste your money on something I've been doing for forty years."

He had his nurse strap a sanitary towel across my arse and off I went to a meeting at Deane Brunson's office. I was walking like Hopalong Cassidy and when I explained what had happened, Deane cracked up. I didn't sleep that night for pain which seemed worse than before. Next day I returned to Dr. Naumoff's surgery. He had me on the couch again and once more I felt an excruciating pain:
"What are you doing?" I said
"I missed a bit yesterday, but I think I've got it all now". he said.

On my way home from Salisbury I kept noticing a little bar and restaurant just off the Brookshire Freeway near the Graham Street exit. One night I took this exit which brought me right to the bar at the corner of 10th Street and Graham Street. To my delight they sold Guinness so I sat there and had one or two and talked to the owner's wife, Iola Douglas. This little bar, The Pioneer Restaurant, became a regular stopping off point for me on my way home. I soon got to know the Douglas family, "Preacher" Douglas, his wife, Iola, son Junior and daughter, Sherry. Preacher

owned the block of property in which his restaurant was situated and also ran a night time cocktail bar upstairs called the Gold Room. Shortly after I met him he opened a second restaurant on Statesville Avenue called The Burger House. He built this new and included a shop next door to his restaurant which he let to a grocery store. He also had a workshop behind the restaurant from which he operated his main business which was the supply of pool tables and video game machines. These were located in bars and shops throughout Charlotte and he split the takings with the owner of each location. I became good friends with Preacher and admired his business acumen. As he used to say:
"It isn't easy for a black man to be successful in this town.'

He put two video game machines in each of the 3 Guys' Stores and I even had a couple at home into which my children and their friends put their allowances. I would get half the takings so I kept giving the kids their own money back. I became very attached to Preacher's daughter, Sherry, and she and I had a liaison that only ended when she got married and moved to Lexington. The following St. Valentine's day I asked Iola for Sherry's address and sent her a dozen roses. When I got home that night Sue said Sherry Douglas's husband had been on the phone six times about me sending flowers to his wife. Sue insisted I call him. The conversation was heated:
"Why have you sent flowers to my wife?"
"It's an English custom to send flowers to people you love"
"You can't send flowers to someone else's wife. I've a good mind to come down to Charlotte and give you a good hiding."
"I'm sorry you are so insecure in your relationship with Sherry that you are worried about her receiving flowers from an admirer"
"Insecure in my relationship, I'll insecure you – I'm on my way to Charlotte right now and I'm bringing my gun"

I didn't get much sleep that night but, thank God, the guy never showed up.

On the subject of liaisons I started having an affair with a twenty four year old girl who worked in the accounts department at 3 Guys. He name was Susan Tyree and she was tall and shapely

with long legs and enormous breasts. The first time we went out was to a shagging competition in Salisbury. I didn't know that shagging referred to dancing to beach music and as I was dancing with Susan I said to her:
"When and where do we start shagging"
"We're shagging now" she said.
So different from the home life of our own dear Queen.

For Christmas and the New Year Sue and I and the children flew to Ireland and after a couple of days in Dublin we went to Ballymaloe House. Unbeknown to Sue I'd arranged for Susan Tyree to fly to London on New Year's Day and I was to meet her at Heathrow Airport. New Years Eve was a big night at Ballymaloe House and as well as the Allen family and Jim Whelan our friends Mike Johnson, John Hussey and his wife and Dr. Derry McCarthy, with who we had become friends on previous visits, were there. On New Years Day I told Sue I was going to England to see my mother and would return in three or four days to fly back to America with the family.

I spent a couple of days in London with Susan Tyree and then took her to my home town, Bradford. We went to see my mother who said:
"Susan, you have really developed an American accent"
I don't know if she was playing games or really did think that Susan Tyree was my wife Sue.
We went to the Delvers pub where we met my brother, Michael. He took one look at those big breasts and immediately took one in each hand and gave them a squeeze. We left promptly and went to York for a few days. There was very bad snow and the airports were closed for a couple of days so I phoned Sue in Ireland and told here I'd fly back from England to the States. I flew back with Susan Tyree on Concorde but didn't enjoy the experience because I had an upset stomach all the way.

In March, 1982 Peter Thornton came over to stay with us and we agreed to have a long weekend in New Orleans. Sue and I had visited New Orleans the previous summer and had been enchanted by the French Quarter, which seemed to combine all the best qualities of an American and a European city. We loved the street life; the jazz, the secluded gardens and the restaurants. We went for a cruise on a paddle steamer on the Mississippi and had our portraits drawn by an artist in Jackson Square. We drank in Pat O'Brien's Hurricane Bar, ate breakfast at Brennans, lunch in the Court of Three Sisters, drank coffee in the Café du Monde, got drunk in the Old Absinthe House and listened to jazz in Preservation Hall. We enjoyed the superb cuisine at Leruth's Restaurant.

Peter and Sue flew to New Orleans on Thursday and I was to join them on Saturday. Instead I went to Jacksonville, Florida with Susan Tyree and stayed on the beach at the Turtle Inn. For some inexplicable reason I kept calling Sue in New Orleans and telling her where I was and with whom. This was a cruel thing to do and served no purpose other than to hurt my wife. When Peter and Sue returned to Charlotte, Peter looked me in the eye and said: "You rotten bugger"

The affair with Susan Tyree got very serious and we decided to live together. I told Sue, who was very hurt, but asked for a formal separation agreement. We rented a house on Mariners Cove Drive at Lake Norman and Susan Tyree and I moved in together. Within days the romance began to disappear. The clandestine affair, the trips away together, the excitement of finding somewhere to live had obviously fanned the flames of passion. Now we were in a settled situation the excitement was gone. Everything was very civilized with Sue. I had the children every weekend and we all (including Susan Tyree) got together once a week for dinner and went to watch the Carolina Lightning soccer games. After a few weeks I realized I was desperately missing Sue and the kids so I went to see her and told her I'd made a mistake and asked if I could come back.

"Gary" she said " I'm having a really good time without you, Wade and Darryl are looking after me and we sit on the screen porch drinking wine and smoking pot and everything is very relaxed. I'm going to lots of parties and I don't want you back

until you are absolutely certain that it is what you want to do, and that you will not leave again. You can come back in six months."
I continued living with Susan Tyree although I knew that soon I would be leaving her and going home to Edgehill Road.
Sue went with the boys on a cruise to the Bahamas that summer and they also took a trip to England. I started to have a clandestine affair with my own wife. Sue used to meet me in a room in the Ramada Inn on Kings Drive. I had created a very complicated life for myself. As well as working very hard I was living with Susan Tyree, having an affair with my wife, cheating on them both with Sherry Douglas and regularly seeing a high class hooker called Margot.

Eventually the day came for me to return home. I told Susan Tyree I was going back home and helped her to find a flat, gave her the furniture I had bought and a little cash to help her with the move. I loaded up the car with my clothes and personal possessions and went home. Sue said:
"What are you doing here?"
"I'm moving back in"
"No you're not, the six months isn't up until tomorrow. I'm having a party tonight and you're not invited. Come back tomorrow".
Off I went and spent a lonely night in a motel.

I had become good friends with a poet, Chuck Sullivan. I first met him in the Brown Derby Restaurant and Bar on Kings Drive. We immediately got on and I took him home for dinner. He gave me a couple of books of poetry he had written "Vanishing Species" and "A Catechism of Hearts" which I read with great interest. Chuck was a New York born Irish Catholic. He had been to college on a basketball scholarship at Belmont Abbey near Charlotte. All his poetry reflected his Catholicism and his endless search for truth, beauty and grace. The poet to whom he probably owed the most was T.S. Elliot. One night I was in the bar eating some oysters; a woman sat next to me and looked at my oysters and started telling me what was wrong with how the oysters had been prepared and presented. I told her to mind her own fucking business and a

blazing row ensued. Chuck was a few feet away and his eye caught mine and he shouted to me:
"What's the problem, Gary?"
"It's this big titted monster interfering and annoying me" I replied.
"That's my wife, Chris," said Chuck with laughter in his eyes.
From then on his wife was known to me and Chuck as the BTM.

In the spring of 1982 we went to the World's Fair in Knoxville, Tennessee. We booked into the only hotel we could find with vacancies and soon found out why – it was a Temperance Hotel – my worst nightmare. The World's Fair was very disappointing but the Chinese Pavilion was reputed to be excellent. Naturally, there was a two hour line to get in so I got James who was thirteen years old to act like a spastic. James is a natural born actor and he put on a bravura performance as we strolled to the front of the line and were admitted with no wait.

In July Sue and I went on a cruise to the Caribbean and Mexico. We visited the Mayan city of Chicen Itza and on the way our coach stopped at a roadside market. I ordered a bacardi and coke and was about to drink it when Sue said:
"Gary, don't drink that, it's got ice cubes in it so it's like drinking water. You know how we were warned on the ship not to drink the water."
"Bollocks" said I and I downed the drink in one swig "you see, I drank it before the ice had the chance to melt".

How wrong I was. I spent the next two days aboard ship in the lavatory. I got so sore I asked to see the ship's doctor. His only remedy was to apply cornstarch and surprisingly it gave almost instantaneous relief. While we were on our cruise, James had gone on a trip to Germany, Switzerland and Italy organized by Elizabeth Ross an art teacher at CPCC. James was terribly homesick and kept calling us on the ship's telephone. He made us feel very unsettled but after a couple of days he stopped calling and we were able to relax and enjoy ourselves. Later in the summer Sue and the children went to Disney World and stayed in one of the treehouses with Diana Rusmissil, secretary to Rick Rickenbaker.

CHAPTER TWENTY

"I'd rather see a parson run over" Harold

In late 1982, A.G. became bored with the business just as he had in England and New Zealand. He had proved his point and successfully established a profitable supermarket operation in the place where it all began, America. He returned to his tax-haven home on the Isle of Man where he owned the largest private bank, Celtic Bank, and a property investment company, Anglo International Holdings, with a large portfolio in the United Kingdom. His initial investment in the New Zealand business had been repaid to him so he owned that business free and clear. He decided it was time to cash in his chips and put all his money and energy into the U.K. property market. He had said his ambition was to make a million on three continents, now he was about to turn that dream into reality by selling his New Zealand and U.S. companies.

He had appointed Trevor Wilson as President of the U.S. operation and he hired George Ball, a New York investment banker, with the firm of Donaldson, Lufkin and Jenrette, to find a buyer for the company. In spring of 1983 Bruno's Inc., an Alabama grocery chain expressed interest in the company and in July signed a contract to purchase 3 Guys. The completion date was set for August 14 and Jim Scowcroft, the solicitor who ran his companies in the Isle of Man when A.G. was absent in America, came over to make sure everything went smoothly. The day before the deal was to be completed Brunos' attorney called Deane

Brunson and said the deal was off. No explanation was ever given as to why the deal did not proceed and A.G. started a lawsuit against Bruno's which was eventually settled out of court with a substantial sum being paid to him.

George Ball suggested we look into carrying out a Management Buyout which were all the rage at the time. The six of us in senior management positions with 3 Guys set up a company, Rowan Management Group, and instructed George Ball to find a lender so that we could buy the company from A.G. George structured the deal in two parts. The warehouse complex was to be sold to a property investment group CPA4 with 3 Guys taking a lease-back and simultaenously General Electric Credit Corporation were to loan us the money to buy out A.G. and provide us with a revolving line of credit. The U.S. deal was concluded in November, 1983 and fourteen months later A.G. sold his New Zealand operation to a competitor, Progressive Enterprises for NZ$42.3 million. By this time A.G. had parlayed his £14 million obtained from the sale of Kwik Save into a £300 million property empire. He was fast becoming a major player in the U.K. property market.

At Christmas, 1983 the whole family went to St. Petersburg in Florida hoping for a little sun. We drove down and stayed in an apartment we rented. It was one of the coldest spells on record in Florida and we suffered a power cut in our apartment building which left us without heat. We met up with some friends, Ken and Violet, to whom A.G. had introduced us in Charlotte, but who now lived in Florida, and went out with them to a restaurant for Christmas dinner. The weather was so bad that after Christmas we packed up and came home foregoing five days of our planned vacation.

In Spring of 1984 we were having a cook out in our backyard and were sitting round the pool eating burgers when I heard a loud cracking noise coming from the house. I went to investigate and discovered that there was a fire blazing fiercely in the kitchen. The sound I had heard was the glass in the windows cracking because of the intense heat. Sue had put on a pan of chips and we had forgotten about them. Simon was in the house and after I made sure he was out safely I went to a neighbor's house and phoned the fire brigade. The fire was quickly extinguished but the whole house was badly smoke damaged. We moved into temporary accommodation at the nearby Manor House, at the expense of the insurance company, and by the time all the repairs to the house were complete six months had elapsed. For Fathers Day 1984 Dominic wrote me a poem as follows:

Destruction

*I see a terrible thing
destruction of things
of things that cannot
be replaced because
of sentimental value*

*And trees trying to
survive in the wind
I hear people crying
because their house is gone
where would they go?
and hearts pumping trying to see
what will happen next*

*People trying to pick up
what can't be replaced
I smell quietness
tears dropping to the ground
the fragrance of perfume
that has been washed away*

My 40th birthday was on 25th February 1984 and Sue confided in me that she was organizing a 'surprise' party for me and wanted to know what I wanted for my birthday:

"First," I told her "I want the party to be in the library at Nicklebys and I want only our closest family and friends to be there. Second, I want Chuck Sullivan to write me a poem. Third, I want Tommie

Making Hen's Meat

Robinson to do a painting or drawing for me, and finally at midnight I want my favorite hooker, Margot to come to me gift wrapped in a red ribbon and sit on my knee".

Sue delivered on everything I wanted. The owners of Nicklebys provided all the food and wine for the dinner free of charge, Tommie Robinson did me a portrait of my three children, Chuck Sullivan wrote me a poem which he read after dinner, and Margot duly appeared at midnight. When Sue asked Chuck to write a poem for me he said he couldn't just write poems to order but if something happened which genuinely inspired him then who knows maybe a poem would be forthcoming. Chuck always carried a notebook with him and every now and then you would see him jotting a note, maybe what someone had said or something he had just seen or just a thought passing through his mind. One day I met him in Mac Mac's bar in Elizabeth and as we were drinking and talking our conversation turned to radio programs we'd enjoyed as children. I mentioned the ventriloquist, Peter Brough, and then decided to go one better and told Chuck there had been a juggler on BBC radio. Chuck made a note of this and here is the resulting poem that Chuck read at my birthday party:

The Juggler on the Radio
(for Gary at 40)

In a new country a world away
the Yorkshire man at 40 remembers
pressing
the doubtless witness of his child's ear
to the light behind the face of the radio's
tiny cathedral
and recalls his faith
a tough act to follow

What the child knew was the pure
sound of syllables juggling
a magic beyond his sight three four and
finally five
duck pins or swords of fire

Gary Spence

> *the weight & size & edge*
> *of a world of objects caught*
> *up in the motion of all things*
> *tossed in the air each the ward*
> *of sure hands speaking*
> *the unseen balance of deeds*
> *only a child could believe*
>
> *Now and then amazed we still dream*
> *the show we believed as children before*
> *T.V.*
> *even on this sharp waking edge*
> *of our 4th decade of mysteries*
> *hearing now through a sound*
> *ever more darkly we chance to take*
> *for better or worse*
> *those old unseen hands at the tricky*
> *performance of their word*
>
> *God bless the dial-lit spinner*
> *of 40 plates at once*
> *our turning years on their thin sticks*
> *have wobbled in time*
> *like phantom Wedgwood plates*
> *at great risk and yet each crisis*
> *has seen them be spun back to spinning*
> *straight*
>
> *Or so we have heard and so still listen*
> *to the envisioned sleight-of-hand*
> *that blesses the blind balance*
> *of going where we know we are*
> *at the vaudeville mercy of the child*
> *who makes belief real*
> *in the juggler on the radio*

The Juggler on the Radio became the title of Chuck's fourth book of poems and he was also featured reading it in a public TV program about his poetry called Longing for the Harmonies. Sue and I were interviewed for this program.

In March I went to London for a few days with James and took the opportunity to renew my British passport and to get a B2 Visa at the US Embassy in Grosvenor Square. My immigration status had become rather complex. I had first come to the US on an E2 (Investor) Visa based on A.G.'s investment in 3 Guys. This visa expired on September 12, 1983 and could not be renewed because A.G. no longer had this investment. We had an immigration lawyer, Robert Fraade working on the case and while he was putting together an application for a new E.2 Visa, based on our new investment in 3 Guys, he had suggested I get a B2(tourist) Visa as a holding operation.

Finally, in August, 1984 the new E2 application was ready to be presented. This could not be done in the US – application could only be made at a US Embassy. Because Robert Fraade had a lot of middle eastern clients who he was meeting in Nicosia, Cyprus, he asked me to meet him there at the Hilton Hotel on August 14th, 1984.

Len Clark, one of the other investors in 3 Guys, traveled with me and we met Robert Fraade as arranged. He told us to see him in the lobby of the hotel at 8.30 a.m. on August 16th. There were at least thirty people waiting in the lobby to see him and he gave everyone a numbered ticket. Len and I got tickets one and two. Fraade then led all thirty of us through the streets of Nicosia like the Pied Piper of Hamlin. When we arrived at the Embassy there was a line two blocks long and my heart sank. I thought we were going to be in line all day in the stifling heat of a Cyprus August day. But Fraade led us straight to the front of the line. He had picked up the tickets the night before and Len and I were the first two people into the Embassy. Thirty minutes later we had our visas and having paid Robert Fraade his fee of $8,000 we headed back to the hotel to see if we could get a flight to London as we both wanted to spend some time in Yorkshire with our families before going back home to the US. All the flights to London out of Larnaca Airport were booked for the next three days; we tried every alternative routing up to and including flying to Moscow, but without success. Finally, Robert Fraade called someone he knew and miraculously two seats became available on the next flight to London.

Meanwhile, back at 3 Guys, people were jumping ship at an alarming rate. Trevor Wilson, the Gubay appointed president and leader of the buyout team, resigned and went to live on the Isle of Man; he apparently had some new found wealth as he bought himself a magnificent house and a Rolls Royce and has not worked since. Next to go was John Halpin, the computer specialist, and then a real body blow was inflicted on us by Bobby Fogle, the meat and produce concessionaire, when he pulled out of all the stores on a months notice.

We brought in George Ball, the investment banker, as President of 3 Guys and hired experts in meat and produce to run these departments. Suddenly this was a very different company to the lean mean fighting machine we had inherited from A.G. and the company began to lose money. The next blow was when Winn Dixie, one of our competitors, cut their prices by 10% across the board. This price cut was aimed at Food Lion (formerly Food Town) but it hit hard at 3 Guys. We immediately lost 10% of our sales and despite an aggressive TV and newspaper advertising campaign were unable to win these customers back. We could cut prices and lose profit or leave our prices unchanged and continue to lose volume, an impossible dilemma. Under pressure from me and the other directors George Ball resigned and I reluctantly took his place as President. George was convinced we were headed for bankruptcy and if he was right I had landed myself in a very hot seat indeed.

On St. Patrick's Day, 1985 I went to Nickleby's at lunchtime and drank a few pints of Guinness. When I got home Sue was in the kitchen cooking bacon and cabbage and Deirdre Mistri was there. The phone rang and I answered it. It was my brother Michael. He hadn't called me once in the fifteen years since I had left Bradford so I knew it was something serious:
"Dad's dead" Mike said.

Making Hen's Meat

I burst into tears and said :
"I'll have to call you back".

Deirdre put her arms round me and held me tight while I sobbed. The look of anguish on her face told me that she felt my pain. I called Mike back and he told me that after dinner that day father had said he didn't feel too well and had gone to bed for the afternoon. At tea time mother, who was so ill that she was confined to the ground floor, asked John to make a cup of tea and take it up to Harold. When he went up with the tea it slowly dawned on him that father was dead. He called an ambulance and called Mike, but nothing could be done. Father had had a massive heart attack in his sleep and died very quickly. I decided to fly over to England immediately and told eighteen year old Simon I wanted to take him with me. I phoned my secretary and asked her to get on to the firm's travel agent and organise some tickets for that day's flight to London. Simon and I went to pack and the travel agent phoned to say we were booked on the 5.30 p.m. flight to Gatwick and we should check in at 4 p.m.. By now it was 3:30 p.m. so we went straight to the airport stopping only to pick up some cash from one of the 3 Guys' stores.

Before we landed at Gatwick we got the pilot to radio ahead and arrange for a car and driver to meet us. On the four hour ride to Bradford we talked about choosing a University for Simon to go to in September. He had applied to Georgetown, Vanderbilt in Tennessee, and the University of Virginia and had been accepted by all three subject to graduating from high school with a satisfactory GPA. All of Simon's classmates were planning to go to Carolina – the University of North Carolina at Chapel Hill and his girl friend Ellen had her heart set on N.C. State although she was still two years from her high school graduation. Carolina was the traditional school for Myers Park students to aspire to but I was rather pleased that Simon wanted to go somewhere different, and perhaps better; it reminded me of my choice of Carlton Grammar School when everyone else was choosing Belle Vue. The only downside was that the fees were much higher out of state.

Finally we arrived in Bradford and just before we got to the family house I got cold feet about seeing mother. I was certain she would be distraught at father's death and I didn't know what I could say to her to comfort her without breaking down myself. I decided that a few pints of good Yorkshire ale would be in order to give me some Dutch courage, so I directed the driver to the Delvers pub. Simon went into the pub to see if brother Michael was there and sure enough, he was. We transferred our bags to Michael's car boot and paid off the driver.
"You've got here quick." said Michael "There was no need to rush, there is going to be a post mortem because dad died so suddenly, so we're planning the funeral for Thursday."
Finally, I went with Simon to mother's with considerable trepidation. She behaved perfectly normally, neither she nor John seemed to be grieving. They were very matter of fact about the situation almost as if it was commonplace for your husband and father to die. There was no sign of tears and very little sign of remorse or sadness.

Simon and I spent the next few days seeing our relatives, Mike and his wife Liz and their three almost grown up children, Mark, Richard and Heather, Uncle Jack (my mother's brother) and his wife Auntie Alice. Their children Bruce and Stuart were married and living away, Bruce in Lancashire and Stuart in the Channel Islands. Stuart had a succession of wives, five in all I think. When I asked Uncle Jack why his son had got married so many times he said:
"Happen he likes wedding cake"

We went to the National Museum of Photography in Bradford city center and the Hockney Gallery in Saltaire. We visited the Bronte Museum in the parsonage at Haworth and drank in the Black Bull and the White Horse. We rode the steam railway from Haworth to Keighley and back. This line had been saved by Bob Cryer who organised the Keighley and Worth Valley Railway Preservation Society, bought the track from British Rail, bought engines and carriages from various sources and with volunteer workers ran a profitable enterprise. We hired a car and drove on the M62 to Prestwich to see Sue's parents, Rene and Reuben. As usual I

Making Hen's Meat

slipped Rene £50 when Reuben wasn't looking. He would have died rather than accept money from me.

Finally, Thursday arrived and we rode in a limousine the two hundred yards from 12 Ashwell Road to St. Barnabas Church. The church was packed with at least three hundred people. It was amazing how many people thought enough of my father to attend his funeral. Three hundred people! – I don't know thirty people and I can only think of three or four outside my family who would come to my funeral. The passing of my father was something of an event in Heaton. He had lived in Heaton for almost all of his seventy years and the whole village turned out to say farewell to him. The vicar, Rev. Hollis, spoke warmly of my father and talked about seeing his van parked outside the Delvers and Kings Arms and about him working for the Bishop. He had confirmed my father into the Church of England just a few years before his death and said that father had challenged him on matters of theology at his confirmation class.
"Who was I to argue. Harold spent much more time with the Bishop than I did".
Outside the church everyone wanted to shake hands and say how sorry they were that Harold had died. I had grown to look very much like my father and Mrs. Peebles said:
"Your father will never be dead, as long as you are alive".
The family then went to Nab Wood Crematorium and there was a short service followed by the cremation. Harold's ashes were later interred in Heaton Cemetery in the grave in which my maternal grandparents were buried.

After the cremation mother went home and Simon and I and my brothers, Mike and John, went to the Delvers where Harold had drunk every day since he was sixteen, apart from when he was away in the army. The pub was packed with people who had been at the funeral. It seemed they had all taken the day off work. At 3 p.m., closing time, the door was locked and when the police knocked on the door and they were told it was Harold Spence's funeral party they said alright. People were playing darts and dominoes and reminiscing about father and the other old Heatonians. The feeling was that this was the biggest funeral in

Heaton since Bob Nellist died. Seven years later Simon wrote a poem for my 48th birthday and this is how it goes:

7 Years Passed

*4,000 miles away
on Irelands Saint's Day
lying with girl in arms
he hears the news*

*A long way from home
at his place of birth
he returns with father in hand
brown land from the past
cousins, aunts, uncles are there
tales are told and stories remembered*

*A gardener, a sower of the earth
dim memories remain of a man
at Saint Barnabas
the vicar speaks
of a proud man
who near to the end
aware of his mortality
came closer to the divine*

*A father cries
we move on a black tide
to the hot oven of the body's end
dust to dust it is finished
all over at Nab Wood
the wake commences
at the Delvers we are locked in
a strange group of family and friends
joined together at Harold's resting place in life*

*A noise commences
of life going on
pint glasses clinking*

> and dominoes falling
> broken only by stories of time passed
>
> A drunken lot we leave sodden
> to face the night each alone
> but joined by memories
> of an afternoon passing
> in the Delvers drinking like
> Harold so many times before

Simon, Sue and I went to look at Universities and after seriously considering Georgetown finally settled on the University of Virginia. It has a beautiful campus in a little gem of a city, Charlottesville, situated on the edge of the famous Blue Ridge Mountains of Virginia. Standing on the Lawn looking at the Rotunda it is possible to think that one is at an ancient British University. Thomas Jefferson did a very fine job. Simon enrolled in the Business School with his goal a degree in Business Administration and was to start his freshman year in September, 1985.

We went for our summer vacation to Garden City, near Myrtle Beach in South Carolina. We stayed in Becky Sippe's house which she loaned to us. Ellen Barnett, Simon's girlfriend, went with us. On Monday morning the phone rang and I answered it. It was Becky Sippe. She had been at our house feeding the dog and cats when Sue's sister Carol had called from England urgently looking for Sue. Sue's mother had had a heart attack and died. Carol phoned a few minutes later and told Sue the details; in the middle of the night Rene had gone to the bathroom and had fallen off the toilet dislocating her shoulder. Reuben took her to the emergency room by ambulance and they set her shoulder and put her arm in a sling. She was discharged from hospital and sent home. Within fifteen minutes of arriving home she had a heart attack and died. We said we would come at once and we agreed that Sue, James and I would go, leaving Simon, Ellen and Dominic at the beach.

We flew from Myrtle Beach to Charlotte and that night flew from Charlotte to London. We rented a car and drove to Manchester and went straight to Aunt Hesse and Uncle Sidney's house in Prestwich. When we arrived there was a Rabbi present and everyone was praying. In the Jewish religion burial has to take place within twenty four hours of death. By the time we arrived Rene had already been buried in New Blackley Jewish Cemetery. We all stayed the night at Reuben's and the next morning Sue's sister Carol and her husband Simon returned to London. We invited Reuben to come back with us to Charlotte for a few weeks and then Sue James and I flew to Dublin for a few days as Sue needed to get a new passport at the British Embassy and both she and James needed to get E-2 Visas at the U.S. Embassy.

On the way back to Charlotte Reuben developed a terrible rash on his chest and we took him straight to hospital where he stayed for a few days before coming home with us for three weeks rest.

CHAPTER TWENTY ONE

"I went to the pictures tomorrow
I took a front seat at the back
A woman gave me a banana
I ate it and gave her it back"

Harold

Things at 3 Guys were going from bad to worse. When we took inventory in the warehouse we found we had 'lost' $1,000,000 of groceries. We called in our auditors and they sent a specialist in forensic accounting. They never discovered what had happened. I do not believe that there could have been a theft of this magnitude. My suspicion is that the inventory taken by us at the time we bought the business was over stated by $1,000,000.

A.G.'s remaining real estate holdings in North Carolina were also sold successfully. The Tyvola Road center was sold to a Texan, J. D. Sims, who converted it into an office park. Jerry Rodgers, a developer from Pittsburgh bought the North Tryon Street and Wendover Road Centers and Food Lion now occupy the Wendover Road Store and Big Lots the North Tryon Street store. U-haul bought the Albemarle Road store and turned it into their main depot for Charlotte. The center in Kannapolis and a store in Greensboro were also sold. Altogether, between real estate sales and the sale of 3 Guys A.G. collected approximately $30,000,000 on an investment of about $20,000,000 which is a great return by any standard. Due to the way in which he had arranged his affairs the tax paid on this $10,000,000 profit was just $12,000. But for him the best was yet to come. A.G. had brought his pounds into the US at a rate of $2.13 = £1 sterling. He took his money out at a rate of $1.50 = £1 sterling, so he profited very handsomely on the exchange rate variation.

Our line of credit from General Electric was a percentage of our inventory so with $1,000,000 inventory reduction we had to reduce our borrowing overnight by $800,000. I talked things over with Jim Ward, 3 Guys' accountant, and he said to me:
"Gary, it's time to take this sucker down"
We called a board meeting and there was some opposition to my proposal to put the company into Chapter XI bankruptcy but I pointed out that in our accountant's opinion we were insolvent and our attorneys advised that it was a crime to trade whilst insolvent. The vote to file for bankruptcy was unanimous.

We flew to Atlanta and told G.E.C.C. what was happening and also advised CPA 4, the landlords of our headquarters complex. We called in our attorneys, Robinson Bradshaw and Hinson, and filed in federal court for reorganization under Chapter XI in November 1985. I called George Ball the day before we filed and apologized to him; I told him he was right and I was wrong about 3 Guys' future or rather lack of a future.

It is a matter of fact that generally speaking the later the 3 Guys' store opened and the further it was from our warehouse in Salisbury the lower the sales volume and profitability. The first ten stores we opened were our best stores both for sales volume and profitability. No one has ever satisfactorily explained this phenomenon but I believe there are two principal factors. First, the opening of the initial ten stores was very much under the personal supervision of A.G. He would almost live in each store that opened, for between four to eight weeks, and only move on when the next store opened. His attention to detail meant that the managers and staff of these stores received exceptional training. The second factor is that the stores director and area managers spent less time in stores that were far distant from Salisbury. They would go there less frequently and when they did go would arrive later and leave earlier than if the store was near to home. Some of the stores, such as Fayetteville, Cary and Martinsville, Virginia were a three hour drive away. Add to this that the further away the store the higher the distribution cost and it is clear why we closed the stores furthest from H.Q. first. By the end of December we had closed twelve stores, seven in South Carolina, one in Virginia and four in eastern North Carolina. In January, 1986, we closed an additional seven stores leaving us with ten stores, all in North Carolina and all within eighty miles of Salisbury. It did seem that these ten stores which had high volumes and excellent management could form the nucleus of a successful business but they could not sustain the overhead of a central warehouse. I and three of my colleagues put together a proposal to buy the assets and leases of these ten stores for $2,200,000 plus inventory and negotiated an agreement with a cooperative, Associated Grocers, to supply the stores. Associated Grocers had a warehouse in Charlotte and served three hundred independent grocery stores. We felt that they would be able to supply us as cheaply as our own central warehouse because we proposed to 'loan' them one of our chief buyers.

No sooner had we put this proposal forward to the Bankruptcy Court than I received a phone call from Consolidated Stores of Columbus, Ohio(who trade as Big Lots) expressing interest in buying all the assets of 3 Guys. I met their representatives the next day and took them to our warehouse and gave them a look at six typical stores. They met with me and our attorney, Tom Hinson, and made a cash offer of $3,700,000 for the leaseholds and equipment in the twenty nine stores and for the equipment, but not the leasehold, in the warehouse. Additionally they would buy all the inventory wherever situated. To prove their good faith they wired $1,000,000 into our attorney's trust account and this was received before they left Charlotte. It was obvious that this offer was better for the creditors than my group's offer so I felt duty bound to clear the path for Consolidated by withdrawing the offer. Landlords' approval to Consolidated becoming their tenant was required and a few refused; there were one or two other stores that Consolidated did not want and in the end the proposal that went to the Bankruptcy Court was for Consolidated to buy twenty of the twenty nine leases. They left their offer unchanged, however, at

$3,700,000. On February 28th, 1986 the Bankruptcy Court approved the buyout offer and we closed the remaining ten stores and the warehouse and head office and terminated all employees except Jim Ward, the accountant, and a skeleton maintenance staff. Consolidated then reopened twenty of the stores under the name Big Lots and sold off the groceries from all the stores and the warehouse. They then commenced their regular business of selling general merchandise purchased at close out sales and from bankruptcies of other retailers, wholesalers and manufacturers. Many of the 3 Guys' managers and staff were hired by Big Lots. As part of the deal Consolidated were to pay me $50,000 to act as consultant for one year and this payment was approved by the Bankruptcy Judge. The payment was made to our attorney at the closing of the sale and immediately paid to me.

Following the sale to Consolidated we were able to repay GECC in full. They were very happy. They said I was the best bankrupt they had ever dealt with!

CPA4, the owners of the warehouse complex asked me if I could find a tenant for them. I approached Food Lion whose distribution center was also in Salisbury and was able to conclude a deal with then at a rent of $700,000 per annum. The fee paid to me for this letting was $42,000.

About a month after the sale to Consolidated. Sol Norfluss, President of Big Lots, called me and asked me when I was coming to work for them. I said I wasn't and he said they had paid me $50,000 and expected me to work for a year. I said he could consult me but if he wanted me to work on a regular basis he would have to pay me a salary or fees. He asked me to visit him in Columbus, Ohio, and I flew there a few days later. The upshot of the meeting was that I would work under the supervision of their Real Estate Director, Jerry Large, securing locations for them in the Carolinas and Virginia at a salary of $50,000 per annum commencing immediately. I was beginning to think that bankruptcy wasn't too bad; I had $92,000 in the bank and a job at $50,000 a year as a direct result of the bankruptcy.

My car, a 240GL Volvo, was now owned by Big Lots but they sold me it at the bargain price of $2,000 (it was worth about $10,000) and also sold me my office furniture for $1,000. I rented a serviced office on Trade Street in uptown Charlotte and was back in business in a matter of a couple of weeks.

CHAPTER TWENTY TWO

"God nivver made half a day" Harold

The saga of our immigration status continued. I had my E-2 Visa issued in Cyprus and in 1985 Sue, James and Simon had also had E-2 Visas issued in Dublin. Dominic needed an E-2 Visa so in February 1986 we flew to the nearest place with a U.S. Embassy, Nassau in the Bahamas, and Dominic was issued with his visa at the U.S. Embassy.

In the summer of 1986 the whole family took a vacation in Ireland and England. Simon had finished his freshman year at the University of Virginia and was still dating Ellen who had completed her junior year at Myers Park High School, so we took her on the trip with us. James was at Myers Park High School having moved from Charlotte Country Day and Dominic had transferred to A.G. Junior High.

We flew from Charlotte to New York and Ellen was very excited. Not only was this her first trip outside of America it was also her first time in an airplane. From New York we flew to Dublin on Aer Lingus. We were met by a driver from Murrays of Ballsbridge having hired a Mercedes from them. All our bags had been mislaid in New York so we arrived at Jury's Hotel with nothing but hand baggage. We went down to Grafton Street and bought ourselves a change of clothing.

After a couple of days in Dublin we went to Ballymaloe House in east Cork. The route we took was over the Vee and through

Ladysbridge and Castlemartyr. As soon as we arrived Simon took Ellen to explore Ballymaloe's grounds and James and Dominic went off with two of their Ballymaloe friends, Ivan and Sacha Whelan. Sue and I found Jim Whelan and he didn't take much persuading to go with us for a drink to The Goal Posts in Shanagarry and then to the Holiday Inn in Ballycotton. We found accommodation for our driver, Seamus, in a hotel across from the Holiday Inn and then he joined us for a few pints. He could really down the pints; he was what Jim Whelan described as "an impressive drinker".

The next morning we were picked up by our driver at 10:30 a.m. and headed into Cork City for the day. I noticed that our driver, Seamus, had the shakes so I told him to stop at the first pub in Midleton. I was ready for a pint myself and, while Sue and the kids wandered down the Main Street, Seamus and I made short work of three pints. Seamus was steady as a rock after these drinks and this was to be our pattern for the rest of the week. Seamus could only drive normally if he had not less than three pints and not more than five. We explored West Cork and took Ellen to Valencia Island, Ballydehob and Kinsale.

On Friday morning we flew from Dublin Airport to Leeds/Bradford Airport where we were met by a driver with a mini-bus which my brother Michael had hired for us. He took us to Haworth where Michael had booked accommodation for us at the Black Bull Hotel. The rooms were so tiny that we had to book an extra room to keep our suitcases in! When I asked Michael why he hadn't booked us in at the White Horse across the street, which was a much better hotel, he said:

"The White Horse, you're right, I meant to book you in there. Sorry but I was close, I knew it was an animal and a color"

The next day was Mike's eldest son, Mark's, wedding to Janet, who he'd been dating for years. This was the real purpose of our visit. The wedding was held at St. Barnabas Church and the reception was at a fine restaurant near Keighley. We gave them a wedding present of hand-blown glassware from Simon Pearce's studio in Shanagarry near Ballymaloe. After a couple more days visiting relatives in and around Bradford we took the train to

London where we stayed at the London Tara Hotel in Kensington. This is a first class hotel owned by Aer Lingus, the Irish airline. We often stayed there because it was well located and was a little bit of Ireland in London.

I was doing lots of deals for Consolidated and they asked me if I would cease being a salaried employee and instead became an agent for them working for fees. I agreed and pointed out that, in most cases, I would be able to obtain my fee from the property owner and Consolidated would only need to pay me when this was not possible. I passed the necessary examinations and got myself licensed as a Real Estate Broker in North and South Carolina. I moved out of the downtown offices and started operating Spence Real Estate Services from home.

By this time we had sold 810 Edgehill Road and moved to a smaller house at 616 East Kingston Avenue in the Dilworth area of Charlotte. We had vastly improved the Edgehill Road house following the fire and we sold it for $225,000 and bought the house in Dilworth for $110,000. With Simon away at University we did not need as much space and after the experience of the 3 Guys' bankruptcy we wanted to control our living expenses.

James was due to graduate from High School in 1987 but we could not get him to talk about which University he wanted to attend or what subjects he wanted to study. He was very good academically but also had a leaning towards the arts. At Charlotte Country Day School he had played the lead in a production of The Tempest and a drawing he had done won a Congressional Medal of Honor Award and was displayed for a year in the House of Representatives in Washington. At Myers Park he was enrolled in a photography class and was showing real talent. He had won two Kodak Medals of Excellence. One day he came home from school with a check from the Savannah College of Art and Design for $10,000, made payable to themselves. Representatives of SCAD had visited Myers Park and Byron Baldwin, the photography teacher, had shown them samples of James' photography. They were so impressed that they made the $10,000 scholarship award without interviewing James. It all seemed too good to be true.

Making Hen's Meat

Sue had taken and passed her Real Estate Salesman's examination and was working selling houses for Harding Real Estate. The nearest bar to us was a gay bar called Oleens and I had become an habitue. Two or three nights a week they had drag shows and I became friendly with and attracted to the transvestites. Sue used to come to the bar with me occasionally and one night she was talking to Greg, the bar manager, when he mentioned that he and his partner, Karl, were interested in buying a house. Sue successfully secured a house for them and this opened the flood gates. Sue became the realtor to Charlotte's gay community and became very successful and earned big fees. As my office was at home Sue and I reversed roles and I began to do most of the cooking. We hired Linner Locklear, one of the transvestites, to clean the house for us once a week. Linner was far and away the best house cleaner we ever had. He needed no supervision whatsoever.

In May 1987 James graduated from Myers Park High School and in the fall he commenced attending SCAD where he was enrolled to become a Bachelor of Fine Arts specializing in photography. We went to Savannah with him and fell in love with the city. It far outshines New Orleans or any other place we had ever visited in the USA. The old town was perfectly preserved with thirty Georgian squares and SCAD was housed in a series of historic buildings ranging from the old City Jail to a Masonic Temple and the Railway Station. We were to become frequent visitors to Savannah and we also discovered Tybee Island, Savannah's beach community, which was to become our vacation spot for many years to come.

I was very active for Big Lots and was securing stores in Virginia and Georgia on their behalf, as well as the Carolinas. I also did some site finding for Marci Imports, a company that sold imports from the orient, similar to Pier One. In 1987 I secured six locations for them in the Carolinas. I spent quite a lot of time with the founder of the company, Stan Atkins, who was another whirlwind like A.G. He expanded too fast, however, and was unable to supply and manage profitably all the stores he had leased. In the end Marci Imports went bankrupt and my fee payments ceased. I also did a tremendous amount of work looking for sites for a Texan developer, J. D. Sims, who had moved his operation from Dallas to Charlotte and for whom Deane Brunson had become the in house attorney. All this work came to nothing when they too filed for bankruptcy. Thank goodness I had Big Lots as a client as without them I would have had nothing.

Once again we were concerned about our immigration status because our new E-2 visas, which were related to my investment in 3 Guys, would soon cease to be valid because of the bankruptcy of 3 Guys. The bankruptcy judge had ordered me to stay in the jurisdiction during the bankruptcy, because of my position as debtor in possession, so there was no immediate panic, but certainly in the next year or two there was a need to do something. There was an amnesty for illegal immigrants which we investigated, but found we did not fall within its provisions. The problem was that we had entered the USA and lived there perfectly legally. It seemed strange that someone who had entered the country illegally qualified for a Resident Alien Card (Green Card) but we did not. Then the government announced a lottery for Resident Alien Cards. There was a quota for each country and, for Ireland, which was our last previous country of residence, the quota was four thousand. We made five separate applications, one for each family member, and to our surprise all five of our applications were chosen in the lottery so the whole family could now go through the process of actually obtaining the cards.

We had to return to Ireland to make the application and had to produce a sizeable dossier of information for all five members of the family. We all flew to Ireland on December 5th, 1987 and attended at the US Embassy and were told that our applications were approved but we had to pass a medical before being issued with the necessary paper work for admission to the USA. Our existing visas were stamped "CANCELLED WITHOUT PREJUDICE" so, temporarily, we could not return to the States. We went to the Blackrock Clinic for our medicals which were very thorough and included HIV and Aids tests. The results were not due for a week and we went to Ballymaloe House to kill time.

On our return we were all given a clean bill of health and returned to the US Embassy where we were each given a small card which we had to show the Immigration Officer at our point of entry to the USA. The Immigration Officer then had to make the decision whether or not to admit us for a temporary stay pending the actual issue of the Green Card. We returned to Charlotte on December 20, 1987 and our passports were stamped "TEMPORARY EVIDENCE OF LAWFUL ADMISSION FOR PERMANENT RESIDENCE" A few months later we all received our Green Cards and were pleased to have at last become Resident Aliens with the right to live and work in the USA indefinitely.

CHAPTER TWENTY THREE

"he doesn't know if he's on God's earth or Fuller's"   Harold

Marion Tucker who, with her husband Charles, owned Nickleby's and the Lamplighter asked me if I would pay my monthly bar bill in cash direct to her; if so she would give me a 20% discount. This was an arrangement which suited us both; Marion got cash about which her husband, Charles, knew nothing and I only had to pay $800 for a $1,000 bar tab. One day I was in the bar at Nickleby's and asked the bartender if he would cash me a check for $100. He agreed and I put my hand in my pocket for my check book only to find I had left it at home. The bartender said he would put two $50 bottles of Champagne on my bar bill and gave me $100 in cash. Later I realized that the $100 would only cost me $80 due to my 20% discount arrangement with Marion. Thereafter I was constantly drawing cash and having it put on my bar tab. If I could buy a dollar for eighty cents I was laughing all the way to the bank.

One evening Sue, Deirdre and Marion had a girls night out and went for dinner to the Lamplighter. About 10.30 p.m. they joined me in the bar at Nickleby's. For some reason Marion did not have a car and Charles was at home for the evening. I offered to drive Marion home and Sue and Deirdre left together. About 11 p.m. Marion and I left Nickleby's and as soon as we were in the car I asked her how she felt about a quick assignation. She was all for it so I took her to the Ascot Inn where they had rooms with heart shaped jacuzzis, water beds and cheap champagne. We had an

uproarious, hilarious sexual encounter and about 1 am I took Marion home. The next day the bartender at Nickleby's told me Charles was gunning for me. Apparently he had phoned Nickleby's about 11.15 p.m. the night before and asked if Marion was there only to be told she had just left with me. When I dropped Marion at 1.15 a.m, he had been watching from the front window. Marion, instead of going in through the front door, went round the back of the house and climbed in through an open bedroom window, an action which served to compound her guilt. As she did so Charles switched on the light and asked her why she had lied about going out with Sue and Deirdre when she was really on a date with me. A furious row ensued which ended with Marion telling Charles that if he mentioned the subject again she would leave him. When Marion told Sue about the event later she said:
"All I can remember is flashing lights and water beds."
There were no flashing lights.

I was worried about what Charles would say or do when he saw me and started carrying a cheese knife in my pocket for protection. I have no idea what I would have done with it if Charles had attacked me, but it comforted me when sitting at the bar at Nickleby's to put my hand in my jacket pocket and feel the knife. Finally, after about two weeks, I walked into Nickleby's and Charles was there.

"Come into the library, Gary" said Charles "I want a word with you."
When we were ensconced in the library Charles looked me in the eye and said:
"I'm going to forgive you this one time, Gary, but if I ever hear of you fucking my wife again I'm going to be quite angry."
With that we returned to the bar and had a drink together.

My eighty cents on the dollar deal was nothing compared to the arrangement Sue made with Marion. They went into business together as caterers and called themselves 'Tucker's Fine Foods'. Their food costs were zero because they took everything they needed from either Nickleby's or the Lamplighter. Even their serving dishes, table cloths and napkins came from one of the restaurants. All the food was prepared in our kitchen and delivered in Sue's wagon. Dominic worked as a server, as did James and Simon when they were home. This was a very profitable little enterprise.

March, 9th, 1989 was Dominic's sixteenth birthday and after a family dinner he went out with his friend, Mark Sippe, who was seventeen and had the use of a car. I was awakened by the phone ringing at 4 am. It was a police officer to tell me that Dominic had been arrested for possession of marijuana and was in the Mecklenburg County Jail along with his friend Mark. I laughed out loud with relief. When I first heard it was the police on the phone I thought he had been in an accident. Becky, Mark's mother, was out of town so I went down to the jail to see if I could get them both released. The arresting officer took great pleasure in showing me a little pipe with a small quantity of marijuana in the bowl which he had found in the car. I told him he ought to find something better to do with his time such as catching real criminals. They released Dominic but to get Mark released I had to go before the magistrate and convince him that I was acting in locum parentis. Our next door neighbor, Karen Combs, was an attorney and I asked her to see what deal she could get from the District Attorney. She must have either been very persuasive or owed a favor because she got the charge dismissed and the arrest expunged from the record. Dominic had to work washing up at the Dilworth Diner for about three months to pay Karen's well deserved Attorney Fee.

In May of 1989 Simon graduated from the University of Virginia. The whole family traveled up for the ceremony as did his girl friend, Ellen, and her family. The night before the graduation we went out for dinner together and gave Simon his graduation presents. We gave him a University of Virginia watch and a framed piece which a calligraphist had done up for us. I had found the piece in a one hundred year old edition of UVA's yearbook, Corks and Curls. It was about the honor of graduating from Virginia, and here it is;

> Virginia writes her highest degree on the souls of her sons.
> The parchment page of scholarship-the colored ribbon of a society – the jeweled emblem of a fraternity-the orange symbol of athletic prowess-all these, a year hence, will be at
> best the mementos of happy hours-like the withered flower a woman presses between the pages of a book for sentiment's sake.
> But –
> If you live a long, long time, and hold always honesty of
> conscience above honesty of purse;
> And turn aside without ostentation to aid the weak;
> And treasure ideals more than raw ambition;
> And track no man to his undeserved hurt;
> And pursue no woman to her tears;
> And love the beauty of noble music and mist-veiled
> Mountains and blossoming valleys and great monuments-
> If you live a very long time and, keeping the faith in all these things hour by hour, still see that the sun gilds your path with real gold and that the moon floats in dream silver;
> Then –
> Remembering the purple shadows on the Lawn, the majesty of the colonnades, and the dreams of your youth, you may say in reverence and thankfulness;
> "I have worn the honors of Honor; I graduated from Virginia."

In the summer Simon and Ellen went on a tour of Europe using a European rail pass. They visited England, Ireland, France, Switzerland and Italy. Simon had been recruited by Andersen Consulting's Charlotte office whilst at UVA, as had his friend, T.J.

Demas, who had graduated from Carolina. Simon and T.J. bought a house together at 1816 Thomas Avenue in the Plaza/Midwood area and moved in during July 1989. They rented out a room to an old school friend of James, Tim O'Boyle. In September James went back to Savannah after the summer holidays and Simon and T.J. went to Chicago to Andersen's boot camp.

A hurricane, Hugo, was heading for the USA and was predicted to make land fall at Savannah, on 21st September then turn northwards and travel up the Atlantic coast. We talked to James on the phone and he told us it was very exciting in Savannah, many people were evacuating and those who were staying were boarding up their windows and generally preparing for the worst. I insisted he come home to Charlotte well out of the way of the hurricane's predicted path and reluctantly he agreed. Hurricane Hugo made an unexpected maneuver and instead of making land fall at Savannah hit Charleston then instead of turning north barreled on inland and headed straight for Charlotte. I woke up in the middle of the night and could hear the wind shaking the windows and rushing through the trees and went downstairs, poured myself a drink, and turned on the radio. Then I discovered Charlotte was in Hugo's path and was expected to be hit at 4 am. I woke the family and told them to come into the dining room and get under the dining table. They each brought a blanket and were soon asleep again. I couldn't sleep. I was excited at the thought of seeing what it was like to go through a hurricane but I was also frightened. When the storm hit I was amazed by its ferocity. The noise was like a freight train rushing through the house. The devastation was unbelievable. I went out the front door to see what was happening. Charlotte is a city of trees and they were falling like matchsticks. I saw one fall onto one of our cars. Debris was flying through the air and I quickly went back inside. The radio station went off the air; their transmission tower had been toppled. By the time the storm had blown itself out an estimated one million trees were down.

Finally, about 9 a.m., we ventured out and the street and yards were full of trees and tree limbs, the power was out, the phones were out, the whole city had been beaten to a standstill. About 10 a.m. Tim O'Boyle arrived, he had spent two hours finding a way across the city from Simon's house. He told us a tree in Simon's yard had been blown down, narrowly missing the house. I went over to Thomas Avenue and we arranged for a guy with a truck and chain saw to cut up the tree and remove it for $80.

James went back to Savannah and I realized that I had to relocate temporarily to somewhere with power and phones so I could keep my business running. We drove north on I-77 and when we got to Exit 28, near Lake Norman, we stopped at a Holiday Inn and found that they had rooms and that everything was working, including the phones. We rented two rooms, set up our fax machine and typewriter and were back in business. The next day we went back to Kingston Avenue and took coffee, doughnuts and ice for all our neighbors. Our cat, the Phantom, ran from under a bush towards me, then ran back under the bush and towards me again. She kept doing this until I realized she wanted me to look under the bush. There were three newly born kittens. Naturally, we named the male Hugo. It was three weeks before the phones and power were restored enabling us to return to East Kingston Avenue.

By 1990 I had found over a hundred locations for Big Lots and as well as deals in North and South Carolina, I had secured sites for them in Virginia, West Virginia and Georgia. I had also visited upper New York State and reported to them on available sites. In early 1990 Jerry Large, Real Estate Director of Big Lots became elusive. I tried over and over again to speak to him but without success. Finally, he called me and told me we had been too successful at finding sites and the company had decided to call a halt to expansion as they had problems with distribution and store management to resolve before they opened any more stores. This was a body blow because my only other clients, Marci Imports and J. D. Sims & Co. had both filed for bankruptcy.

I began to feel ill again; dizzy spells and deep depression, difficulty breathing and chest pain. I figured this was all psychosomatic and related to my business problems.

Just when I was close to desperation the phone rang; it was A.G. He was in Charlotte at Arnold and Betty Benton's house, would I pick him up and take him to Kannapolis, where his last significant piece of real estate in the States was located. I picked him up ten minutes later and spent the day with him. After we had been to Kannapolis we went to Perrin Place where he had lived in Charlotte and he told me he was about to build some houses overlooking the harbor in Douglas, Isle of Man and he was going to base the design on Perrin Place. He would like me to try and get him floor plans of the Perrin Place houses and make a video to give to his architects. Finally we headed for the airport and I told him I needed a job and he said he would think about it and let me know. At the airport we hugged each other and there were tears in my eyes.

I managed to get floor plans of Perrin Place and as a house was up for sale I was able to get inside to make a video. A.G. invited me over to the Isle of Man for a few days and I took the video and plans with me. He had bought the remains of an old mill, Crogga Mill, in Santon, Isle of Man and had built a magnificent house for his new bride, Carmel, who he had met in Ireland. In the grounds was a pond stocked with trout and a five hole golf course which he had built for Carmel who was an avid golfer. Overlooking the harbor he had built an office building and shops, called Anglo International House, and his property company, Anglo International Holdings occupied the top two floors. On the ground floor was the bank which he owned, Celtic Bank.

He and his co-directors, Andrew Thomas and Peter Willers showed me the plans of a development in Cape Town, South Africa. This was a retirement community the developer of which had filed for bankruptcy and A.G. was thinking of buying the assets from the receiver. The plans envisaged four hundred houses of which two hundred had been built, in addition to central community facilities for the use of all the homeowners. A.G. said he was fairly certain he was going to buy the retirement community and needed someone to supervise the remaining building work and then manage the center. He offered me the job and I said I would have to talk to Sue but is sounded like a good idea to me. A.G. gave me £500 for the few days I had spent with him and I returned to Charlotte.

A few days later A.G. called me and said he was going to South Africa to try to finalize the deal and he wanted me to go with him. The following week I was back in the Isle of Man and going through the files on the South African development when I came across a flyer promoting the development which contained the words "Underwritten by People's Bank" It seemed to me that if the development was underwritten then when the developer went bankrupt it was up to the bank to complete all the central facilities promised by the developer. A.G. and Peter Willers were very excited when I pointed this out:
"It's all those years in America that's made you see this legal angle that we all missed" said A.G.
They called their lawyer in Cape Town who said he would check the deeds to the houses to see if there was an underwriting clause and would investigate the possibility of a class action law suit on behalf of all the residents who had been induced to buy by the words "Underwritten by People's Bank." The following week A.G., Andrew Thomas and I flew to Cape Town and on arrival we went to A.G.'s house, which he had bought as a holiday home two or three years previously. Cape Town is magnificent. It is a linear city situated between the ocean and Table Mountain. Wherever you live in Cape Town you are no more than a mile or two from the beach. We went to a restaurant and ate lobster for 28 rands each, the equivalent of about $6!! We were watching whales basking just off shore and I looked at A.G. and said:
"I don't think there is any doubt that I could live here"

We spent a week in a succession of meetings; with solicitors, with the residents, with banks, with building contractors and with the receivers and their attorneys. By Friday the deal was virtually done. All the major obstacles had been overcome and it was only a question of drawing up the final paper work. We were due to fly out on Saturday so on Friday night we went for dinner with our solicitor to finalize and formalize his instructions. Over dinner A.G. started talking about the political situation in South Africa with considerable foreboding; finally he decided not to proceed because of what he saw as an uncertain political future for South Africa. I was terribly deflated, I'd spent the whole week getting psyched up about moving there with Sue and now it was all for nothing.

On the flight back I sat in the smoking section and A.G. and Andrew Thomas sat up front. Andrew came and slipped into the seat next to me,
"I've been talking to A.G. about finding something for you to do" he said "I have come up with an idea. A.G. has £40,000,000 in cash and he wants to invest this in property in the United Kingdom. He already has property holdings valued at over £300,000,000 and these properties are generating cash faster than we have been able to re-invest. How would you like to go back to Bradford and set up your own property agency and find sites for us."
I was taken aback but said that I would consider anything and I appreciated him trying to help me. When we got back to the Isle of Man I called Sue and talked it over with her and she agreed with me that we should give it a shot. I could move over to England more or less immediately and Sue and Dominic would follow after his High School graduation in May 1991.

I asked A.G. what the deal would be and he said they would loan me the money to open an office and they had vacant space which I could occupy in a building called Stanhope House in Shipley, near Bradford. They would advance me whatever was needed including £25,000 per year for myself. I would be given 10% of the profit on every property I bought less a pro-rata share of the amount of the advances. I asked for this to be spelled out in a letter and before I left to return to the US I had the letter in my pocket.

CHAPTER TWENTY FOUR

"she's got a face like a torn clog" **Harold**

In the middle of October 1990 Sue and I flew to England and took delivery of a Volkswagen Passat Wagon that A.G. had bought for me and started looking around for somewhere for me to live temporarily. Sue was going to come and live with me in June, 1991, after Dominic had graduated High School and it was most likely Dominic would come with her, so I needed to find a house for us all. We couldn't find any suitable temporary accommodation, so it was agreed that I would move into the family house at 12 Ashwell Road and live with my brother, John, for the next six months. John was living alone because mother had become too ill for him to nurse at home. She was in a nursing home called Maylands on Parsons Road. This is where father used to garden for the Craven family.

No sooner had I settled into Ashwell Road than mother died. The funeral was at St. Barnabas Church and she was buried in the same grave as her mother and father and we also took the opportunity to inter father's ashes on top of her coffin. Mother had been ill for years and it was amazing she had lived to the age of 75. John had not worked full time for many years and was receiving disability benefit. His benefits and mother's pension provided enough for him and mother to subsist. They had no mortgage to pay because I had paid this off in 1980. It was a blessing for John that I was there now because I could share the household expenses with him.

A.G. had a small office in Walkden near Manchester where Keith Melia and two assistants and a secretary were located. They kept an eye on A.G.'s property holdings in the U.K. for him. Keith had arranged for the one roomed office in Stanhope House, Shipley to be decorated and furnished so I had a very smooth transition. I put up my shingle, Spence Realty Ltd., and had some notepaper printed and was in business. It was a strange feeling. Just me in one room with £40,000,000 to invest. Geoff Mason of Mason Owen & Partners, Chartered Surveyors, had first met A.G. when he had four stores and had been responsible for the acquisition of every store site from then on. Even when A.G. sold Kwik Save the company had retained Geoff's services and they now had over one thousand stores. Similarly he had been involved in all A.G.'s ventures overseas to a greater or lesser extent. But his main task had been investing in U.K. property for A.G. and he had built up a portfolio of shopping centers and industrial and office premises worth £300,000,000. Not wanting to in any way upset Geoff, A.G. had obtained his agreement to me opening up in Bradford. It was agreed that Geoff's imprimatur had to be on any site I found before Anglo International Holdings would buy it.

I sent out a letter to all the leading property agents in the north east and midlands describing the type of property I was looking for and emphasizing that I had the cash available. I received lots of details through the mail but only one agent came to see me, Roger Woolhouse, of Donaldson and Sons. He put one of his young surveyors, David Brackenridge, on my case and within weeks we had our first deals under contract, the purchase of two locations in Bradford which I felt could be let to a grocery discounter either Netto, new to the British market, or Kwik Save. A.G. was on holiday in South Africa but Geoff spoke to him and he approved the deals. One purchase was £1,000,000 and the other £350,000, both from Bradford Co-op. We quickly followed this up with the purchase of a small retail/warehouse complex in Saltney, North Wales, for £1,600,000. Keith Melia was sent to do a report on this property for the directors of Anglo and he described it as 'dog shit alley'. I was very pissed about this and vowed to get my revenge on Keith one way or another. As the saying goes 'every dog has his day'.

Gary Spence

When A.G. came back from South Africa another Liverpool agent, John Taylor, arranged for him to meet the managing director of Netto to discuss several deals. Geoff Mason had stood aside from any dealings with Netto because of his involvement with Kwik Save. A.G. had a very successful meeting with Netto and agreed terms to lease six stores to them. In the course of the meeting he mentioned the two sites in Bradford and asked if they wanted to lease them; they replied that they wanted to buy them and A.G. said he would get me to sign the contracts over to them in return for an agency fee of £10,000 to me and £10,000 to John Taylor. I was disappointed to have lost my first two deals but it was nice to be putting £10,000 in the bank so soon after opening up for business.

I was involved in a big deal on the Isle of Man, which involved assembling a site on which to build a Resort Village which eventually included a two hundred acre site, a one hundred roomed Radisson hotel, a state of the art leisure center, an eighteen hole golf course, a driving range, tennis courts, a multi purpose sports hall, together with garages and workshops and one hundred and fifty houses. Site assembly and obtaining planning permission took a year and a half and then A.G. set about his biggest ever building job, The Mount Murray Hotel and Country Club and Resort Village. He dammed a river to create three lakes which he stocked with fish, he bought the stock of a bankrupt nursery in Leeds and Sue and a team of laborers dug up and shipped to him thirty thousand trees which he planted on the golf course. He excavated an ampitheater to house the tennis courts and the rock he excavated was crushed in an on site crushing plant and the resulting aggregate was used as a foundation for the roads and for drainage under the golf course greens and tees. The hotel bedrooms were built to look like a group of Manx cottages in the local vernacular style. The country club and leisure center were built in the style of Baillie-Scott, the renowned arts and crafts architect who lived on the Isle of Man and built many houses there. All in all this was A.G.'s finest achievement and it paid off handsomely for him. The Isle of Man government had passed legislation that made all profits from new investment in tourism tax free for a period of ten years. They amended this law specifically at my request to include all expenditure on the golf-course and sports hall. As this tax relief could be used against all profits made by the group of companies which had made the investment in tourism A.G. saved £1,000,000 a year for ten years. He had spent £15,000,000 but after tax relief his net investment was only £5,000,000. The value of the property is probably £20,000,000 conservatively so in effect A.G. made himself £15,000,000

When I had lived in Bradford previously my favorite pub had been the Delvers but it just didn't 'fit' me anymore and I began drinking in all the pubs in Heaton and Manningham until I found one I could call home. Eventually I settled on the Melborn in White Abbey Road, a tough neighborhood that had a big Irish population. The landlord was Eamon and he hailed from County Mayo. He had made the pub a mecca for live music and he himself played the guitar and sang, mainly country and western songs. On Saturday night there was usually a rock band and on Sunday there was traditional Irish music. On Monday night musicians playing a host of instruments formed a circle and took it in turns to perform. On Thursday night the Topic Folk Club, now run by Phil and Finola Hingstone, met at the Melborn and Friday was open mike night. There was a house band who played rock 'n' roll and usually performed on Friday and Saturday nights and Sunday afternoons. This pub became my home from home and if I had too much to drink, which was often, I would phone my brother, John, and he would come in a taxi and drive me home.

I found a house I liked, 8 Rossefield House, Park Drive, Heaton, at a price I liked even better, £80,000 and I got Sue to fly over to look at it. She liked it too so we went ahead and bought it. I put all my own money - £30,000 - into the house and A.G. loaned me the other £50,000. Sue and Dominic had sold the house on East Kingston Avenue and were living temporarily at Becky Sippe's until Dominic graduated. I put John to work to look after the garden because I knew that once I stopped living with him his disability pension would not be enough for him to live on.

In May Dominic graduated from Myers Park High School and Sue and he moved to Bradford. He could not get into an English University without 2 'A' level G.C.E's so he enrolled at Bradford College to study 'A' level Economics and History. Because he wanted to try to pass the exams in one year he entered the revision course, which was really designed for people who had failed the exams after a full course of study. James also came over from Savannah for the summer and he and Dominic spent a lot of time together in the Yorkshire Dales. For James' 22nd birthday on August 14, 1991 we took all the family to the Bronte Birthplace in Thornton, a suburb of Bradford. This restaurant had been opened in the house where the Bronte family had lived before moving to Haworth. Deane Brunson was over from the States and Sue's father had come from Manchester.

As well as bringing our furniture from the States we also brought two cars, not because they were valuable but because they were almost worthless. The cars were my 1983 Volvo, which had one hundred and twenty thousand miles on it but was running perfectly and Dominic's 1984 Peugeot 505 which also had high mileage but was running well. It was quite a performance getting them through customs and registering them in England. We had to have some minor modifications made to them to comply with British law including having the headlights re-aimed. The Volvo became Sue's car and Dom kept the Peugeot .

I was shocked on returning to Bradford to discover that my childhood heritage had been destroyed, a victim of the demolition contractor's ball and chain. The Baptist Church and Sunday School had been demolished and my first school, St. Barnabas, was also gone. Heaton's village hall, St. Barnabas Hall, had been demolished and so had Carlton Grammar School. Busby's Department Store had fallen victim to the redevelopment craze, along with Kirkgate Market, the Central Library and the Mechanics' Institute. It was as if every landmark of my childhood had been eradicated without protest; I felt very let down by Bradford and Bradfordians.

Making Hen's Meat

On the positive side Bradford's oldest building, the Paper Hall, which had been derelict for generations, had been lovingly restored and Undercliffe Cemetery had also been saved from a property developer by a grass roots campaign. The Alhambra Theater had been restored and improved and the National Museum of Photography, Film and Television had opened in an office building across the street from the Alhambra. The Little Germany district of Bradford, including the Civic Theater, was in course of restoration and Salts Mill had been saved by the efforts of Jonathan Silver and had become the home of the largest collection of David Hockney paintings in the world as well as an active business and retail center. Finally, the Wool Exchange had been converted to retail use, and its demolition averted.

As the year progressed I bought more properties in Smethwick, Wickford, London, Stoke on Trent, Whitefield, Leeds and Bradford, and became heavily involved in preparing plans for the refurbishing of these properties. I appointed Trevor Waller of Waller & Partners to do the architectural work on the properties I had bought. Trevor had been with Arndale at the same time as John Fell and I back in the 1960's. His wife was called Maureen and was a former beauty queen. Trevor and Maureen and Sue and I often went out for dinner together, usually at Trevor's expense. We became particularly fond of a restaurant in Bingley called Christopher's.

CHAPTER TWENTY FIVE

" he's only as tall as a couple of piss-pots" **Harold**

In May of 1992 Sue went back to the States for James's graduation from SCAD. Becky Sippe went with her from Charlotte to Savannah. James was to receive a Bachelor of Fine Arts Degree but because most of the professors and lecturers were on strike there was no official ceremony. Some of the students and lecturers got together and organized an alternative ceremony in which James participated. The lists of graduates and prize winners were in the Savannah News and Becky Sippe noticed that James had won the award for Outstanding Student in Photography.

James decided after graduation that he would like to give England a try so he sold his Audi 5000 and with the proceeds bought himself a ticket to London. He quickly got a position as a freelance photographer for the Bradford newspaper, the Telegraph and Argus, but this did not provide sufficient income for him and he started looking around for a full time job. He applied for a job in Edinburgh printing black and white photographs at Quantum Labs. He was an excellent printer, having worked in his vacation for Quality Chrome in Charlotte and having helped to run the photo lab in Savannah. He traveled to Edinburgh for the interview and Sue went with him. He got the job and they started looking for a flat. Rents in Edinburgh were high and it soon became apparent that James would not be earning enough to rent a flat without a room mate. I had heard that in Scotland there were no GCE exams consequently the requirement to have a pass in two

Advanced level subjects for admission to university did not apply. I therefore suggested to Sue that she check out the universities in Edinburgh to see if Dominic could be enrolled based only on his American High School Diploma. Sue found that Napier University would accept Dominic in principle so he caught the first plane to Edinburgh and joined Sue and James. He enrolled in a course in Estate Management at Napier University and while he was in Edinburgh he and James found a flat and signed a lease. Unfortunately the company James was working for fell on hard times and in December his job was eliminated so he returned to Bradford to live with Sue and I. Dominic remained in Edinburgh for three years.

I was asked by A.G. to play a more active role in managing his U.K. properties and with this in mind set up a company called Land & Property Management Services (UK) Ltd. owned jointly by Geoff Mason and I. We hired the existing employees in Walkden, Manchester and I began to spend a day a week there. By 1993 I was very busy indeed. I was going to the Isle of Man a day a week to assist A.G. with the Mount Murray development and was in Walkden one day a week. In addition I attended Anglo International board meetings once a month in a consultative capacity. We also had a monthly meeting at Geoff Mason's office in Liverpool to review all the work he was doing in leasing, rent reviews, purchases and sales on A.G.'s behalf. My role had been expanded so that as well as being responsible for the day to day management of all the U.K. properties I was also responsible for the project management of all the new building work which was running at the rate of about £10,000,000 per annum. To make things easier for me I got A.G. to agree that I could switch architects and began using Waller & Partners of Bradford for all the work on his U.K. projects.

When I traveled to the Isle of Man I flew either Jersey European from Leeds/Bradford or Manx Airlines from Manchester. If there were two or more of us flying we would use A.G.'s plane and flew out of Blackpool. We had hired the Sports Turf Research Institute from Bingley near Bradford to design the golf course and one of their architects, Dewar Wishart, used to fly over to the Isle of Man with me most weeks. The fare to the Isle of Man was very expensive and for many years Manx Airlines had enjoyed a monopoly and although Jersey European had started flying two or three routes these were from places Manx did not service. We realized that the only obstacle to the success of the Mount Murray Hotel would be the high cost of flying to the island. We needed to be able to offer a package that included airfare. Accordingly I had discussion with both Manx Airlines and Jersey European but the only discounts they would consider were for last minute flights, when they would be flying with empty seats, or if we chartered months in advance. This was obviously not satisfactory so we began to investigate running our own airline to service the hotel. We discovered it was possible using Shorts Commuter Aircraft to fly from England to the Isle of Man for £20 and make a profit. Manx were charging over £100 return at a time when flights to the U.S. were available for £200 return. At this time I was well known to Manx radio and the local newspapers so we had no difficulty getting maximum publicity about our proposed airline. Manx Airlines were suddenly chasing me, and they offered us discounts that made it unnecessary to go into competition with them.

On February 26, 1993 Sue and I went to Paris for four days to celebrate my forty ninth birthday. We went on a cheap package tour and soon found out why the price was so low. The so called 'Paris Airport' our flight landed at was just across the channel and we had a two hour bus ride to get to Paris. We stayed in a very pleasant little hotel in Montmartre and spent four days walking around Paris. We went to the Louvre and to Versailles and of course we explored the Left Bank; we drank and dined and had a good time. We had some very good food and some terrible food. In one bistro the waiter didn't speak any English and with my schoolboy French, now more than a little rusty, we had difficulty with the menu. I ordered what I thought was sausage only to be presented with a sack filled with fat and entrails and Sue ordered what she thought was pork and got pigs feet. We paid the bill and left without eating.

When I came back I went to see my doctor, Doctor Bowring, to get my prescription for Ativan.

"This practice no longer prescribes Ativan or any of the benzodiazepines" declared Bowring.

I felt panic and fear building in me as I stuttered

"Why not?'

"They have been found to be addictive and, between doses, patients are in constant withdrawal and feel dizzy and sick. Patients are starting law suits against doctors who prescribe Ativan for them and our malpractice insurers will no longer cover us unless we stop prescribing."

"I've been on these or similar drugs for twenty years" I said "If you cut me off, I'll commit suicide"

"I won't cut you off suddenly I'll reduce the doseage and taper you off over a couple of months and I'll send you for some therapy"

He sent me to The Bridge Project and I spent an hour with Ian Fuller every week from March 18th to July 8th. At Easter we went to Whitby for a few days with James and Dominic and on our last day I quit taking Ativan. Within a few days I was feeling very ill indeed. Not only did I feel dizzy but there was a whirring in my brain as if a video had been put on fast forward. I felt as if my brain was trying to process all the information it had received in the preceding twenty years. I could not stop this brain activity for long enough to catch hold of a single thought. I told Ian at the Bridge Project how I felt and he said I must see my doctor right away. To my surprise Dr. Bowring was most sympathetic and prescibed me a non-addictive tranquiliser.

Most of A.G.'s building work in the U.K. had been carried out by David Ashton of Ashton & Co. Since I had become responsible for new building projects I had introduced a new bidder, F&R Construction, and they had beaten Ashton hands down on every job they bid. They were currently building two developments on Edge Lane, Liverpool and a retail park in Walkden for A.G. and carrying out a major refurbishment on one of my projects, Wira House in Leeds. The only project Ashton was left with was the refurbishment of the old Arndale Center in Walkden and he had totally sub-let that contract and was working for a fixed fee. The job was running behind schedule and when the final certificate was issued by Land & Property Management, the client, Anglo International, deducted the penalty specified in the contract for late completion and Ashton received nothing. His sub-contractor started a law suit against him and he called in the receiver.

James had tried hard to get a job in Bradford but nothing suitable could be found so on April 29th he returned to the States to stay with Simon until he got on his feet. At the end of May Simon and Ellen flew to Puerto Rico to meet friends with whom they were going on a sailing trip. On the first night Simon and Ellen were in the old town of San Juan watching the sunset when Simon went down on his knees and proposed marriage which Ellen accepted. They set the wedding date for April 23rd, 1994 and Simon invited me to be his best man.

On one of my regular trips to the Isle of Man I became ill on the flight from Leeds/Bradford airport. I had a pain in my chest and felt as if I were choking. I couldn't seem to get my breath. It was a full blown panic attack and was accompanied by a terrible dread of flying. Fortunately one of the air hostesses was a trained nurse and she took me to the back of the plane and let me lie down across two seats. She loosened my tie and undid my collar and held my hand while she directed me to take slow deep breaths. When we arrived at the Isle of Man they let me get off the plane first and there was an attendant waiting with a wheel chair. I felt a lot better as soon as the plane landed and declined the wheel chair but as I walked towards the terminal it dawned on me that in a few hours I would once again have to board a plane for the return journey and a feeling of dread enveloped me again. Chris Barr, a solicitor who worked for Anglo International, met me off the flight and was very concerned when I told him what had happened. Micky Cannell, a property manager with Anglo, arranged for me to see her doctor and he gave me a thorough examination and said he believed I had had a panic attack. He gave me a few tranquilizers and suggested I take a couple before my return flight.

The following week I was driving on the M-62 motorway to see Geoff Mason in Liverpool when I got caught in a traffic jam. I experienced exactly the same symptoms as on the airplane. I felt like a rat caught in a trap. Everywhere I looked there were stationary cars and there was no escape. I seriously considered abandoning my car and 'escaping' on foot. Fortunately the traffic started moving again and I took the first exit and started looking for a hospital. I phoned Geoff and told him I couldn't make it to his office and gave up looking for a hospital and made my way home on the old roads not daring to get back on the motorway. For the next few months I got Sue to drive me around as somehow I felt a little better if I was not alone in the car. We tried driving on motorways but whenever we did I had a panic attack so we had to take the old slow routes.

I was now in real trouble. My job required me to look for sites and visit building projects which meant a lot of driving. I also had to go regularly to the Isle of Man by plane. Geoff arranged for me to be excused from attending board meetings but I still had to fly at least twice a month in connection with the Mount Murray project. I used A.G.'s plane whenever I could and I felt much better in this small private plane. If the plane was not available I would fly from Blackpool instead of Leeds/Bradford. This reduced the flying time from forty minutes to twenty minutes and was just tolerable. I went to see Dr. Bowring and asked him to refer me to a psychiatrist. He referred me to Dr. Amal Beaini and I had my first appointment on January 10, 1994. He was very understanding and did not seem surprised by my symptoms. He did not engage in psychoanalysis preferring to treat the symptoms with medication. After experimenting with various drug combinations we finally settled on Prozac, Trazadone and Librium. I was still drinking excessively and was in the Melborn every night. I only seemed to feel well under the combined influence of the drugs and alcohol.

In March, 1994, Dominic came to Bradford for his 21st birthday party and we had a dinner for him at the Dubrovnik Hotel. All the family were there and so were Gordon and Maureen, who were the landlord and landlady of the Beamsley, a pub on Heaton Road that we frequented.

In April we all flew back to the States for Simon and Ellen's wedding. I was very anxious about being best man although Simon had assured me I wouldn't have to make a speech. The combination of flying and fear of the wedding put me in a terrible state by the time we arrived in Charlotte. Peter Thornton came over for the wedding and stayed with Becky Sippe. The rehearsal dinner on April 22, was held at the Crossroads Restaurant on Providence Road and, as promised by Simon, there was no pressure for me to make a speech. Chuck Sullivan spoke and recited one of his poems and Donald and Debbie who were good friends of Simon and Ellen also read a long poem they had written. Sue, who was tipsy, made a nice little speech. The wedding was held at Myers Park Methodist Church. I had to stand at the front of the church with Simon to await Ellen's arrival and I had a dizzy spell. The ceremony lasted about forty minutes but is seemed like an eternity to me. I was close to having a panic attack and was sweating profusely. After the ceremony I was outside the church when I saw our friends Wade and Darrell, who had traveled from Richmond, Virginia for the wedding. I rushed towards them but when I was about ten yards away I choked up and felt as if I couldn't breathe. I turned around and struggled back to Sue. It took about ten minutes to calm me down. Things were getting serious if the sight of two old friends could put me into a panic.

We rode on a hired double decker bus to the reception at The Reid House in Matthews. The reception was held outdoors and the weather was perfect.   We danced and talked and enjoyed wonderful food.   Simon and Ellen went to Ireland for their honeymoon and stayed at the Park Hotel in Kenmare and Ballymaloe House.   We went back to England and joined Simon and Ellen at Ballymaloe for the last few days of their honeymoon.

CHAPTER TWENTY SIX

"correcto profundo, as they say in Wales" **Harold**

In February, 1995 Sue and I went to Hackness Grange for my birthday. We had grown to love this little hotel situated close to Scarborough. While it wasn't up to Ballymaloe standards it was very pleasant and relaxing. There was a lake in front of the house and after breakfast we would feed the ducks then collect a couple of golf clubs from the house and have a game of pitch and putt. In the afternoons we would go to Scarborough or Whitby or walk by the river in Forge Valley.

I was still operating out of the Shipley offices and Sue was working virtually full time as my unpaid secretary. I was spending more and more time in Walkden where we now had a staff of six managing A.G.'s properties. I came under a lot of pressure from Geoff Mason and Peter Willers to move to Walkden and finally made the move on April 18, 1995. A.G. owned a row of old mill cottages on Bolton Road, Walkden and I got Peter Thornton to tart one of these up and we moved in; we were only two minutes walk from the office. Peter had agreed to supervise a job for me in Liverpool and he moved in next door so that he would only have a thirty mile journey to work, rather than a sixty mile drive from his home in Yorkshire. We kept the house in Bradford and spent the weekends there and occasionally would spend a Monday or Friday at the Shipley office, until we finally closed it completely.

Our project manager, John Lambert, had caused me a lot of grief. He just didn't seem able to work with builders and architects to get

Making Hen's Meat

projects completed in a timely fashion. His site meetings would last eight hours and although his minutes and reports were excellent he just lacked that certain something that I possessed that made people want to please you. I never once lost my temper with John but he had seen me really lose it with other people on more than one occasion. On my first day in Walkden John called me on the intercom.
"I'm not feeling well, I'm going home" he said
"What's wrong with you" I enquired
"I think I've got malaria" he said.
Malaria, in Manchester, I didn't know whether to laugh or cry. I never saw John Lambert again – he obviously didn't like the idea of having me in the same office as him.

In May Dominic graduated from Napier University with a B.Sc. in Estate Management and I offered him a job working in Walkden for Land & Property Management which he accepted. I asked him if he would like a trip to the States as a graduation present.
"I'd rather have a week in Amsterdam with you than a month in America on my own" he said.
I didn't feel like flying so we booked on a ferry from Hull in Yorkshire to Rotterdam. When we arrived in Rotterdam there was a bus to take us to Amsterdam but I said to Dom
"Let's take a taxi"
We got into a Mercedes taxi and I said to the driver
"Take us to Amsterdam"
"You can't afford a taxi all the way to Amsterdam" he said
"Oh, yes I fucking can" I replied.
So off we went and an hour and a half later we were walking towards the red light district having dumped our bags in the hotel. On our way towards Dam Square we were passing an Irish pub when who should we see but Peter Headland, who was our new project manager – John Lambert's replacement. He had told me he was going to Paris for the weekend, obviously he was embarrassed to say he was going to Amsterdam where both marijuana and prostitution were legal.
"Good morning, Peter" I said without breaking my stride.
Soon Dom and I were in Dam Square one side of which is occupied by the Hotel Krasnapolski.

"That's where we'll stay if we come here again" I said to Dom.

On the way from Dam Square to the red light district we stopped in a tiny pub which we named the Smallest Pub in the History of the World. We bought beers and took them to a sidewalk table. As I sat there a feeling of all consuming peace enveloped me; a feeling I've had only a few times in my life. I felt totally and utterly relaxed; all my cares and woes had disappeared in a twinkling.
"I'm home at last" I said
"I know exactly what you mean" said Dominic.
We sat there in silence drinking our beer; although we were silent there was a deep feeling of communion between us.

Why is it that certain places make you feel instantly happy and others have either no effect on you whatsoever or a negative effect. I seem to feel at my best in cities on the coast with a harbor or a river and I am always happier on the east coast than the west. In England I feel at home in Whitby, Scarborough or Bridlington, but not in Blackpool, Morecambe or Grange-over-Sands. In Scotland, Edinburgh entrances me whilst Glasgow impacts me in a negative way. In Ireland I am most happy in Dublin and Cork. In the States I feel great in New York, Baltimore, Wilmington, Savannah, St. Augustine and New Orleans, but Los Angeles and San Francisco leave me cold. I think it's the quality of the light that determines where I feel in harmony with the world.

After a few beers we walked into the red light district and stopped at a café that sold marijuana . We were amazed to have a menu brought to us which described the types of marijuana, their country of origin and had a sample of each weed attached. While Dom smoked a joint I went into a nearby second hand bookstore and browsed for half an hour. We walked around for a while and then agreed to split up so we could sample the delights of the red light district without any embarrassment. We agreed to meet up in a biker bar called Excalibur which we had spotted while walking around. I was wandering around a produce market when I spotted Dom out of the corner of my eye. I called out to him .
"Dom, come here and have a look at these magnificent parsnips"

"Right this minute, I've got something more important on my mind" said Dom.

On September 1st, 1995, James and my friend, the poet, Chuck Sullivan, arrived at Manchester Airport. Chuck had never been to England or Ireland, the country his forefathers had hailed from, so I had organized this little trip as my way of saying thank you for the Juggler on the Radio. We went straight to Wira House in Leeds where we had an opening party planned for Monday night. We had received from James over a hundred of his photographs and these were on display down the main corridor of the building. I wanted James to identify the location of each picture so we could prepare a brochure before Monday. I think James was taken aback by the quality of the exhibition, never had so much of his work been hung in one location.

On Monday night we had our opening party and from a business point of view it was a good night and a bad night: the good part was that we finalized deals to lease over 7,000 sq. ft. of space in Wira House; the bad part was that David Ford of F&R Construction told me he was filing for bankruptcy the next morning at 9 am and work on all the sites would have to cease. He was building for us in Leeds, Manchester and Liverpool on seven separate projects. James' exhibition was a great success and a few days later I received a letter from Roger Suddards the Deputy Lieutenant of Yorkshire which read as follows:

> *"My dears*
> *What a very good exhibition of James's photographs. We were very keen on the photographs and thought they were excellent and we liked the idea of the exhibition in your splendid new premises.*
>
> *I am so glad to see that you have settled firmly in the UK. It was good also to see that all James's photographs were of the UK!*

It was so nice to be with you and the family and I congratulate you on having a first class son with real artistic talent. He did a splendid job.

Many thanks.

Yours sincerely,

Roger.

David Ashton had got over his bankruptcy and had started up again as Crowngrade Construction. He was carrying out a couple of small jobs for us and I phoned him and asked him if he would like to take over all F&R's projects. I arranged to meet him and his right hand man, Dave McGibbon, at my office in Walkden at 7 am the next morning. Ashton asked me to bring F&R's project manager to the meeting as he planned to hire him. The next morning we all met at my office and laid out plans for keeping the jobs going. All F&R's site agents were hired by Ashton so there was no break in the construction process, and we hand delivered a letter to David Ford terminating all of F&R's contracts.

James and Chuck teamed up with my old friend, Johnny Milnes and spent a few days touring Yorkshire. We then went to Edinburgh for a few days and saw all the sights. At the weekend we drove through North Wales and had a night at St. Tudno's Hotel in Llandudno, then caught the ferry at Holyhead for Dun Laoghaire in Ireland. Chuck was very excited to be sailing to the land of his forefathers and as we sailed into Dun Laoghaire the most magnificent double rainbow appeared in the sky. Chuck and I were both choking back tears; it was a very poignant moment. The next morning I hired a car and took Chuck on a one day tour of Dublin; we went to the US Embassy where Chuck left a copy of his latest book of poems "Longing for the Harmonies" for the Ambassador, Jean Kennedy. Then we went to Malahide and Howth Head and from there to Glasnevin Cemetery where we paid homage at the republican plot and again at Brendan Behan's grave. From there we took a drive through the Phoenix Park and then went to the G.P.O. and Trinity College. Finally, we went to

Making Hen's Meat

St. Patrick's Cathedral and then had a drink in the Stag's Head and Neary's and Davy Byrne's and returned to the Burlington Hotel in time for dinner.

The next morning we drove to Ballymaloe House where we had rooms booked at Darina Allen's Cookery School. The following day we set off to visit the City of Cork but as we were driving though Midleton we spotted Dr. Derry McCarthy crossing the street. When he heard that Chuck was a poet he insisted on taking us to lunch at Carrigtwohill Castle. First he had to deal with the dozen patients waiting to see him. He walked into the waiting room and said.
"Good morning, how are ye all?"
"Fine Doctor"
"I'm well Doctor"
"Fine"
"Well, so I am "
'I'm fine Doctor"
"I'm well"
"Well then" said Derry, "If ye are fine and well, ye can all feck off".

We never did get to Cork that day. After lunch in Carrigtwohill Castle we came back to Derry's house and drank whiskey while Chuck read poems. Derry made a phone call and arranged for Chuck to meet a poet friend of his in Cork the following day. The next day we did get to Cork and while Chuck had his meeting with the poet I went to Fallon's Bookshop on Oliver Plunkett Street and bought an armful of books about Ireland or by Irish writers to give to Chuck. Then we headed for Dingle where we stayed at the Sceilig Hotel. On the way back to Dublin we spent the night in Adare, surely the prettiest village in Ireland. Then it was back to England and home to America for Chuck and James.

In February, 1996 for my fifty second birthday Sue took me to the Sharrow Bay Hotel in the Lake District. We stayed in a house in the grounds but ate dinner in the hotel. The food was magnificent but we found the décor to be overdone, it was all gilt and ormulo, but very gay as it should have been for the owners and, as far as we could tell, all the staff were gay themselves.

I was still having panic attacks despite the medication prescribed by Dr. Beaini. I was also constantly running short of breath and having frequent chest pains. Finally I made an appointment to see a heart specialist at the Yorkshire Clinic, Dr. Chris Morley, on March 15th, 1996. After a series of tests he diagnosed me with cardiomyopathy with significant congestive failure. The ejection fraction of my heart which should have been 60% was down to 30%. My cholesterol and triglyceride levels were very high. He prescribed Ramipril and Digoxin and Frusemide. As there was no other obvious cause he told me the cardiomyopathy was the result of excess intake of alcohol and I needed to quit or cut down to no more than two or three units a day.

On March 22nd Sue's sister, Carol, called to say she had just had a phone call from Reuben to say he had fallen two days previously and could not get up. He had just managed to crawl to the phone. Sue and I went round to his house which was only a twenty minute drive from the Walkden office and after talking to Carol again agreed to get an ambulance and have him taken to the Yorkshire Clinic. The doctors said he had badly sprained his ankle and had Pagdets Disease, a common ailment amongst older people, which was a degenerative bone disease and he was suffering from dehydration. He stayed in the clinic for a week and then in a nursing home for two weeks recuperation. On discharge from the nursing home we brought him to John's house at 12 Ashwell Road. We had converted the front ground floor room to a bedroom for him, and as there was a bathroom on that floor he would not have stairs to climb. We knew he would not be able to live by himself any longer and felt that John and he would be good company for each other and we would be able to see him on the weekends. His house in Manchester was put up for sale.

I got a call from James, who was working in a photo-lab in Charlotte, to say he wanted to go to graduate school to get a Master's Degree in Art History. He wanted to teach at a college or university and could not do so without a Masters Degree. He wanted to know if I would finance this venture. I told him I thought he should come to England to do his Master's, he could stay with us so the only expense would be the fees. Furthermore, he could get the degree in one year in England instead of the two years it would take in the States. He applied by mail to Leeds University and Manchester University and was accepted by both. He opted for Manchester with a course commencement date of September, 1996.

On July 4th, 1996 Simon and Ellen and Ellen's parents, Bobby and Gina arrived in London for a two week trip to England, Scotland and Ireland. I had taken a six seat station wagon to London for them to use and I had a cab driver meet them with it at Gatwick Airport. After a couple of days in London they came to Bradford for a few days. We had a party in a restaurant out in the wilds near Haworth to celebrate our thirtieth wedding anniversary and all the family were there. As a surprise I gave Sue a Toyota MR6 sports car which had been bought with Sue's share of the proceeds from the sale of her fathers house. Then Sue and I, Simon and the Barnetts went to Scotland where we celebrated our anniversary again. Simon and the Barnetts took the ferry from Stranraer to Larne and then drove down to Dublin and to Ballymaloe House. Sue and I flew to Ireland on July 14th and spent a couple of days at Ballymaloe with them.

James came to enroll at Manchester University and we rented a house for him on Bolton Road, Walkden next door to the house we occupied. In November Sue went to Charlotte to visit Simon and Ellen and Dominic and I went for a week to Amsterdam. This had become a second home and over a two year period we made about ten trips there and always stayed at the Hotel Krasnapolsky.

I had managed to cut down my drinking a little and when I had an echo test in October the ejection fraction had improved from 30% to 50%. I stupidly went on a real bender as far as drinking was concerned. I was drinking at lunch times and most nights Dom and I would end up in Bradford at the Beamsley or the Melborn, leaving Sue and James in Manchester. This drinking pattern was asking for trouble so far as my heart was concerned but I was running wide open and drinking more than ever.

Dominic met a girl called Marina in the Melborn and took an immediate liking to her. She was twenty six and had been previously married. She had three beautiful daughters who were being raised by her mother in Hull. Her mother was Irish and he father was from Somalia. Her grandfather had been the Chief of Police in Mogadishu. Marina was a heroin addict and she was in the government methadone program. This permitted a doctor to prescribe methadone, a synthetic form of heroin, to a registered drug addict. Most doctors did not prescribe methadone as a matter of principle, but there was a doctor in Bradford who did. Marina lived in Bradford because both heroin and methadone were freely available. When she was drugged up, which was a lot of the time, Marina could be a right royal pain in the arse, but when she was 'normal' she was an amusing and vivacious companion. I could see how Dominic was attracted to her. She moved in with us and would travel about between Manchester and Bradford with us. She often used to come into the office and eat lunch with Dominic. In December Simon went to Europe on a business trip and came to England to visit with us for a long weekend. He tried to like Marina, but like James could see she would only be trouble in the end for all of us, especially Dominic.

At Christmas Sue, James and I went to Amsterdam and on December 27 Sue and James flew to Athens to do some research for James's dissertation. He needed in particular to visit the cemetery at Kerameikos. They had a successful trip visiting the cemetery and also the National Museum and the Acropolis Museum.

CHAPTER TWENTY SEVEN

"it looks as if a dog's been scratching" Harold

In January of 1997 I asked Dominic to leave Land & Property Management and find a job elsewhere. This was at the prompting of Geoff Mason who didn't like my son working with me. As both Geoff's sons were with him in Mason & Partners I never understood the logic of this but had little or no choice but to go along with it. I spoke to an old acquaintance, Robert Allen, who was the senior partner in the Bradford office of Eddison's Commercial, and he interviewed Dominic and gave him a job. Soon after Geoff Mason and A.G. parted company after a thirty year association.

Dominic and I had persuaded Marina to seek treatment for her addiction and I arranged with Dr. Beaini for her to be admitted to the Harrogate Clinic where he was medical director. She was admitted on January 12th and was there for three weeks. At first the treatment seemed effective but after a while it was obvious she was drugging again. We had several episodes when she overdosed and had to be rushed to the emergency room of the Bradford Royal Infirmary.

There was a strict rule laid down by A.G. that competitive bids had to be obtained for anything bought on his behalf. This ranged from pencils for use in the office to multi million pound building contracts. There were no exceptions except with his specific consent.

One day John Peers phoned me and said that the cost of fitting out a small shop in Acton looked high. We had paid David Ashton £15,000 for this work. John asked me if I had obtained prices. I said I was almost certain we had but would have to check with Damon

Matthews, who was our quantity surveyor. I asked Damon and he said he hadn't got prices as it was unnecessary, Ashton had won a contract to carry out a major refurbishment of a shopping center in Wickford and the work in Acton had been carried out at the same rates as the work in Wickford. Damon was confident that the price was very competitive. This was a good explanation and I should have told John Peers what Damon had told me. Instead I asked Damon to fake a bid list for me to send to John Peers. He refused. So I asked Terry Gill at Waller & Partners to fake a list of bids. He refused. Foolishly on March 13, 1997 I had Sue type up such a list on Waller & Parners notepaper showing Ashton as the low bidder and had this faxed to John Peers. John was unconvinced and asked me to send him all the original bids. The game was up and I told John what I had done. Half an hour later A.G. came on the phone and said:
"I think its time for you to go the same way as Geoff Mason"
"Are you telling me I'm sacked?" I asked
"I suppose I am" he replied.

There was nothing else he could do . I would have done the same. Strictly he couldn't sack me because I owned the company but all he had to do was cease giving me any work and I would be out of business in next to no time. I told Sue what had happened and she said
"What are we going to do?"
I thought about this for a micro second and replied
"We are never going to change his mind so there is no point in thinking we can tough it out. I think we should pack up and leave now"
I phoned the house and asked James to bring an empty suitcase round and we packed our personal possessions and drove to Bradford. John Peers phoned my mobile and asked me and Sue to meet him at the office in Walkden at 9 am the following day.

Sue, Dom and I went to the Melborn that night and got drunk. I was very worried. I had no money and didn't know where I was going to get a job. Additionally A.G. owned the house in Walkden, and had a mortgage on the house in Bradford. I woke up about 2 am with chest pain and having difficulty breathing. I woke Sue up but she said
"Go back to sleep, Gary, you can see a doctor tomorrow"

"The way I feel right now, Sue, there may not be a tomorrow," I said "I need to be in hospital."
Sue phoned the Yorkshire Clinic and they woke up Dr. Morley who said I should be admitted immediately. Sue drove me to the hospital and I was put in a room with a window into the nurses' station. The duty doctor came to see me and gave me a thorough examination and hooked me up to a heart monitor. Sue phoned John Peers' house on the Isle of Man to tell him we wouldn't be able to see him but his wife said he had flown over the night before and was already in Manchester.

Dr. Morley came to see me in the morning and gave me an echo test. My ejection fraction was down to 12% and there was considerable dilation of the heart muscle. He told me I was lucky to be alive. He prescribed a combination of Ace inhibitor, diuretic and Digoxin. I received a phone call from John Peers asking me to return the company car and mobile phone by the next day, Saturday, and to vacate the two houses on Bolton Road by the following Tuesday. David Brackenridge called me to say that he had heard from Larry Grayson, the janitor at Wira House, Leeds, that he had been told by Anglo that I was no longer allowed on the property and the locks were to be changed. I also heard that the locks had been changed at the Walkden offices. I did not even have a key to the offices as we had 24 hour security and they let me in and out after hours. It seemed that Anglo were over-reacting, but I discovered the reason; they had found a totally empty filing cabinet in my office and assumed that, for whatever purpose, I had 'stolen' the files. In fact on A.G.'s instructions the files which had belonged to a former employee, Phil McPartland, had been sent to Ken McAvoy, Anglo's consulting engineer, in Dublin. James and Dom took the car back as requested and moved everything out of the Bolton Road houses and brought it to Bradford. The only person from Anglo (apart from John Peers and Peter Willers) to phone to ask how I was doing was Rosalie Quirk and I was very grateful for that call. On Saturday, 22nd March, John Peers came to see me in hospital and gave me £1500 in cash and I resigned from the various Anglo Companies of which I was a director.

Dr. Amal Beaini and his wife came to visit me and Dr. Beaini said:

"Why not take a real time out, come into the Harrogate Clinic when they're finished with you here and let's try to get to the bottom of your problems."

I agreed with him and on Monday 24th March I was transferred by ambulance from the Yorkshire Clinic to the Harrogate Clinic.

I had to hand over all my medications when I arrived and I was shown to a private room on the second floor. I was soon in need of a Librium and went to the nurses' station and asked for one. I was told I couldn't have any medication except as prescribed by Dr. Beaini. I pointed out that the medication I had given them was prescribed by Dr. Beaini but still they would not give me a Librium. I completely lost my temper and demanded that they get Dr. Beaini to come and see me right away. I went back to my room and telephoned Sue in search of a little sympathy. Whilst phoning her I leaned on my television which was wall mounted; my weight was too much and the TV crashed to the floor. A couple of nurses came running into my room having heard the crash. I told them it was an accident but I don't think they believed me.

Dr. Beaini was in my room in a matter of minutes and handed me a couple of Librium to take. He said he was very disappointed by my behavior, he had been telling the staff to 'expect a star patient'. He said there would be daily group therapy sessions and some kind of group activity every afternoon. He expected me to participate fully. I was to stay at the hospital and not make any visits home. Phone calls should be restricted to family and under no circumstances was I to take calls from Marina. If I got angry in the future I was to walk away, there were to be no more incidents with the staff. He then prescribed Trazodone, Librium, Tritace and an antibiotic, plus a daily B1 injection. I think he figured that should keep me quiet. He also released the medicines prescribed for my heart by Dr. Morley.

On Wednesday, 26th March, Sue and I received our regular pay checks and on Thursday, Dave Allen, one of the staff at Walkden, brought all my remaining personal possessions from Walkden to Bradford and on Friday came to visit me. I soon got into the routine of the hospital and began to participate in the group therapy and the daily outings. The food was good and plentiful and I had a visit everyday from Sue. James and Dominic also came to see me as did my nephew Richard. On Sunday 13th April I heard that Ken McAvoy, Anglo's consulting engineer, had had a heart attack. I had been giving him a very hard time recently and was concerned that the stress I had caused him might have contributed to his heart attack.

Although I was keeping my anger in check I was hypercritical of everything about the hospital and my room in particular. I was used to doing "snagging lists" or "punch lists" on building projects and effectively I did this on the hospital, Dr. Beaini said I was not to make any more criticisms and he gave me a post it note pad and told me to write out my complaints and stick them all up on the wall of my room. I had no choice but to do this which made me feel very foolish. One Sunday I went home against Dr. Beaini's instructions. When I opened the fridge I found beer and wine and in the dining room were some bottles of liquor. I went absolutely crazy at Sue and threw all the bottles out onto the street.

In the room next to mine was a young woman, Karen Kuculchki. She was very withdrawn and I barely knew her until mid-April when she became more talkative at group therapy and started taking pride in her appearance. She was brushing her hair and putting on makeup and seemed to be making some progress. On 22nd April she sat next to me at group therapy and insisted I participate to the full in trying to solve the problems of various members of the group. That evening she came to my room and asked for a cigarette. I gave her a pack of cigarettes and some chocolate. She talked and talked, an avalanche of words. She told me she was twenty seven years old and from Washington near Newcastle. Her husband was Japanese and worked at the Nissan car factory. She was a heroin addict and regularly smoked two ounces of pot a day, took four doses of methadone and took any other drug she could get hold of from Valium to crack cocaine. She told me she had children but couldn't look after them and had been working as a prostitute to support her habits. She hugged and kissed me, then cried and asked me to hold her. She said she was afraid and unless Dr. Beaini would give her either pot or methadone she would have to discharge herself and go back to being a prostitute. Her husband didn't really want her back; he had told here that if she were Japanese she would have killed herself before bringing shame on the family. She asked me to tell the nurses what she had said and I did and soon afterwards Dr. Beaini phoned her and said he would come to see her next morning. She seemed calmer and we went outside arm in arm to look for the comet Hale-Bopp streaking across the night sky on its four thousand year journey. We hugged and kissed and then went to our rooms to sleep.

Next morning Karen was in my room at 7.30 am and we smoked a cigarette together; she told me she was afraid and needed to talk. I said I had to get weighed and do a few things and I suggested she go back to her room and wait for me. When I returned she was waiting by her open door and asked me to come in. She held me and kissed me and cried and told me she was afraid. She asked me to stay with her until Dr. Beaini arrived but I said I had to make a phone call and I left. I didn't come back right away but went to eat breakfast. After breakfast as I approached her room I was told by the day nurse not to go in; then I saw paramedics arrive followed by Dr. Beaini. I knew something terrible had happened but went to group therapy. The counselor received a call to go upstairs and she came back looking shaken. She told us Karen had hung herself in her room before Dr. Beaini had arrived, but was not dead, and had been taken to another hospital.

I felt overwhelmed with guilt; Karen had asked me to stay with her until Dr. Beaini arrived and I selfishly had gone to make a phone call and eat breakfast and in that brief period she had hung herself. I wept. The whole group wept. Many people in the room had or were having suicidal thoughts; some had harmed themselves before. What shocked them, they said, was not that she had attempted suicide but the method she had chosen. I couldn't comprehend this and thought: "Christ, did they want her to fucking crucify herself?"
Subsequently I realized that what shocked them about hanging was that it was not so much a cry for help as a decision that it was better to be dead than alive.

Dr. Beaini joined the group and told us he was shaking and nervous about facing us. He explained Karen's situation; he knew everything she had told me and none of us should feel guilty; especially not me. He took me in his arms and then moved around the group talking and consoling us. Two days later Karen Kuculchki died. Somehow

Karen's death sealed a bond between the members of the group and rapid improvements were obvious in the condition of several patients. We felt that Karen had died for us; that she was at peace so we could be at peace. I thought her death was a testimony against an evil system of government that peddles methadone through the National Health Service, much of it then being sold at black market prices. I hated a government that would rather build prisons than hospitals, to train warders rather than doctors or nurses. The day after Karen's death I wrote this poem:

KAREN KUCULCHKI – A CELEBRATION OF HER DEATH

Karen, we weep not for you
but for ourselves for there
but for the grace of God we go
You were the young one
The blonde one
The Geordie lass
With three children and with
Everything to live and to die for.
You were smoking pot and
Drinking black market methadone
And popping any pill you
Could lay hands on.
But we saw the changes
The magic being worked by Amal Beaini and his staff
The sparkle in your eyes
The hair brushed neatly
We saw you getting better by the day
You were helping others, coming back to life
I felt your hugs and kisses
And I listened to your
Stories and I held
You while you wept and trembled.
Easter had just gone and Spring had come and
Summer Time begun
Summertime and the living or dying was easy

> *Hale-Bopp that comet visitor in the night sky that*
> *would only be seen*
> *From earth every 4000 years*
> *Was beginning to fade*
> *And you decided to get aboard*
> *To free your spirit by hanging*
> *From the neck until dead.*
> *This was no cry for help*
> *This was a brave decision*
> *To release your spirit from*
> *The prison it was trapped in.*
> *Your death has made us cry and*
> *Our spirits are suffused with*
> *A special bond with you and each other.*
> *You did not die in vain*
> *Your death has made us strong*
> *For your courage and your strength*
> *We salute you Karen Kuculchki*
> *Cosmos mariner; destination unknown.*

After Karen's death Dr. Beaini agreed I could go home for a long weekend, and on Friday evening John Peers came to the house in Bradford. He wanted me to sign the accounts of Land & Property Management for 1995- 1996 which I did and he gave Sue and I salary checks for April.

On Sunday night Marina overdosed and was taken by ambulance to the Bradford Royal Infirmary. Late Monday night she had herself sectioned into a mental hospital, Lynfield Mount. The next morning at 10 am the police arrived, she had been subpoenaed to appear in court as a witness. When I told them she was in Lynfield Mount and had been sectioned one of the officers said:
"That's very clever of her. This means we can't touch her even with a subpoena; the case has been adjourned three times, the judge won't adjourn it again and without Marina we will lose the case."
At 7p.m. Marina made a miraculous recovery and had herself de-sectioned. That evening I returned to the Harrogate Clinic and three days later on May 1st I was discharged

While I was in the clinic Simon and Ellen phoned me from the States every day. Sue told them it was unnecessary to come over and they said they would pay for Sue and I to visit them for a period of convalescence. Sue explained that I didn't feel I could fly on such a long journey. Simon and Ellen offered to pay for Sue and I to travel to the States and back on the ocean liner, Queen Elizabeth 2. This was a tremendous thrill and we found that the next transatlantic sailing was on June 6th with a return date of August 18th. We busied ourselves with preparations for this trip of a lifetime and planned a schedule for when we were in the States to include a week staying at Marion Tucker's on Lake Wylie; a week in Blowing Rock in the Blue Ridge Mountains and a week at Tybee Island near Savannah, Georgia. We also planned to hire a car and make a long drive back to New York visiting places we had not been to before, Nashville, Tennessee, Denver, Colorado, Chicago and the Finger Lakes area of New York State.

About a year previously I had been arrested in Bradford for drunk driving. I had been drinking in the Melborn and on the way home stopped in the West End pub on Lumb Lane where I was very friendly with Christine, the landlady. When I left the pub I bumped into a guy I knew and asked him if he had any marijuana because I knew James and Dominic wanted some. I bought an ounce from him and put it in my trouser pocked. I had only gone a couple of hundred yards when I noticed a police car was following me and he put on his blue light and pulled me over. He gave me a breathalyzer test which was positive and arrested me and placed me in the back seat of the police car. Another policeman drove my car to the police station and we followed in the police car. I knew they would ask me to empty my pockets at the police station so I needed to get rid of the ounce of pot. The best I was able to do was to get it out of my pocket and leave it on the back seat of the police car. I was taken into the police station and they took a blood sample and gave me half of it so I could have it analyzed by an accredited analyst. Because I was still over the limit on the breathalyzer I was put into a cell and told I would be re-tested every hour and released when I tested negative. I hated being in a cell and was very worried that they would find the pot in the police car and charge me with possession.

Eventually they let me go at 4 am and I drove home. Sue, Dominic and James were in Manchester and as I didn't feel like driving I phoned and asked Dominic to come and pick me up. I didn't want to remain in Bradford in case the police found the pot with my finger prints on the wrapper and came looking for me. I appointed a solicitor, Bassra Singh, to represent me and as a conviction would mean the loss of my license we decided to plead not guilty. He had somehow managed to keep the case going for over a year obtaining adjournment after adjournment but the time was fast approaching when I would have to face the music. He managed to get one last adjournment because of my trip to the States but the definitive date for the hearing was set for September 8th at 9.45 am.

I obtained prescriptions for three months supply of medications from Dr. Morley and Dr. Beaini and had a final check up with each of them. Dr. Beaini added Seroxat to my medication and both doctors gave me letters to be handed to doctors in the States if I needed medical attention whilst there. Both stressed the need to stay off alcohol if I was to have a permanent recovery. I had an echo test and my ejection fraction had improved from 12% to 35%. The magic of medicine and abstention from alcohol could clearly be seen in those figures.

On Thursday, June 5th, 1997 we took the train to London where we changed stations and took a train to Southampton. We stayed the night at the Forte Post House Hotel and Sue's sister, Carol, and her husband, Simon, joined us at the hotel and stayed the night. We went for dinner and I had just one glass of wine. The next day we boarded the Queen Elizabeth 2 and were shown to our cabin on five deck where our luggage was already awaiting us. The one thing you can say about the QE2 is that it is big. It is like a small town but even with two thousand passengers and fifteen hundred crew it never seems crowded because there are so many public rooms and so many simultaneous activities. It is the world's first totally cashless society; on boarding you register a credit card and then simply sign for all purchases against your room number. You don't need to spend anything because all the meals and entertainment are included in the fare. Inevitably you do spend money; drinks are not free and although I drank a lot of non alcoholic beer I was also having a few pints of beer when Sue wasn't around and a glass or two of wine with dinner. I believed I could drink in a controlled way, become a social drinker and, if this were possible, I should be able to enjoy the pleasure of drink whilst maintaining good health.

There was a Steiner Spa on board and I spent a lot of time and money having all kinds of relaxing and de-stressing treatments. I really enjoyed the experience, not least because the spa was staffed by a group of very pretty young girls.

We were assigned to the Mauretania Restaurant and the food was truly excellent. There were several other restaurants open to everyone so it was possible to eat all day long if you wanted to. There was an array of bars and amongst our favorites were the Crystal Bar, The Yacht Club, The Chart Room and the Golden Lion Pub. We became friendly with one of the entertainers, Cathy Caine, who played keyboards and sang in the Golden Lion every evening from 7 p.m. to 9p.m.. Every day we received a program of the day's events and activities and over breakfast we planned our day. Sue would usually go to a movie while I went to the spa and we went to concerts and lectures. As well as a movie theater and ballroom there were many smaller areas set aside for special activities. We went to cookery lectures and demonstrations by Gary Rhodes and Nanette Newman and bought both their latest books and had them autographed to Simon and Ellen as a little thank you gift for the trip. As well as restaurants, bars, casino and spa, a swimming pool and hot tub, there was a full range of exclusive and expensive shops. We spent a lot of the day sitting on deck and enjoying the sea breeze and the view of the ocean. It is a strange feeling to travel for six days and nights without seeing another ship; to be so far from land that you never see a bird; to have the excitement of seeing a whale alongside the ship.

On the third day we received a notice in our cabin which read;
"We have secured your porthole cover, in the event the glass of your porthole becomes shattered in heavy weather, which could cause flooding in your cabin"
We assume this in one of the perils of being on deck five almost right on the waterline. For two days it blew a gale and even a ship the size

of the QE2 was not immune from the rocking and rolling motion engendered by the high seas.

As we approached Newfoundland we were warned to expect fog but none materialized. On the morning of the seventh day we glided into New York Harbor and felt this was the way to travel. There's something about taking six full days and nights to get from England to America that seems right. Because we had changed the clocks one hour for each of five nights there was no time change on arrival in New York. It was 7.30 a.m. but we did not disembark until 9.30 a.m. Immigration officials had traveled on board QE2 and we had cleared immigration three days before our arrival in New York. We collected our bags and took a taxi to Penn Station where we boarded the Metroliner for Baltimore. Simon was working in Baltimore and had the use of a luxury flat overlooking the inner harbor so he had invited us to spend a week there with him before journeying on to Charlotte.

Simon met us off the train in Baltimore and to my surprise I had difficulty walking. On the train journey from New York to Baltimore my right foot had swollen up and become painful. By the time I got to the apartment I could barely walk and the pain was excruciating. I managed to get an appointment with a podiatrist and he diagnosed gout. He prescribed some pills and in two or three days the swelling and the pain were gone. Simon had to work each day at Domino Sugar Company so Sue and I had the apartment to ourselves. There is a system of water taxis in Baltimore harbor so Sue and I traveled everywhere by water not by road. It seemed appropriate after a week at sea. Ellen flew up from Charlotte for the weekend and we had a great time together. I didn't get the opportunity to drink because Simon, Ellen and Sue were always with me. I must have drunk hundreds of bottles of non-alcoholic lager. On Saturday 21st June, we drove back towards Charlotte but stayed the night with our old friends, Wade and Darrell, in Richmond. We had dinner with them at their house and held hands and danced around a great oak tree in their front yard to celebrate the Summer Solstice. We stayed the night in the Ramada Hotel, which Darrell had booked for us because they didn't have room for three of us in their house. We had a pleasant surprise on Sunday morning when we discovered that Darrell had settled our bill.

The next eight weeks were ones of total rest for Sue and I . We spent a week at Marions house on Lake Wylie just south of Charlotte. She was getting ready to sell up and move back to England. She was lonely in America since Charles had died a few years earlier, and had met a man called John on her last trip to England who she was going to live with. We also went with Simon and Ellen for a week at Tybee Island near Savannah. We were sad that James and Dominic were in England and not there at the beach with us; we began to understand how much Simon and Ellen missed us. As Simon said:
> "The kids are supposed to leave the parents not the parents the kids."

We went to Blowing Rock in the Blue Ridge Mountains for a week and stayed at Ellen's great aunt's house on Misty Mountain. We began to entertain the possibility of moving back to America and started looking for a Bed and Breakfast to buy in the Boone or Blowing Rock area. We found that everything was way outside our price range.

When we returned to Charlotte we talked to Simon and Ellen about the possibility of moving back to America to live. They were excited at the idea and said we could stay with them at Thomas Avenue until we found a place of our own. Once we had decided to return to the States we scrapped our plans to go to Nashville and Chicago figuring we would have the rest of our lives to make that trip.

We were due to sail from New York to England on QE2 on Monday 18th August checking in not later than 11 am and with a sailing time of 12.30 p.m.. Sue wanted to get the Amtrak train to New York on Saturday 16 August, have Sunday night in New York and be certain of being in good time for checking in for QE2. I said I thought it was a waste of money to pay for a hotel in New York and we should catch the New Orleans – New York train, the Crescent Express in Charlotte, at 12.30 a.m. on 18th August and arrive in New York at 9 a.m. leaving us two hours to get to QE2 which would be berthed only a ten minute taxi ride away. We were at Charlotte Station at midnight to catch the train but were told it was two hours late. It finally pulled into Charlotte station at 3 a.m. and Sue became very agitated at the possibility that we would miss the QE2. We had a sleeping cabin on the train but Sue just couldn't sleep because of her fear of missing the ship. I told her not to worry, if we missed the ship we would charter a helicopter and soon catch it. There was a helipad on the deck of the QE2 which had been installed when she was used as a troop ship in the Falklands War. The worst scenario was that we would have to stay in the States for another few months, which was fine because we had nothing else to do anyway. Finally she nagged me so much that I went to talk to the conductor and he confirmed that the arrival time would be after 11 a.m; there was no chance of the train making up any time and if anything it was likely to get even further behind schedule. I asked if there was any way possible he could get us there on time and gave him $20 to help his thinking process. He talked on his radio phone to someone in Washington and told me they would take us off the Crescent in Washington and transfer us to the high speed Metroliner which would have us in New York by 10.30 am. Sue finally calmed down and when we arrived in Washington there was a guy waiting for us in a motorized trolley and he whisked us and our baggage across half a dozen rail tracks and had us on the Metroliner in under five minutes. Another $20 for him and $20 for the conductor on the Metroliner and we were on our way at high speed to New York.

The trip back on QE2 was uneventful; we felt we were becoming old hands at transatlantic ocean travel. Whilst on board we investigated the best dates for a return trip and found that the cheapest date by far was to sail on the first leg of a round the world cruise departing Southhampton on 15th December and arriving New York on 21st December. There would be very few passengers on board; the bulk of them would board in New York. We booked our one way passage in the very cheapest cabin but arranged that when we boarded in Southampton we would be upgraded to more sumptuous accommodations. We had discovered that the purser had been at school with my nephew, Mark Spence, and the upgrade was courtesy of him.

As soon as we arrived back we put the house up for sale and busied ourselves getting rid of all the items we did not want to ship to the States. Dominic moved to an apartment with Marina at Melbourne Villas on North Park Road, Bradford. I was due back in court on 8th

September but obviously wanted another adjournment. I did not want to lose my driving license until I was back in the States. Apparently the court had had enough of my delaying tactics because not only did my solicitor not get an adjournment but a warrant was issued for my arrest without bail. I was to spend the next three months hiding whenever the police came to the house looking for me. Sue always told them I was in America but on one occasion James answered the door and told them I would be back in a couple of hours. When they returned Sue asked them which Gary they were looking for as both her husband and son were called Gary. They said it was a fifty three year old Gary so they assumed it was her husband.

"Oh he's in America" said Sue "and I'm joining him there in a few weeks, the other Gary, my son, Dominic Gary, is the one who is due here soon".

On the weekend of 13th September Sue and I took the ferry from Holyhead to Dun Laoghaire to have a farewell visit to Dublin. We went to all our old stomping grounds but felt very sad at the thought it might be years before we had the chance to return again. Two weeks later we took James on a trip to Bath, a place I had never visited before which I wanted to see before leaving England for what I thought may be the last time. On 7th October James submitted his final thesis to Manchester University and the following week James, Sue and I took a trip to the Lake District. We stayed in a delightful hotel called Underscar Manor overlooking the town of Keswick. I took a side trip by train to Edinburgh and while I was gone Sue and James climbed the nearby mountain of Helvelyn.

In early November we found a buyer for the house, who was an American lecturing at Bradford University. I made a final visit to Dr. Beaini and Dr. Morley and got them both to write letters enclosing my medical records to a doctor in the States. An echo test revealed my heart's ejection fraction was up to 50% which is close to normal. On 17th November James got his results from Manchester University; he had been awarded a Master of Arts degree in Art History. I spent some time inspecting the records of burials in Heaton Cemetery in an attempt to piece together a family tree and spent time in the dales visiting Dacre Banks where my maternal grandfather had been born and Eastby where Mark Newbould was from.

Making Hen's Meat

On 29th November we had a leaving party at the Melborn Hotel. Six bands played free of charge; Twister, Avalon, the Full Mash House Band, Somebody's Brother, The Whitfield Family and Eamon & Friends. We laid on food for about a hundred guests. In the afternoon there were fresh salmon sandwiches, pork and stuffing sandwiches, black pudding, dripping on bread and an assortment of other foods. At night we served beef stew and French bread. Eamon gave me a card and when I opened it there was £100 inside. They put up a plaque to remember me by in the pub. Dominic spent a lot of the afternoon talking to Finola Hingstone and ended up going home with her. He had been trying to break up with Marina for some time and Finola coming into his life finally enabled him to terminate that relationship. Dominic moved into Finola's house in Thornton and we were glad to see him settled in a job and a relationship before we left England.

On 5th December James flew back to America where he was to stay with Simon and Ellen until he found a job and somewhere to live. On the same day Sue and I drove to Liverpool to meet John Peers of Anglo at the offices of Davies Wallis Foyster, their solicitors. We had reached a settlement with Anglo whereby they would forgive all my debt to them including the mortgage on 8 Rossefield House. We received a release from the mortgage and rushed back to Bradford to deliver it to our solicitor, Tony Emmott, thus enabling him to complete the sale of the house. On Tuesday we moved out of Rossefield House and into the Victoria Hotel in the center of Bradford for our last few days in England.

Mike and Rosie came to see us at the hotel on Thursday, 11th December and on Friday his son Mark, and his wife, Janet, came to say goodbye and to get my signature on some documents in connection with the transfer of money to the States (Mark was a banker with Barclay's Bank). On Saturday we said our last farewells to all the crowd at the Melborn and Peter Thornton and Johnny Milnes came to say au revoir. On 14th December Dominic and Finola drove us to Manchester Picadilly Railway Station to catch the train to Southampton. We stopped on the way at the Jewish bakery near Sue's old home and bought bagels, chopped liver and chopped

herring. We borrowed a knife and ate them right there, sitting in the car outside the shop. It was a tearful farewell at Manchester Picadilly and I remember saying to Dominic and Finola;
"Look after each other".

BIBLIOGRAPHY

I am indebted to the authors of the following books, all of which served me well as aides-memoire.

- "Sam Chippindale.... Shopping Center Pioneer" by Zita Adamson.
- "Retailing on Three Continents, the Discount Food Store Operations of Albert Gubay" by Dennis Lord, Warren Moran, Tony Parker and Leigh Sparks.
- "Gerry Healy – A Revolutionary Life" by Corinna Lotz and Paul Feldman.
- "North Carolina's Historic Restaurants" by Dawn O'Brien.
- "Myrtle Allen's Cooking at Ballymaloe House" by Myrtle Allen.

I am grateful to Chuck Sullivan for permission to reprint several of his poems in this volume and for writing the notes on the back cover, and to Hamish Hamilton, publishers of Malcolm Muggeridge's "Affairs of the Heart" for permission to quote from that book, and to the National Museum of Photography, Film and Television, Bradford, England for permission to quote from "Stone Walls, Grey Skies" by George Tice.